AF464786

Karl Bädeker.

Karl Baedeker I [there were four], 1801-59, had four children, Anna, Ernst, Karl and Fritz. The latter [1844-1925] took over the firm, then *his* son Karl [b.1876], followed by *his* son Karl Friedrich [1910-1979]. The last of the line was Florian [b. 1943] who died in a car accident in 1980.

Baedekeriana

An Anthology

Michael Wild

The Red Scar Press

Baedekeriana

First published by The Red Scar Press
in March 2010

ISBN 978-0-9565289-0-2

Introduction

Like many of you, I have been collecting the old Baedeker guides, (in my case since the age of sixteen, or so.) My early set, culled from various secondhand bookshops, was modest at first, but then, as I kept a weather eye open for more and more titles, it began to grow. Inevitably, I started with the more available ones: *Belgium and Holland, Northern France, Paris, North Germany, South Germany,* and the Italian guides, most of which, in the 1960s, sold for a few shillings. I had only to open a copy of one of those raspberry-red little bindings, to feel that I was among friends.

What intrigued me, when I dipped inside, were the apparently low cost of travel in the late nineteenth century, and the remarkable wealth of detail concerning hotels, means of transport (almost always trains), things worth seeing, and precautions to be taken.

Thanks to visits to Hay-on-Wye and more specialist dealers, both here and abroad, the common European titles were soon joined by *The United States, Canada, Lower Egypt, Greece* and the reprint of *Russia.* My world was beginning to expand as quickly as my available cash diminished!

A few years later, when the little red books were becoming much less profuse on the shelves of secondhand bookshops, I came to the conclusion that Baedeker guides of the ancient vintages must now be rather rare. Taking the plunge, I spent much time visiting bookshops and book fairs and reading antiquarian press adverts, and soon had enough stock to set up a one-man mail-order business, ("Only Baedekers"), issuing lists twice a year and finding a remarkable number of interesting contacts (at home and abroad), all of whom were as keen on Baedeker as I.

Because I am something of a writer as well, it did not take me long to realise that the wealth of information about Karl Baedeker and his dynasty was worth reading. What were the stories behind these books? How exactly was the material researched, and by whom? What happened to the firm in Leipzig during World War II? This was a seminal area, well worth following up.

And so, in 1986, the first glimmers of ***Baedekeriana*** appeared, and, from now on, the lists were accompanied by a booklet containing the articles and anecdotes about Baedeker that a small but devoted readership eagerly lapped up, twice a year until 1992, when I retired from teaching, gave up bookselling and no longer had access to cheap photocopying.

Now, some twenty years after I began, it occurred to me that I might use the more sophisticated methods of desktop publishing to issue this present volume, which, while it contains much of the old ***Baedekeriana*** material, offers it in a format which might better grace the shelves of those kind enough to want it.

The name ***Baedeker*** is, of course, a protected registered trade-mark. In those far-off days, I was given permission by Dr Florian Langenscheidt (whose firm acquired the registered name of Baedeker) to use the name ***Baedekeriana***, provided that I sent him copies of my booklets for his archive. Nowadays, the editorial office and company, trading under the name "Mairdumont", is located at Ostfildern-Kemnat, and in the capable hands of Chief Editor Rainer Eisenschmid. When planning this book, I wrote to them, and was delighted to receive permission to go ahead, and, as before, include generous excerpts from my own translations of certain of the guides which never appeared in English. You will not need to dig very deep in this text, to find them!

I must also mention the names of past friends, acquaintances and contacts whose contributions to ***Baedekeriana*** down the years were invaluable, and of whom further acknowledgment is made in the text:

[The late] Karl Baedeker, Mr John Gretton, Dr Roger Hickley, Herr Alex Hinrichsen, Dr F.Langenscheidt, Mr W.B.C.Lister, Herr Reinhard Öhlberger, Mr Harold Otness and Herr Hans-Werner Renner.

The articles are not always printed here in chronological order. I have used some editorial discretion in this regard, but have provided an index at the back, to make items easier to locate.

Hermann Augustine Piehler, 1888-1987

[Taken from *Baedekeriana* no. 8, Autumn1987]

The name of H.A.Piehler is to be found in the Preface of many an English-language Baedeker, for the very good reason that, from mid-1911 onwards (shortly after acquiring his degree), he was appointed to be Baedeker's English writer. If Baedeker is often praised for the excellence of his English style, the compliment is largely paid to Piehler. "The writer is H.A.Piehler, B.A., F.R.G.S., who for many years has taken part in the preparation of the English editions of Baedeker's Handbooks, and who, in the course of recent motor-tours aggregating over 10,000 miles, has personally visited almost the whole of the districts described." (Baedeker's *Great Britain,* 8th ed. 1927).

How he came to be Baedeker's man in Britain was let out in the recent *Daily Telegraph* obituary (4.7.87), which says that while Piehler was sampling Europe, he went to Leipzig and, "walking along a street, happened to see Baedeker's nameplate, so dropped in and asked for a job."

Despite his German-sounding name, "Gus" was in fact born and educated in England, the son of a naturalised German. He possessed, not surprisingly, a remarkable talent for languages, notably French and German, and did a great deal of translation during his long life.

At the outbreak of the First World War, he refused to change his name (unlike some members of his family, who became "Peeler"), and was refused entry to the Services. By the Second World War, however, his true worth was finally recognised, and it was as colonel in the Intelligence Corps that he played a significant role, firstly as a "screener" of aliens interned in the Isle of Man, and secondly as a member of the Allied Control Commission in Germany, vetting books this time, to see which were suitable for post-war German readers. Baedekers were quickly restored as wholesome reading *(Leipzig, ein neuer Führer von Karl Baedeker, 1948)*, though, with "Gus" busy in Germany, *London* 1951 was updated by "E.F.Peeler", (Edward Peeler being his younger brother).

One of Piehler's less tasteful tasks was to adapt the volume which appeared in Britain as *Germany* 1936, with its references to Nazism and the Third Reich, but this element was kept to an absolute minimum. As Reinhard Öhlberger says, in his article entitled *Berlin im Spiegel des Baedeker,* (which appears in English, on page 24), it was not possible in the 1936 (German) Baedeker of Berlin, to avoid political allusions in the historical sketch. (See also my article on *Das Generalgouvernement,* starting on page 14).

Hermann Piehler probably had more direct knowledge of Baedekers and the Baedeker dynasty than anyone else alive now. It is with deep regret that we say farewell to a cultured and generous man, English to the marrow, but stubbornly European and outward-looking as well, without whose dedicated and great work the name of Baedeker might still be virtually unknown on these shores.

D.D.A.C.

Mr Alan Sillitoe states that the 1939 edition of our Germany *(in German) had the swastika on the jacket. From this your readers may gain the impression that we were in the habit of adorning our books with that symbol. The facts are that this particular volume was selected by the German Automobile Club as their club guide and that part of the edition had a jacket showing the club's emblem (which at that time of course incorporated the swastika). Similarly, the preface ending with the then customary hailing of Hitler was not the firm's preface (which is also there) but that provided by the Automobile Club's president for the club edition. A glance inside this volume will quickly show that the text was as factual and unbiased as that of all preceding editions.*

KARL BAEDEKER (From *Time and Tide*, 16th November 1961)

The might of the house of Baedeker

by Joachim Ahlemann

From Baedekeriana *no. 8, (Autumn 1987), this article appeared in the* Neue Literarische Welt, *Darmstadt on 12th April 1953. My own translation.*

It was quite unintentional, I admit. I had dared to alter the date of origin of a painting by a second-rate master of the Siena school from 1472 to 1473. After I had spent two whole days brooding over all manner of histories of art and early editions of Baedeker's *Italy,* I made this decision which was to have such severe consequences. I could quote Vasari, Winckelmann and Gregorovius. Full of the confidence which intensive work on source material gives one, I handed my proof sheet back to Hans Baedeker, the chief editor of the house.

Not long afterwards, the girls' telephone rang. The young editorial staff on the ground-floor of the sober rented office on the corner of Nürnberger and Brüderstrasse in Leipzig (now in ruins) still had no telephone. The firm, scorning all vanities and modern innovations, had not yet been able to make up its mind about this. It preferred inconspicuousness, which manifested itself for example in the fact that there was no large plate on the front of the house to declaim that here were the offices of a world-famous publishing house. On the front door was merely a white name-plate, hardly bigger than a visiting-card, bearing the name 'Karl Baedeker'.

Besides, the brothers Hans, Ernst and Dietrich (known to all as 'Dietz') would never have agreed to such a disruptive upheaval as the installation of a house telephone, with all its lines, would have caused. The often tense relationship between the three brothers had its reefs, past which the employees did not find it easy to navigate unscathed. For weeks at a time, the bosses communicated tersely by notes, a practice which generally caused further errors and rows. Newcomers never learned to cope.

So there I was, sitting very dispiritedly up in Hans Baedeker's room, and he was holding my proof before me – and scolding. My timid references to the authorities I had quoted were dismissed by my superior with a wave. There existed in the Vatican, unbeknown of course to me, an autobiography by that master (whose name escapes me), wherein the date of origin of his painting was irrefutably fixed for all time. Vasari, as I must surely know, had not been excessively thorough in his researches, and his successors had merely copied him without question. It was shattering, the way the boss knew such things. The regard in which the house of Baedeker was held was based upon such attention to tiny details and the greatest possible exactitude, which was why every well-travelled person used the red guides, whether it be for the sights of Venice or those of Jerusalem!

'Oh yes, Jerusalem,' said Hans Baedeker. 'We once made a slip, before the First World War, such as can all too easily happen when the information about hotels is constantly changing. But,' he continued, with a quick threatening look in my direction, 'that is not to be regarded as a precedent for any kind of laxity in this instance.'

Against the last of the few hotels which had the honour to be mentioned in Baedeker, stood the remark: "Arab proprietor". Now, before the war, there were very few first-class hotels in the Holy City of three religions. This doubtless well-run establishment was included in them. The nationality of the hotelier was of no consequence to German priests. The comment was directed only at the exclusive international travelling public, and not intended as derogatory in any sense.

The owner got to hear of the remark, however, and sued the firm of Baedeker. In Leipzig there was consternation, and all the files were examined. Not one individual, but several authorities had contributed to this announcement. A tiresome and expensive lawsuit followed, mounted first in Alexandria, then London. The house of Baedeker fought on all fronts, supported by outstanding lawyers. But it lost, for the hotel owner produced a passport declaring him to be Maltese, i.e. a true British subject. Admittedly, there has been the craziest imaginable mixture of races in Malta from time immemorial, with Arabs strongly represented, but this held no validity in the judge's decision, and the firm of Baedeker was then liable to pay all the costs of the case, and to delete the derogatory words from all of its books.

This meant that the volumes *Palestine* and *Mediterranean* would require a reprint of the relevant page about Jerusalem. Volumes already dispatched were recalled from the bookshops. The already bound books had to be ripped open, re-stapled and rebound. The expense was horrendous, and the chagrin huge in proportion.

But now the firm did something which the astute judges in neither Alexandria nor London could have foreseen, let alone the Maltese hotelier: in the reprint, the hotel was totally deleted! And there was no power on earth that could compel the firm of Baedeker to set anything down in its books that it did not want. The corrected guides were issued. The public bought and used them, staying at the hotels named in Jerusalem. Not, however, at the hotel of the Maltese. It was not in Baedeker: it did not exist.

The effect was amazing. Within a short time, petitions arrived from the hotelier and his lawyers. The opposition declared itself ready to shoulder all the costs if only, *please!*, the hotel be reinstated in the guides. They would do *anything.* They were prepared to bind themselves to pay any amount of compensation, but… 'We too had our pride,' said Hans Baedeker contentedly, 'and we declined all these offers. The hotel subsequently went bankrupt and the owner became destitute. That's how great our power was!'

Without realising it, I had begun to stoop. After all, did I not know, from my own observations, how widespread the red guides were, whose name had become an idea, an ideal even? For, on a random check, 29 out of 30 travellers from all countries who entered San Marco were equipped with a Baedeker, and only one had the brown Meyer. And *he* was a German teacher, with an ancient edition!

Venice

by James Morris

being the author's comments on Baedeker's advice

From this truly magnificent book about La Serenissima (first published by Faber in 1960), these extracts (which Jan Morris kindly allowed me to quote) contain interesting references to Baedeker:

"Venice was founded in misfortune, by refugees driven from their old ways and forced to learn new ones. Scattered colonies of city people, nurtured in all the ease of Rome, now struggled among the dank miasmas of the fenlands, their 'malarious exhalations', as Baedeker was to call them, fussily adjusting his mosquito-net 1,400 years later".

"The pigeons are fed twice daily at public expense, besides being stuffed to excess by indulgent tourists ('those whose ambitions lean in that direction,' as Baedeker loftily observes, 'may have themselves photographed covered with birds')."

"Baedeker reported in 1914 that there was a resident Anglican chaplain in Venice, a Scottish minister, an Italian Episcopalian Methodist church (it still exists, behind the Piazza), an English nursing home, two English doctors, and a seamen's institute presided over by Mr Fussey."

On the cries uttered by the gondoliers: "Baedeker, frankly defeated by the whole system, merely records the unpronounceable exclamation 'A-Oel!' – which means, he says bathetically, 'Look out!'"

On drinking water: "It is stored in reservoirs near Sant' Andrea, and is so good that even Baedeker was prepared to commend it."

"It is ninety miles around the perimeters of the lagoon but it is still all Venice: tempered, watered, vulgarized, often neglected, but always tinged with the magic of the place – 'a breath of Venice on the wind'. Only fifty years ago most of the lagoon shore was untouched by progress, sparsely inhabited, scarcely visited by tourists from one decade to the next. The old guide books speak tantalizingly of unspoilt strands and virgin beaches, and make it sound as though a trip to the villages on the rim of the lagoon required a sleeping bag and a bag of beads. Today, Herr Baedeker would find it much more suitable for delicate constitutions, and could safely advise that stomach pills, portable wash-basins and topees will not be required."

"The canals of Venice are lined with accumulations of garbage, and nothing is more strongly worded, in the whole range of travel literature, than Herr Baedeker's warning: '*Oysters* should not be eaten at Venice.'" (*Northern Italy,* 14th ed. 1913.)

* * *

"In the Book Bazaar in Istanbul I inquired about the prices of the three Baedekers that one shop had (being attracted by the *Belgique et Hollande)*, and discovered he was asking 50,000 TL per copy (no doubt bargaining would reduce this price, but I'm not sure how much). That represents over £40. I looked at two English-language ones (1903/1904 of *Spain* and *N. Italy),* not in particularly good condition. Turkey is your market, except that I can't imagine who *buys* them there."

(Dr Anne Powell, Freiburg-im-Breisgau, 1987)

Das Generalgouvernement

The Generalgouvernement

Traveller's Handbook

by

KARL BAEDEKER

With 3 maps and 6 town plans

LEIPZIG · KARL BAEDEKER · 1943

'For the traveller returning home to the Reich from the East, the Generalgouvernement provides a concept which is already strongly redolent of the homeland. For the traveller leaving the Reich to travel East, it is the first greeting from the Eastern world.'

Generalgouverneur Reichsminister Dr. Frank on the 23rd of October 1942'

Some years ago, Jerrold Packard of the USA had in his catalogue the following item for sale: 'Das General-gouvernement: 1st and only German ed., 1943, 3 maps and 6 plans, 264pp., $550. Fine cond., with only a slight stain on the back cover and cover tips a bit worn. This guide was printed for German occupation forces in Poland. "Das General-gouvernement", the German newspeak *name for the truncated Poland, was taken from the pre-World War I Russian title for the area, when it was part of that empire. It is a rare and fascinating look at this German rump-state. There is a long introduction giving the German view of affairs. Not likely to be available again in the foreseeable future, as very few copies are in existence.'*

My correspondent Harold Otness, from Ashland, Oregon, copied some pages and sent them to me. I have translated some of them, and give you this extract. Baedeker at his most tendentious and sycophantic, even allowing for the incredible red tape prevailing then – but, after all, his editorial freedoms were severely curtailed.

"The Governor-general, Reichsminister *Dr. Hans Frank* provided the inspiration for this new volume in our collection. The Editor accepted with enthusiasm the task of producing a Handbook which would give the reader some idea of the labour involved in restoring things to normal, and the rebuilding which, under difficult war conditions, has been achieved (or is in hand), since the German Reich assumed control over the Vistula basin, 3½ years ago. The region and its cities have taken on a new aspect, the widely scattered beauties of nature and the innumerable (often buried) vestiges of early German culture and pioneering, above all, the achievements of German architecture, have become more easily accessible. Our new guide will assist not only the traveller but everyone concerned with this area, to find these things, even in the remoter districts, to acquire a proper insight into land and people, and become conversant with the historical context.

The work was put into the hands of my colleague of many years' standing, *Oskar Steinheil,* who, on the invitation of the Governor-general, and with his assistance, was able, for the purposes of this book, to travel all over the region in the autumn of 1942. He was given information and valuable material by the authorities in Cracow, Radom, Warsaw, Lublin, Lemberg etc.; *Herr H.H. Stallberg,* chief adviser on tourism in the government of the Generalgouvernement (main information dept.) made available for our use a copious work of his own on the subject. We should like to take this opportunity to thank all concerned. We were also able to peruse the available literature.

Besides the descriptive text, the reader will welcome the introductory essays contributed by experts in the various fields: on the history of art, by *Prof. Dr. Dagobert Frey* (Breslau); on landscape, people and economy by *Dr. Ernst R. Fugmann* (deputy head of the topographical section of the Institute for German Involvement in the East, at Cracow); on the history of the Vistula region by *Dr. Erwin Hoff* (history section at the same Instititute); and on the legal status and administration of the Generalgouvernement, by *Dr. Albert Weh* (director of the judiciary office in the government of the Generalgouvernement).

The maps and plans were compiled from the most recent official information. The spelling of place-names in the text and maps follows the enactments of the 15th of August 1941 and the 20th of May 1942 by the government of the Generalgouvernement.

It is impossible to achieve literal exactness in every mention in a traveller's Handbook which must give information about things that are so subject to change, especially during war-time and in a newly opened-up region where so much is still coming into being. The Editor always welcomes any corrections, suggestions and possible improvements, all of which will be conscientiously examined.

Karl Baedeker, Leipzig C1.

(After the usual list of routes and maps, the Introduction proper begins).

A. PRACTICAL NOTES

I. Entry

a. Passport, customs and currency regulations

The Generalgouvernement (hereafter "GG", tr.), as an 'adjacent territory' to the German Reich, is separated from the latter by a police, customs and fiscal frontier. Even Germans therefore require not only an official identity document with photo (such as a passport), but an entry permit also, which is issued by the police authority in the place of residence upon proof of the need to enter the GG. This 'need' can be confirmed in the case of duty trips by the relevant agency; in the case of business trips, by a supporting letter from the appropriate industry chamber or chamber of commerce, or by the State Food Office (for members of the working class). Those intending to stay for health reasons (e.g. at a spa) require an official medical certificate stating the necessity to take a cure at a spa or health resort in the GG, also for visiting workers (including soldiers) stationed in the GG, and for visiting war graves. The entry permit is valid for a limited period only (generally up to 3 months) and is checked, along with the identity document, at the frontier. It must also be handed in temporarily at the hotel where the first night is spent in the GG.

Customs regulations have recently been considerably relaxed. Hand luggage is normally not examined now by Customs. Information may be obtained from the Customs Offices and the information points mentioned on pp. XVI/XVII.

Currency regulations must be strictly observed. Unless he has special permission, the traveller may import or export only 10 RM [Reichsmark], or 20 Zloty. The movement in either direction of larger sums is subject to official approval. In the case of business journeys, the appropriate chamber or Food Office will issue, on production of the entry permit, a supporting letter to permit the necessary currency to be obtained; by virtue of this letter, the exchange office will allow the traveller to receive the relevant type of currency (Zloty) from any exchange bank. Visitors to spas and health resorts in the GG are granted permission by the exchange office to acquire the necessary currency (at present up to 1000Zl.), on production of an official medical certificate; those wishing to visit the graves of their relatives killed in the war are likewise permitted 1000 Zloty if the relevant authorisation is produced. When crossing the frontier, one must produce the sum of money as well as the permission, or receipt from the exchange bank.

It is expedient to get the bank to hand over a small part of the currency in small change, which is useful to have at one's disposal after crossing the frontier. Reichsmarks may be used as payment in the GG only up to a maximum of 10RM.; higher amounts must be offered to the issuing bank or to an exchange bank. There are severe penalties for changing Reichsmarks into Zloty anywhere else; only the Ostbahn (Eastern Railway) is allowed, at some stations, to accept Reichsmarks when tickets are purchased, or to exchange the same.

On leaving the GG, travellers are allowed to bring unspent Zloty back to the Reich without fresh permission (but they must show the authorisation used when they entered). On arrival in the Reich they must, however, immediately change them back into Reichsmarks at an exchange bank, producing the authority referred to above.

For traffic between the Generalgouvernement and territories further east (Reichs-commissariats Ostland and Ukraine*) special conditions apply.

* *"Ostland" was a jargon term for White Russia. Tr.*

This was evidently not a Baedeker guide as we know it. During the Third Reich, all publications were constantly vetted and censored and, as in this case, twisted and jargonised to fit the needs of the occupying power in Poland. Anyone intending to go to the GG, and reading the above few pages, would doubtless come to the conclusion that his journey was not necessary, after all. Dr Hans Frank, the Governor-general, was arraigned at Nuremberg after

the war, accused of war crimes, and executed. To try to redress the balance, I now present the description of Cracow, with (very faint) echoes of the old Baedeker style...

Cracow

Cracow (212m.), capital of the Generalgouvernement, with 345,000 inhabitants, (25,000 of them Germans), and occupying a built-up area of 169 sq.km. (1942), lies in the SW. part of the Vistula province, about 30 km. from the border with Upper Silesia, in a broad plain in the region of the Carpathian foothills. Most of the town is on the l. bank of the *Upper Vistula,* which receives the *Rudawa* at this point and, to the E., enters the Vistula basin (or depression). The town, run by a civic prefect, is the seat of government for the country, residence of the Generalgouverneur, also the governor of Cracow distr., the distr. Prefect of the province of Cracow and numerous other important authorities. Besides this, it also forms a cultural high-point for the German East, as expressed in the Institut für Deutsche Ostarbeit [Inst. for German projects in the E.]. Cracow owes its eminent position in trade and traffic (from which its manifold industries originated) to its highly accessible position on a major river and at the junction of several railways and roads, among which latter the route from Breslau via Lemberg to Kiev, already famous in the Middle Ages as a 'Hohe Strasse' [high road] has re-assumed considerable significance today.

The history of Cracow, whose name (from the legendary Viking hero Krakus) in any case betrays its Germanic origins, reflects, in a convincing way, the centuries of German development work in the East. As far as prehistoric times are concerned, it is possible to see, within the modern town, traces of the presence of Eastern Teutonic peoples (Vandals) since the IInd c. B.C., and there is also evidence that the further environs of the town, as well as the entire Vistula province, contained settlements of Vandals – and sometimes Goths – into the first few centuries A.D.

– Beneath the shelter of the castle rock (already inhabited in prehistoric times) above the l. bank of the Vistula, a pre-medieval settlement grew up between the VIth and VIIIth c. It belonged in the Xth c. to the Bohemian Przemyslid Empire, and was described at that time by the Arab merchant Ibrahim ibn Jakub as already a place of some importance; he mentions that in Cracow (this name emerges for the first time in the Xth c.), resident Varangian (i.e. Viking) merchants were trading with Prague. A witness to the introduction of Christianity in the second half of the Xth c. is the round chapel of SS.Felix and Adauctus on Castle Hill, the oldest surviving ecclesiastical building in the GG. Towards the end of the Xth c., Cracow also became an important bishopric, which passed to the Polish state at the conquest of these areas by Boleslas the Bold (999), and was then subordinated to the archbishopric, founded in 1000 at Gnesen by Otto III, Poland's feudal lord.

The king now remodelled the fortress and, presumably using the services of German builders, erected the first cathedral around 1010, on whose site a new structure arose in the first half of the XIIth c. At the same time, several churches also came into being (incl. the fortified portion of St Andreas) in the merchants' quarter, which consisted at that time mainly of wooden houses. The settlement's rapidly increasing German population had already been living according to German statute in 1228 under its community leader Peter, when the Mongol invasion (Tartars) destroyed everything again in 1241 (only St Andreas and St Adalbert's survived).

The Germans who were called in to undertake the reconstruction founded a merchant settlement, which was granted German title again in 1244 and, through King Boleslas V, the Modest (1243-79), acquired the privilege of a German town under Magdeburg Law (on the Breslau pattern) in which, according to the articles of foundation, no Pole was to be given the status of citizen. The town was burned down in 1259 during a second Mongol attack, and was rebuilt to a plan executed by German master-builders on the outline that is still visible today in the old town, fortified with a moat and town walls with towers. Through the efforts of its German craftsmen and merchants, it quickly flourished again, displaying the affluence of its German citizens in their magnificent patrician houses and public buildings, among which the Marienkirche [St Mary's] and the Cloth Halls merit special attention. At the coronation of King Ladislaus Lokietek (1306-33) on the 1st January 1320, Cracow became also the coronation place of the Polish kings, who now rebuilt the fortress in Gothic style and erected the third cathedral as their coronation church and burial place.

In 1364, under King Casimir the Great (1333-70), a university was founded (originally in the modern suburb Kasimir), which however declined rapidly after the king's death and was founded anew in Cracow in 1400 (today, the Institut für Deutsche Ostarbeit). It owed its period of flowering (from the XVth to the mid-XVIth c.) to the very large number of German professors and students (sometimes up to 70%), among whom Nikolaus Copernicus, 1491-95, may be numbered. In 1384 the Marienkirche was also completed, the pure creation of German artists, with money from German citizens and, even today, the most conspicuous expression of the proud might of German Cracow in the Middle Ages.

Around 1400, the town was already one of the largest in the E., its inhabitants being 90% German. Because of its favourable position on the navigable Vistula at the intersection of the 'Hohe Strasse' from Breslau via Lemberg to Kiev with the trade-routes N. from Bohemia and Hungary, Cracow became an important commercial and trading town, even entering the Hanseatic League in 1430. The town's period of eminence, which reached its peak in the XVth & XVIth c., is also reflected in the achievements of numerous German artists, who were working then in Cracow. Pre-eminent is the Nuremberg master Veit Stoss (1440/50-1533), whom the German citizens had called to Cracow in 1477 to create the high altar for the Marienkirche, and who did not return to Nuremberg until 1496.

The centre of the Old Town is taken up by the almost square *Adolf Hitler Platz, the former Ringplatz which was laid out, similarly to the Breslau Ring, to the dimensions of 210 X 190m., when the town was reconstructed in 1257. In its very compactness it manages to preserve the image of the typical marketplace found in German medieval E. settlements. In the E. corner of the square, the twin-towered Marienkirche; in the centre, the long Cloth Halls; to the W., in front of these, the ancient free-standing town-hall tower; to the S., the small Adalbertkapelle [chapel of St Ethelburt]; and ancient patrician houses all around.

The *Marienkirche [Cath. Parish church], the finest piece of architecture of the German population of Cracow, in which sermons were delivered in German until 1537, is a triple-aisled Gothic basilica (without transepts) executed in brick, with two characteristic W. towers, visible from many points in the streets of the Old Town. The N. tower bears a conical roof surrounded by 8 pointed turrets (81m. tall). The building was endowed in 1220, had only reached the foundations when the Mongols invaded, but was then continued, esp. in the first half of the XIVth c., with the generous patronage of the German patrician Nikolas Wirsing; the choir was completed in 1384; between 1395 and 1397, the nave was vaulted by Master Wernher from Prague; in 1442, the choir vaulting (which had collapsed during an earthquake) was restored by Nik. Zipser.

The INTERIOR of the church, which we enter through a Baroque vestibule added in 1756, makes a spacious impression, esp. because of the height (28m.) of the centre aisle, but this effect is spoilt somewhat by the wall-paintings carried out in 1889-93 to Matejko's designs, and the over-abundant fittings. The rows of chapels down both sides are XV & XVIth c. and contain numerous tombs of German patricians, esp. from the XVI & XVIIth c., some by Italian sculptors; worthy of special mention is the Boner Chapel (1st chapel on the l.), with the memorial slabs to the merchant Severin Boner († 1549) and his wife, née Betmann, possibly from Hilger's studio in Freiberg (Saxony).

In the vestibule of the penultimate chapel l., the bronze slab of the patrician Emeran Salomon, from Vischer's foundry (1504). At the end of the l. aisle, a carved altar attributed to Stanislas Stoss (son of Veit). On the Baroque altar at the end of the r. aisle, a *stone crucifix by Veit Stoss, whose Cracow masterpiece (created in 1477-89 exclusively from contributions made by German citizens), the famous High Altar, had been demolished by the Poles at the outbreak of the war, and is now being preserved in Nuremberg, the home of the artist. To the r. of the entrance to the choir, a ciborium by Gian Maria Mosca. In the triumphal arch, a great crucifix of 1473, from the studio of Veit Stoss.

In the choir, early Baroque stalls, 1620. The present High Altar (Mater Dolorosa; orig. in the chapel of the Cross in the Cathedral) doubtless originated from a Frankish master at the end of the XVth c. To the r. of the High Altar, several superb *bronze tomb slabs, incl. that of the patrician Peter Salomon († 1506), by the Nuremberg caster Peter Vischer…

In the middle of the Adolf Hitler Sq. are the buildings, 120m. in length, that form the *Cloth Halls, a covered market reminiscent of the cloth halls of Flanders, (Antwerp, Bruges, Ghent), and which developed from a roofed-in lane of stalls. Here, other items were sold, apart from cloth; various shops have persisted, and so have numerous simple stalls, as in the Middle Ages. The building was created in 1391-95 in Gothic style by the town's master-builder Martin Lindintolde, then, after a fire in 1555, it was adapted to the Renaissance style and crowned by a Classical roof with blind arches, doubtless under the direction of the court architect Joh. Frankenstein (prob. from the small Silesian town of the same name).

[Almost Baedeker as we know him elsewhere, but look how he harps, ad nauseam, *upon the German-ness of the place, and never misses a trick when it comes to putting the Poles down.]*

Berlin, as reflected in Baedeker, 1842-1940

by Reinhard Öhlberger

(From *Baedekeriana* no. 9, Spring 1988, and no. 10, Autumn 1988)

(Herr Öhlberger is bassoonist with the Vienna Philharmonic Orchestra, which gave two concerts in the Albert Hall at the end of the Proms season last September. He is a keen collector of Baedekers, and gave talks at the Baedeker symposiums in Coblence and Heidelberg. I am indebted to him for his permission to translate and print this article).

The year 1842 was to some extent a key year for the future success of the publishing bookseller Karl Baedeker of Coblence, in the then Prussian province of the Rhine: the publishing house's hitherto relatively modest and regionally orientated programme of travel guidebooks was augmented, for the first time, by an informative work on a more voluminous scale. (Previous works included: *Rheinreise von Strassburg bis Düsseldorf* – 3rd ed., entirely reworked, of Prof. J. A. Klein's Rhine Journey, 1839; *Moselreise von Trier bis Koblenz,* 2nd ed. 1839; two *Little Handbooks for Travellers wanting to find their way easily and quickly,* for *Belgium & Holland,* 1839; *New Handbook for Travellers, containing conversations & a dictionary, English, German, French & Italian,* 2nd ed. 1840).

With his *Handbuch für Reisende durch Deutschland und den österreichischen Kaiserstaat* [Handbook for Travellers through Germany and the Austrian Empire], Baedeker took the important step towards bigger business; the rapid extension of the central

European railway network and the resulting upsurge in middle-class tourism provided the immediate stimulus to prove himself in the face of competition, and market a better product.

Nach eigener Anschauung und den besten Hülfsquellen [from personal observation and the best sources], as it states on the title page: in the Baedeker family firm, all the possible routes were investigated and the sights listed, wherein their own observations – reconnaissance trips by the firm's boss, later his sons – were mentioned repeatedly as fundamental, and included value judgments about what to see and what was "worthy of remark" (in the 19th c. sense).

From the postulate that one intended to write guides for "travellers with a general education" and thereby drive from the field the products of other firms (overloaded as they were with detail and therefore unwieldy), this colossus of the tourist scene, of undreamed-of influence abroad, established itself here within a few decades. Concerning the state of accommodation around 1880, the editor utters in the prefaces to his books some well-intentioned tips to hotel proprietors. Along with demands for quality in "sleeping and washing arrangements", whose minimum standards the author would have dearly liked to bring into being, it says, among other things: "A great drawback, especially in the more modern houses, is the thinness of the walls and inadequate doors, which allow the lightest noise to pass in every direction, imperilling in most painful fashion the guest's right to undisturbed rest. In the mountains, or in remote districts, where the provision of a hotel is a virtue in itself, one may well put up with this, but not in towns. Nor may such a house, even if all other appurtenances be up to standard, lay claim to the title of a first-class hotel. Soundproofing devices, mats on stairs and passages, carpets in the rooms and, above all, well-fitting double doors, are an absolute requirement" (from *Mittel- und Nord-Deutschland,* 14th ed. 1878).

When it came to classifying the things to be seen on one's travels, according to their importance, Baedeker turned his subjective views into objective value-judgments, putting himself at the disposal of his faithful readership with his proverbial stars, as a standard measure of what merited one's attention. For this, he earned universal gratitude: generations of travellers passed through Europe and beyond, with the red books in their luggage. Baedeker's judgment was indisputable, his reliability in providing information about travel and hotels (itself prone to change) was everywhere praised and emphasised. The fact that the house of Baedeker strove to wield its opinion-shaping power in a responsible way can be deduced from the strict refusal to accept advertisements, for instance, which the contemporary rivals in the guidebook field – Meyer, Grieben, Woerl and Hartleben – were obliged to include.

There is no need to dwell any longer here upon the enormous superiority of Baedeker's guidebook empire, except to remark that the term "Baedeker" in Webster's International Dictionary was simply defined as "guidebook".

Let us now consider the special position which this house occupied in guide-book literature, with its descriptions of the city of Berlin, along with Berlin's place in its publishing programme. The first account of Berlin as "capital of the State of Prussia" in 1842 occupies, in Baedeker, 22 pages in a work 608pp. long, in the above-mentioned guide to Germany and Austria. The volume is modest in scope: a map (on linen) of the post-coach network, and eight small town plans. The plan of Berlin shows clearly that the town, with its 330,000 inhabitants at that time, had not yet fully grown out to its enclosing city wall. But have no fear! "Berlin is constantly expanding. Streets, squares, bridges, monuments arise from year to year. Progress is the basis of the Prussian state, and its traces may be seen in the capital also." (*ibid* p.392)

The success of a travel guide is to a large extent dependent upon its ability to be up-to-date and reliable. In contrast to other publishing houses, the firm of Baedeker, from its earliest beginnings, revised its individual editions very carefully, using an open, clear system (even today) of reworking the data for each new issue – one might well call it a declaration of loyal adherence to the latest available information. New editions of the guides were brought out annually and, till the 1880s, classified as "remodelled", "revised", "augmented" or even "improved". By this practice, Baedeker acquired a good deal of his prestige, and he liked to refer in the Prefaces to his works (with a mixture of conscientiousness and commercial adroitness), to the importance of being up-to-date: "The Editor expressly rejects complaints, as sometimes occur, based upon *earlier editions.* There is no worse form of penny-pinching among the travelling public, than to journey with an out-of-date guidebook. A single copy of the new edition often pays for itself straight away." (From *Deutschland und Österreich,* 15th ed. 1872 etc.)

The invention of the star or asterisk (*) in the guidebook, as a sign of something significant or outstanding, is ascribed to Karl Baedeker. The first ones were awarded in 1846 in the handbook for Germany and Austria (not in 1844, as is stated repeatedly, even in Baedeker's later publications); 24 stars are awarded to Berlin for monuments, buildings and institutions, exactly as many as the imperial city of Vienna received. Baedeker's cornucopia of asterisks opens wider still, of course, for the paintings in the great Berlin collections. Berlin's chief artistic sight – awarded the only double-star in 1846 – were the six panels from the Ghent winged altar by the brothers Van Eyck, a major monumental work of medieval altar-painting. (They had to be returned to Belgium in 1920, under the terms of the Treaty of Versailles).

Berlin's place as a musical city is also given due recognition in Baedeker, even in the early edition. The Singing Academy, the Stern Gesangverein [musical society], the orchestra of the Royal Opera and other organisations contributed to this reputation, which Baedeker defined in 1867: "The achievements of the various institutions in the field of classical music are not surpassed in any other European capital, and are part of the most significant contribution made by Berlin to the arts." And that, although the Philharmonic was not founded until 16 years later!

Getting hold of theatre tickets was not always an easy matter, just like nowadays. For Berlin's opera and theatre, the 1883 (and later) Baedeker guide reports the following procedure: "It is almost imperative to get a good seat early on. If one reserves in advance by post-card, the Royal Theatre box office will keep the desired seats, where feasible. These post-cards must be placed in the special box at the Opera House, door no.7, opp. the Catholic church, between 10 a.m. and noon on the day before the performance. It is advisable to do this in person, since an official sitting in the window keeps a check, to prevent misuse by touts and suchlike. During the course of the same day, the person ordering the tickets will receive the card returned by post, either stamped "confirmed" or with a blue line across it, if the booking is refused. One may send a hotel servant to collect the tickets the following morning. A reserved ticket costs 50Pf. more than one bought at the box office."

The guide to Germany and Austria, ever more copious from one edition to the next, because of the constant increase in data, was soon issued also in separate offprints for the individual areas. One has the impression of a kind of bibliographic fan, with the branching system of part-volumes and other sub-divisions, as Baedeker, with ever greater attention to detailed accuracy, divided his account of the German-speaking countries into several volumes.

The title *Berlin,* as a separate printing from the 18th ed. of *(Mid- and) North Germany,* appeared for the first time in 1878, but it was not until the 4th ed. that it finally became independent as an "extension of the description hitherto found in the traveller's Handbook for *N. Germany"* (whose more succinct account of Berlin was intended for the "hasty" traveller).

At two-year intervals, almost without exception, the new editions came out until the outbreak of the First World War: this was the era of the firm's greatest economic prosperity and of the ever-growing area covered by its descriptions. Baedeker earned his necessary "small coin" from the guides for local tourism. The volumes *S. Bavaria, Tyrol* etc. and *Switzerland* are a good example of this, with their frequent appearances at 2-year intervals: for *S. Bavaria* the even years were chosen for publication, for *Switzerland* the odd ones.

No other Baedeker Handbook attained such a wealth of reworking as did these two lasting successes, with the exception of the guide to Berlin. In this case, it is doubtless not just a matter of paying homage to the imperial capital, but also of addressing the market. In his guidebook programme, Baedeker brought out only three city guides which had long runs: *Paris* (1855-1937), *London* (1862-1930) and *Berlin* (1878-1936). The first two were prompted by the World (or, as they were then termed, "Industrial") Exhibitions, with which the firm undestandably produced guides to coincide (elsewhere, also). It is however probably erroneous to view the Berlin Congress of 1878 as the stimulus for producing the edition; the provisional appearance of the off-print contrasts with the redrawing of the maps in this edition, which must have required a great deal of time.

We now therefore have an account of Berlin spanning various titles, various lengths of book and various languages, which is what one might expect from the constant reworking and augmenting of the material. In addition to Baedeker's complete guide to Germany and Austria which, by the 15th ed. of 1872, had become an extremely unwieldy tome (and was not issued again), and the actual *Berlin* title (1878-1936), there were the guides to *Mid- and North Germany* (later divided into *NW. Germany* and *NE. Germany), Germany in one volume* from 1906, (an attempt to portray the German Empire more succinctly), *Brandenburg* (after World War I) and the *Autoguide for the German Reich* (1938 & 1939, in co-operation with the DDAC), all of which give only limited information about the imperial capital.

The old Baedeker strictly differentiates the Berlin coffee-houses and pastry-shops, perhaps mainly for the reason that smoking was originally banned in the latter. The Viennese-style coffee-house with its puffing newspaper readers only spread in Berlin after the middle of the 19th c., while pastry-shops were already long since established, and run solely by foreigners: the proprietors were called Stehely, Spargnapani, Giovannoli & Josty. The Grisons, especially the rough Upper Engadine – at that time quite free from the blessings of winter tourist traffic – exported several industrious pastry-cooks to Berlin.

From 1860 onwards, it was possible to read in French about Berlin in Baedeker, from 1868 in English also, at that time in fairly bulky guides to the country. *Berlin* as such appeared in French only as separate editions for two special occasions: in 1885 for a geology convention, and in 1908 for the 12th International Press Congress; on both occasions, the book was issued as a complimentary gift from the then organising committee. *Berlin and its Environs* (in

English) came out, nonetheless, six times between 1903 and 1923 as part of the normal publishing programme.

The 21st German edition of *Berlin,* issued for the 1936 Olympic Games, was the last to appear before World War II from Baedeker's family premises (since 1872) in Leipzig. From the short account of Berlin's history as it was set down in the 1936 Baedeker, I quote this extract, whose tone and content were inevitable under the prevailing conditions of the day: "After the (First) World War, a new, somewhat volatile, development of the city began, but it was a partly unhealthy one, lacking as it did any economic stability. In its cultural life, the capital of the Reich soon became a theatre for various influences to meet and do battle, among whom foreign cultural elements came at times strongly to the fore. *National Socialism,* led by Joseph Goebbels, had successfully taken up the fight since 1926 against Marxism and Communism, both of which had developed particularly strongly here. Many National Socialists, Horst Wessel among them, fell victim to Communist attacks. After Adolf Hitler was summoned by Reich President Hindenburg on the 30th January 1933, Berlin became the Führer's official seat."

The Baedeker firm's offices were destroyed by bombs in 1943, along with the majority of data. From 1949 onwards, a new generation of Baedeker guides appeared, emanating partly as products of the family concern, partly from other publishers using the name under licence. Berlin was still – or, perhaps one should say "once again" – on the menu: with a final refashioning of the Berlin Baedeker, in the guise of individual guides to separate parts of the city, and a new Grosse Ausgabe [major edition, 1986], a decisive bridge to the present was built.

In the narrower period (1842-1940) which is dealt with here, it is worth emphasising as a bibliographic statistic that descriptions of Berlin came out almost every year in one or other of the three languages; of these 99 years, 72 carried editions, the only largish gap being the five years during the First World War. If you discount the short descriptions in the main guides, there are still 58 detailed descriptions of the city for the stated period: a dense and, to our modern way of thinking, close-knit mesh of contemporary information, constantly updated.

If one examines the mapwork, as it appears in the chronological sequence of Baedeker's descriptions of Berlin, one likewise finds a development which is ever more intensified and precise in detail. The small town plan of 1842, which is 7.8 X 10.7 cm. in format, is not arranged vertically, finishing in the W. at the Brandenburg Gate, and in the E. with the present-day Jannowitz Bridge: the coverage N-S runs runs from Invalidenstrasse (Rosenthal Sq.) to the Halle Gate. To the right of the plan there is even room for a key with 39 items.

These lithographic plans were not printed on the page itself, but stuck, as separate sheets, to the next page with a thin streak of paste, a labour-intensive but customary procedure, which continued unaltered until the end of Baedeker's "classical" era. Plans and maps on lithographic blocks have the advantage that they can be corrected in detail, totally in keeping with the firm's practice.

One cannot deny that the old-style town plans as used by Baedeker offer a certain charm to the eye: delicately hatched areas for residential quarters, incorporated into a network of streets, sometimes giving way to the squared grid, sometimes surrounding the city centre concentrically, sometimes pushing out to the periphery. Berlin, expanding after the mid-19th c., makes a positively aesthetic impression in Baedeker's lithographic plans.

Enlargements of the plans of the city soon appeared: in 1846 they increased to 12.6 X 16.5 cm., in 1859 to 20.8 X 31.8 cm. (as a fold-out map in several sections). In 1872, an enlarged detailed map of the inner city was added. For the 1878 editions, the maps underwent substantial alteration, as had already occurred in the Handbooks for *Paris, London* and *Central Italy* (from 1855, 1862 and 1866 respectively): a large town plan was included, in three fold-out strips, in an appendix at the end of the book, which formed an easily detachable booklet. At the heart of this rearrangement of the maps for large cities lay a practical question: how to find one's way around without the bother of unfolding a plan in the open air (perhaps even in a wind). Without laying claim to a "patent folding" process, often met with today, the problem was simply but most efficiently solved by the firm of Baedeker and Wagner & Debes'

Geographical Institute, which had, for a long time, provided the maps and plans for the guides.

The strip-maps, a little over 60cm. in length and, in small octavo, 15cm. high, depicted the layout of the city in significantly greater detail than before, being to the almost uncannily precise scale of 1 : 14,283 (previously 1 : 27,800 or, without indication, approx. 1 : 29,000). A general reference plan and a map of Berlin and its environs completed the collection, together with a 7-page index of streets and buildings. The tight grid superimposed on the plans made it easier to find specific places. The extent of the area covered ran N-S from the S. edge of Humboldthain to Kreuzberg or Victoriapark, and E-W from Ernst-Reuter-Platz, the former "Knie", out to a point slightly beyond Oberbaumbrücke [Oberbaum Bridge].

As further editions of the *Berlin* title appeared, the amount of maps steadily grew. Outline plans of museums, a plan of the horse-drawn tramways, a completely new plan of Potsdam (which used as its basis the same lithographic stone from 1880 to 1936), then, later on, (1887), a map of the further environs, followed by a plan of Charlottenburg. The 1900 edition offered the three strip-maps to a new scale of 1 : 20,000, covering a wider area: vertically from Osloer Strasse (then "Kristiania-Strasse") to the N. edge of Tempelhofer Feld (during its transition from barren steppe to airlift airport, it had then reached the stage of parade-ground); horizontally, following the E-W run of the N. Ringbahn [peripheral railway]. A rather unfortunate choice of grid-marking, in the form of squares numbered not entirely logically, must be mentioned as a shortcoming rather than a positive new development.

After this, in 1928, the plan of the inner city was added in a highly detailed 1 : 12,500 scale. The plans of the "villa colony Grunewald" (1910), the "SW suburbs" (1912) and "Westend" (1914) showed the city's energetic spread to S. and W. The "horse-tram plan" had long since had to change its homely title to "tramway plan" and later to "plan of the transport system".

The between-wars editions – 1921, 1927, 1933 in a "small edition" and 1936 – which could no longer maintain the previous revision standard of every two years, display signs of austerity in the stock of maps also. Nonetheless, 1927 was augmented once more, with a plan of the "SW suburbs II" (Zehlendorf, Nikolas-See), including the "Wannsee" [lake] and a plan of the Botanic Gardens.

The final edition of 1936 (no longer linen-bound, but only in card covers) makes a thorough rearrangement of all the maps and plans, by virtue of the material then extant; from now on the editorial part of the guide shrinks from the 210 pages of the earlier description of the city, to 156. There is also a reworking of the cartographic material which throws a wan light over the proceedings: because of the war, and an edict of the 6th of February 1940 concerning map publication, the labelling of potentially important and strategic buildings, installations etc. had to be erased from the plans, along with the layout of the railway stations. This attempt at cover-up however leads to a paradox: on p.65 of the book, the Berlin Funkturm [Radio Tower] is described indeed, and given an asterisk into the bargain, but it is not to be found on the adjacent plan of Westend – unless you know what the red dot in square F4 means!

Such tricks did not, of course, put a stop to the destruction caused by bombing raids. It is a fact that army units used Baedeker's maps as information that was easily acquired and reliable. It is also a fact that there was a stock of Baedekers, ready at hand, by Hitler's sleeping quarter in the Führer HQ "Wolfsschanze". The perverted notion of using, for militaristic and destructive purposes, a travel guide intended to aid tourism and bring peoples closer together, is thus complete: air-raids on London by the German Luftwaffe were known as "Baedeker raids" in current English parlance, just as RAF pilots used a list of strategic buildings and installations in German cities, arranged in priority groupings, entitled *A Bomber's Baedeker.* (From *The Destruction of Darmstadt,* exhibition catalogue by the State Archive of Hesse, Darmstadt 1984).

The power of attraction of the name *Baedeker* as a trade mark had been recognised and exploited earlier by others also. In the case of Berlin, it was the cartographic publisher Alexius Kiessling who wanted to capitalise on the firm's good name by bringing out a

Berlin Baedeker. He did not adhere so ethically to his model's other precepts, however, such as the refusal to accept advertising copy. The "Berlin Baedeker", with its well-arranged ads., cost 2 marks in its illustrated edition, that is to say one mark less than the non-advertising original, and appeared in more than thirty editions, from the end of the 1870s until the First World War. In an age which knew little about protection of trademarks, Baedeker was unable, for a long time, to defend himself effectively against the misuse of his name. Even a law of 1896, concerning unfair competition, did not help the firm much. Baedeker later had more success in actions brought to guarantee the right of exclusive use of his own name. The author Werner Bergengruen learnt to his dismay that his novel *Baedeker des Herzens* [A Baedeker of the Heart], which appeared in Berlin in 1932, struck no pleasant chords at all in Baedeker's heart, and he was forced to undertake an alteration of the title of the second edition to *Badekur des Herzens* [A Spa Cure for the Heart].

Just as the technical and economic potential of the firm of Baedeker underwent enormous transformation during the period we have covered here, so did the manner in which the author composed for his readership the descriptions of itineraries and places. The plain, sympathetic text of the pre-revolutionary (i.e. pre-1848) Baedeker, which did not see itself as a personal description of travel, but tried everywhere to strike a more objective note (e.g. not "this is what I found" but "this is what one finds, or should expect to find"), stands in strong contrast to the data-crammed catalogue of catchwords of the turn of the century and beyond. Now and then we find the most varied half-tints in the writing. Baedeker's style totally breathes the spirit of its age, with an economy that merits our gratitude: the writers never felt themselves in duty bound to emulate the literary festooning so current at the time. Their sentences are clear, if anything on the short side, sometimes with pathos but never grandiloquent. Whether plain or modernistic, it is the utterance which counts, the view, never too verbose nor too terse. The text is always economical, and the two following excerpts may be regarded as fairly typical:

> *Halle Gate with Belle-Alliance Square mark the end of the Friedrichstrasse, 4250 paces long, which cuts right through Berlin from S. to N., ending in the N. with Oranienburg Gate. A*

good walker must step out, if he wishes to get from one gate to the other within the hour.
(1842, *Deutschland und der österreichische Kaiserstaat*, p.406)

The considerable amount of traffic in the cramped Potsdamer Platz is regulated by, apart from traffic police, light signals from a tower. The lively bustle may be conveniently observed from the Bellevue Konditorei (cake-shop), *N. side, the café of Hotel Fürstenhof (S. side) and Josty's cake-shop and restaurant Pschorrhaus (W. side). In the evening, many illuminated signs.*
(1927 *Berlin,* 20th ed. p.164)

If one draws comparisons, on a contemporary plane, between Baedeker's portrayals of Berlin (or any of the German cities) and the rest of the extensive guidebook programmes, a further difference of style comes to light: whatever is strange is seen from the viewpoint of an educated middle-class German; one is surprised or amazed, one finds something peculiar or repugnant. Things which would not be worthy of mention in one's everyday life suddenly move (when one is travelling) into focus as meriting attention, or a remark, or our scorn, or a peril to beware of. The Russian railways, baksheesh in Egypt, Dutch cleanliness or haggling over prices in Italy – all these circumstances of life or of travel, mentioned in the description, notice or tip, suddenly get rather bigger than life size, which is one reason why reading old guidebooks is not only interesting but often pleasurable as well.

That a serious guide such as Baedeker could not (or would not) fulfil all the desires of his travelling public, was quite obvious in the demure climate of the 19th c. Doubly remarkable, therefore, is the following delicate hint:

Popular festivals on a magnificent scale, whose unique goings-on ladies would however do best to avoid, take place during the summer months at Sternecker's Neue Welt (New World), *36c Hasenheide.* (1883).

Cabs, valets, the pneumatic post, advertising columns – all are found in the "Practical Remarks" by Baedeker in his Berlin guides;

a paragraph is even allotted to the "Public Convenience" (privately-run; prop. R. Protz). Even here is testimony to Wilhelmine thoroughness, in dividing the use of the toilet into 1st class (10 Pfennigs) and 2nd class (5 Pfennigs), and to Baedeker's punctiliousness in recording such evidence of class-consciousness (1889).

Baedeker doubtless shied away from too original a view when writing about one's stay in Berlin, and he nearly always managed to draw a matter-of-fact picture of the city, untroubled by any suggestion of the scurrilous. To gain a breath of the charm of the exotic, one need only betake oneself, Baedeker in hand, to the ethnic section of the Art Gallery at the Royal Palace, to marvel at the splendours on display there in 1847:

> *A feather cloak which Kamehamcha, king of the Sandwich Islands, presented to Frederick William III, in exchange for which he received a complete uniform of the 2nd regiment of guards; the Pasha of Shumla's saddle, who was strangled because he surrendered that fortress to the Russians in 1828; model of a Chinese lady's foot; a 3-inch long case in silver filigree, which elegant Chinese ladies wore to protect their finger-nails; the tattooed head of a New Zealander; and Australian necklace of human teeth; a Laço (sling) from S. America; a cigar, 1½ ft. long, such as the women smoke in Lima.*

> (From *Deutschland und der österreichische Kaiserstaat,* 3rd ed. 1847, p.469).

> Everything is to be found in Baedeker!

When Reinhard Öhlberger wrote his informative article, Germany was still divided and the Berlin Wall very much in place, as it had been since its erection in August 1961. My two post-war Baedekers of Berlin tell contrasting stories. The first, the English 7th edition (1965) says, rather woefully, in the Preface: "For political reasons the environs of Berlin are cut off from the capital, and we have therefore had to concentrate on the city itself, which is so disastrously divided by the Wall of 1961 into democratic West Berlin and communist East Berlin". The guide does sport 26 maps and plans, but the former are disfigured by a horrid red line – much in evidence in the strip maps at the back, where it is thick and green – which denoted the infamous Wall.

My other guide is the Allianz Reiseführer *Berlin,* 8th ed. 1992, set out, like the modern-style Baedekers of today, as a Gazetteer with a host of coloured photos, as well as maps and drawings. The Wall has gone, Germany is united again, and the Handbook is a bulky one – 332 pages.

In making mention of these two guides, I have strayed from the strict confines of the original *Baedekeriana* material, but it is necessary, as Baedeker would say, to be *aktuell* – i.e. up-to-the-minute. I wonder if the first Karl Baedeker (1801-59) has been turning in his grave?

The story is told of the German Emperor Wilhelm I who was receiving one morning an important visitor in an upstairs hall in his palace. Suddenly, hearing a clock chime, he broke off the conversation with a brief excuse, walked over to the French window, flung it open and stepped out on to the balcony.

After a few moments, he returned to his guest. 'I am so sorry, but, you see, it says in Baedeker that I do this at eleven o' clock every morning, and so therefore it is expected of me!'

(The following brief item is from Herbert Warren Wind's famous essay The House of Baedeker *in the* New Yorker, *quoted in Baedekeriana* no.9, Spring 1988):

Gisbert von Vincke, a German Shakespearean scholar, was making his way up the stairs to the roof of Milan Cathedral in 1844, when his attention was attracted by the man just ahead of him – a stocky fellow of about five feet seven, with broad features and muttonchop whiskers, who at regular intervals reached into his waistcoat pocket with his right hand, plucked out a small object and deposited it in a trouser pocket. Back at his hotel, von Vincke spotted this man in the dining room and learned from the head waiter that he was Baedeker. After the meal, he introduced himself to Baedeker and asked him if he would be kind enough to explain his strange ritual on the cathedral staircase. Oh, Baedeker said, with manifest pleasure, he had been counting the steps to the cathedral roof. To guard against losing his count, he had taken the precaution of filling a waistcoat pocket with a supply of peas. After every twenty steps, he had transferred a pea from that pocket to his trouser pocket.
("194 steps inside and 300 outside the edifice": from *Northern Italy,* 4th ed. 1877. Could this have been the origin of the six pebbles in the umpire's pocket in cricket?)

The Baedeker-Murray Correspondence

by W. B. C. Lister and M. R. Wild

In Roget's Thesaurus, Baedeker and Murray can be found cheek by jowl under the headings "itinerary" and "guidebook". Many people know that there was some kind of collaboration between the two men in the production of guidebooks – especially the European ones – but who helped whom, and when, has often been a debatable question. By printing here a goodly selection of the extant correspondence between the houses of Baedeker and Murray, it is hoped that the reader will be enlightened as well as entertained on a subject which is of no small moment to those who collect these Handbooks.

The letters which passed between Karl Baedeker I and John Murray III, such as survive, are both enthralling and tantalising: the former, because they throw considerable light upon the ways in which the two publishers helped (and occasionally hindered) one another in the field of guidebook production, and the latter because it is mainly a one-sided correspondence consisting of the letters from Karl Baedeker and his son Ernst, still extant in the Murray archives. The bombing of the Baedeker offices in Leipzig in the war doubtless destroyed John Murray's answers to these letters, through there *are* three by Murray here as well. Bill Lister has done deep research into the Murray archives, and confirms that the letter-books do not contain copies of any other letters to the firm of Baedeker. Most of the letters are, of course, in German (in a very neat hand which, however, was very difficult to decipher in places). One letter, from Ernst Baedeker, is in French; others by him are in English.

Before we look at the correspondence itself, it is useful to examine how Karl Baedeker and John Murray came to collaborate with one another, seeing that they were, after all, rivals in the same field. When Murray's first handbook – *Travellers on the Continent, being a guide through Holland, Belgium, Prussia and Northen Germany, and along the Rhine from Holland to Switzerland* - appeared in 1836, Karl Baedeker I was 35, and had been running his bookshop and publishing firm in Coblence for nine years. Since 1832, he had been selling J.A.Klein's *Rheinreise* [Guide to the Rhine], which he had bought, together with the firm of Röhling. This was not a "Baedeker", and it is dubbed "D 0" in the Hinrichsen notation. Fritz Baedeker was later to describe it as a book "which possessed many of the features of a modern guidebook". "D 1" was a reworking by Baedeker of the *Rheinreise*, and it appeared ("without a year") in 1835, with a pictorial cover. He had the grace to give Klein's name still as the author, and to put his own name as the publisher on the title page.

John Murray's *Handbook for Travellers on the Continent* was not sold by Baedeker in his shop on the Paradeplatz in Coblence until the 4th edition of that book was published in 1843, when Murray sold him 100 copies, followed by a sale of 125 copies of the 5th edition in 1845. After that, the ledgers become unspecific, but there is internal evidence in the correspondence of continued dealing. As Alex Hinrichsen put it, "Baedeker learned to develop an original concept from this, the result being three volumes issued [by him] in 1839: the 3rd edition of *Rheinreise* and the first editions of *Belgien* and *Holland.*" The Preface contained an acknowledgment of Baedeker's obligation to "the most distinguished Guidebook ever published, Murray's *Handbook for Travellers,* which has served as the foundation for Baedeker's little book."

The Rhine guide was in a yellow pictorial cover, and all the information for it had been collected by Karl Baedeker himself. Fritz Baedeker wrote: "It was the sight of the numerous English travellers following the footsteps of Childe Harold with Murray's handbook under their arms, that suggested to him the desirability of providing his German countrymen with similar books for other parts of Europe. The German Handbooks which he then successively published certainly owed a great deal to Mr Murray's books, but included a lot of his own descriptions, and in the important practical points (recommendation of hotels, tips on means of communication, etc.) were completely independent. My father, indeed, spent his life in traversing and re-traversing the countries treated of in his Handbooks. His obligations to Mr Murray were for many years – indeed, I believe, till his death – frankly and fully acknowledged in the prefaces of his handbooks."

It was in 1838 that John Murray (who, as we shall see, praised Baedeker's German volumes) brought out the 1st edition of his *Switzerland and the Alps of Savoy and Piedmont,* having issued *Southern Germany (a guide to Bavaria, Austria, Tyrol, Salzburg, Styria etc., the Austrian and Bavarian Alps and the Danube from Ulm to the Black Sea)* the previous year. Baedeker's first *Schweiz* appeared in 1844, his first guide to *Deutschland und der österreichische Kaiserstaat* [Germany and the Austrian Empire] in 1842.

The chart on page 54 shows the dates when the various Murrays (in English only) and Baedekers (in German, French and English) first appeared. This is intended only for comparison, for Murray and Baedeker Handbooks each ran to many editions (up to the First World War in Murray's case, and thereafter in Baedeker's case). Space would not permit a full table which would illustrate Murray's point, made in 1889 at the end of his life, that "although Messrs Baedeker have brought out some 18 different guidebooks, every one of them has been preceded and anticipated by a Murray's handbook for that particular country." As we shall see, this perception was to influence the relationship of the two publishing houses down the years.

It is a well-known fact (and Baedeker was the first to admit it), that Baedeker relied heavily upon Murray's handbooks in the early days. Tourism was developing rapidly, as the railways began to cover Europe, and the traveller's appetite for facts, figures and maps became insatiable. Baedeker's method of personally collecting material and vetting hotels proved to be too slow. Murray was pleased enough to supply material (culled by his large army of authors) and allow Baedeker to use it in German, until relations between the two houses were soured by fierce competition (some quarter of a century after Karl Baedeker I died). As we see from his letters, Baedeker spoke openly about the copious material which he was allowed to use in his early editions (not to mention the famous red cover, which he adopted from 1856, Murray having used it almost from the start).

Friction, however politely disguised in the correspondence, began to show when Ernst Baedeker took over the responsibility for running the firm in 1859. Letters of that time between Murray and Ernst and Karl Baedeker II dwell upon that transitional period (see below).

So much by way of setting the scene: now for the letters themselves. They cover the period from 10th December 1838 to 12th November 1862, and are 24 in number. In reading them through, one is immediately struck by the genuine warmth and cordiality which shine through the crust of polite letter-writing style. Murray and Baedeker were much of an age, and in the same business, both aware of the problems of bringing out handbooks of this kind (and with such frequency) in competition with one another, as well as a multitude of other travel publishers (Meyer, Grieben, etc.), albeit that, during this particular period, the competition between them for the British traveller's market was minimal. The postal service was almost as slow and expensive as it is today(!) It is good to see that they bought each other's books: Murray's edition of Byron as against Baedeker's *Conversation Manual,* and, of course, the Guides themselves, of which each publisher would send off a complimentary copy to the other when it appeared.

Political circumstances and wars remain on the periphery in this correspondence, but they damaged the fortunes of Baedeker more than those of Murray. Baedeker sent his son Ernst to do a stint of apprenticeship with Williams & Norgate in London. We do not know who was responsible at Murrays for transcribing and translating Karl Baedeker's German. In the letters which follow, the occasional place where words were really indecipherable, is indicated with "..."

In the first letter of the collection, dated 10th Dec. 1839, Karl Baedeker makes the first reference to his younger brother Adolph, who had settled as a bookseller in Rotterdam, and was his forwarding agent:

> My dear Mr Murray,
>
> I am sure you will have received the letter which I wrote to you a short time ago. I am using the favourable opportunity which now presents itself, to send you the second edition of the little book, to which you showed favour with such… success, and request similar goodwill for this second edition. I am also enclosing the… calendar, which contains a precise list of the postal messengers in the state of Prussia and the neighbouring countries. I had noted down an extract from it for myself, of which I likewise enclose a copy for you. The first and second pages are taken from the calendar, the third page contains note which I have gathered by making inquiries on the spot.
>
> When will the printing of Southern Germany commence? I have received back my ms. for Austria with many alterations and corrections, but do not yet have the ms. for Bavaria and Württemberg. I imagine however that I might be able to make… improvisations for you now and again. I am only too pleased to devote all my knowledge and my copious notes to your book, if you will send me the monograph or, even better, the proofs, before they are printed. I will look through them, compare, advise and note down variations, as well as I can, and leave it then to you, what you choose to adopt or not. I bind myself to returning the proofs always on the day I receive them. If you send them by steamer to Rotterdam to my brother, he can send them on… volumes. Such despatches take 48 hours to get here from Rotterdam, and this route is also the least expensive. In this way, barely 8 days would be needed, to send corrections here from London, and back again.
>
> The printing of my books will hardly commence before April or May of next year, perhaps even later. I have abbreviated and discarded a great deal which your Southern Germany contains, because it describes foreign parts which may well be of interest to your countrymen, but quite unnecessary for mine.
>
> Do you know "Munich" by Dr Förster, Munich 1838, publ. by the Literary and Aesthetic Institute? It is a very good book. The guide to the Sudetenland by Kern (for Silesia and

the Riesengebirge), on the other hand, is of little use to me. I wrote to you about that in my last letter.

I commend myself to your kind consideration,

Your most devoted

Baedeker.

Coblenz, 10th December 1839.

Here we find stated, in so many words, that not only did Baedeker draw upon Murray's works, but the reverse also happened. It would seem that there was a previous (missing) letter, and that others are maybe missing between the ones printed here. The next few letters indicate the problems of consigning books from England to Germany.

To John Murray's Bookshop in London

Coblenz, the 13th of September 1843.

You were so good as to send me, with an invoice of the 7th of August, 10 Handbooks for Southern Germany, which have only just reached me today, as they were held up for so long in Rotterdam. Messrs. Deutz and Jordan will be so kind as to settle up the amount for me, in this connection.

When you sent me 100 Northern Germany in the Spring, there were also 10 Southern Germany, 2nd ed., in the box, doubtless included in error. Because everyone had the review of the impending new edition, I was quite unable to sell a single copy of this, and thus seek your instructions on this matter.

Do you think that you might be able to use a number of copies of my Manual for Travellers?

With best respects, your servant,

K. Baedeker.

The edition of Baedeker's *Switzerland,* mentioned in the next letter, was of course the German version *(Schweiz)* of 1844. His offer of the *Traveller's Manual of Conversation* has more than a tinge of desperation. Murray and Williams & Norgate seem to have been the only outlets in Britain at that time for Baedeker's Handbooks.

My dear Mr Murray,

If no new editions should be appearing this year, then I request you to send me the following, via my brother in Rotterdam:

20 Switzerland
12 France
2 Central Italy
2 Byron's works in one vol.
2 Moore's " " " "
2 Childe Harold illustrated edition.

In the next few days my new travel book through Switzerland will be finished; last year, I travelled all round that country on a tour of inspection and hope that my book will be able to rejoice in your acclaim, upon which I set great value. Joanne's book is more thorough and better, as might well be expected of a Frenchman, but (…it lacks…) the circumspection and tact, not to include too much or too little, which is the hallmark of your books, and which has awarded you such a fine reputation. I shall take the earliest opportunity to send you a copy of my Switzerland. I should be grateful if the above-mentioned books could be dispatched as soon as possible: I am going to Rotterdam at Whitsun, and can pick them up there myself. Can you not make use of my Traveller's Manual?

Fare you well, my dear sir, and continue to show me your goodwill and friendship.

K. Baedeker . (2.5.1844)

Baedeker's trust in Murray's discretion seems to be borne out in his next letter, where he is openly critical about France. We do know that Karl Baedeker I approved the idea that his sons should don military uniform and, if required, fight for their country against the French. It is also significant that there is mention, for the first time, of the other long-running competitor Joanne, which later became Hachette and now appears as the Guide Bleu.

John Murray Esq., London

Coblenz, June 5th 1844.

Dear Sir,

Our friend Jordan is bringing you these lines, together with the book about Switzerland. The routes which I worked on from my personal observation I have marked in the Contents in pencil. I think, however, that there should be few errors in it, since two of my friends, men of letters and scholarship in Basle and Zurich, have read the ms. closely and made many comments, which I have used. Both know their homeland, Switzerland, from many walks undertaken through it. They have asked me if I feel inclined to produce a volume on France, based on your book. I do not think that such a book would find a rewarding market in Germany. My countrymen on the whole journey little in France, with perhaps the exception of Paris. And anyone who goes to Paris buys a French guide there. In any case, I do not feel inclined to take on such an enterprise. I do not like France, I have not been to Paris myself, and do not feel moved to do so. I should, on the other hand, like to come to England one day, and shall doubtless bring this idea to fruition later on.

I was recently in Holland, to collect material for a new edition, which is to appear this year; I shall permit myself to send you a copy of it later on.

The box of books reached me intact, and I have verified that the contents agree with the invoice. One copy of Childe Harold was unfortunately not pristine, but slightly damaged. One page was stained even, with drops of water, which must have been noticed in London, for the invoice slip had been inserted at that place. It is page Q that is wholly stained, and I beg you to replace this.

I sent the box in transit through Holland, otherwise I should have had to pay the expensive Dutch duties on it. But the costs of sending via Rotterdam are so high, that a pound (in weight) from London to Rotterdam costs 4 pence, whereas from Rotterdam to here scarcely 1 penny. I do not suppose you know of a cheaper route than Rotterdam for the outstanding 12 volumes of France?

In the next few days I shall send to you through the Düsseldorf Steamship Company (which is connected with the General Steam Navigation Company):

100 Traveller's Manual.	100 Thalers	
at 10%	50 "	
	50 "	+ 7½£.

You should not find these difficult to sell. Williams & Norgate take quite a lot of them.

I am deducting another 1£ from the above prices for the card for the covers, so that I am charging you £6.10s. for the entire consignment. The sale price in Germany is 1 Thaler per copy, or 3s.

Fare you well, my dear Mr Murray, with deepest respects,

Your very devoted Baedeker.

For a reason which we do not know, Baedeker seems to have abandoned the intermediary services of his brother Adolph in favour of others. KB I is still tramping around his homeland, collecting data for the printing of the next edition of *Germany* (in German), only 6 months or less from the time of his researches. Could anyone produce a guidebook update as quickly and meticulously today? It may be that the sentiments expressed here, as to the reluctance by Baedeker to produce a guide to France or to Paris could have sown the seeds of a belief in Murray's mind that germinated in the ensuing correspondence.

Dear Sir,

Provided that no new editions should appear before Spring 1846, I request you to send me the following through the good offices of Mr P.A. van Es in Rotterdam:

50 Northern Germany
10 Southern "
25 Switzerland
12 France
4 Central Italy
4 Northern Italy.

If a new edition of Northern Germany should already have appeared, I ask you to send 100 copies of it.

You will have received the 3rd edition of "Belgien". Next month, I shall send you via our friend Jordan the 2nd edition of "Holland", as well as the 5th of "Rheinreise". The 3rd edition of "Deutschland" [Germany] is being printed in the autumn, but I intend to visit beforehand the Harz, the Island of Rügen and the Riesengebirge [Sudeten Mts.].

Please pass on the enclosed…

With my best respects, your very devoted Baedeker.

Coblenz, 28th April 1845.

One wonders if no answer to this was forthcoming from Murray as, in his next letter, Baedeker suggests that someone else has informed him of Murray's new edition of *Northern Germany.* At this time, Murray is much more established in the guidebook field than Baedeker. A waspish note *re* shipping expenses creeps in!

Mr J. Murray of London.

Coblenz, the 6th of August 1845.

According to private information given, Northern Germany has already appeared. I therefore request immediate despatch, but am reducing my order to 60 copies, and ask for the parcel from Williams & Norgate to be included.

Is there any likelihood of a new edition of Southern Germany and Switzerland next year? The copies which I received in May have unfortunately found few purchasers, because people are waiting for a new edition.

I was never charged shipping expenses before.

What were the contents of your delivery on the 20th of June (to the account of the 13th J.) and by whom was it despatched? I do not recall having received nor ordered a later delivery than that of May the 9th.

Regards, your most devoted K. Baedeker.

August 1845 did not seem to be the best month for sending postal items. Baedeker manages however, in the next letter, to curb his impatience, and say some nice things in anticipation of Mr Murray's latest offering.

Dear Mr Murray,

First a postal matter. Your Mr Cooke's letter of August 2nd did not arrive here until the 11th, having travelled via Hamburg: your Mr Day's letter came via France, between the 5th of August and the 10th, when it arrived here. I received your letter of the 9th, by way of contrast, on the morning of the 12th. This seems to suggest that the route via Ostende is the surest and best for the connection with the Rhineland. I ask you to be so kind as to use the latter route always for your future communications.

The 100 copies of Northern Germany despatched on the 4th of August have not yet arrived, so I have written today to Rotterdam, and am very much looking forward to their arrival. At the same time, I am personally looking forward also to seeing an attractive book again. I can imagine that you have devoted a good deal of love to your work on it. I thank you in advance for your mention of my own writings, though I have not yet seen it.

My journey of almost two months, chiefly taken up with visiting Copenhagen, has given me copious material for the third edition of the Handbook, which will commence printing in September. As soon as the new edition is done, I shall not neglect my duty in sending you a copy.

Fare you well, respected sir and friend, and retain your goodwill towards me.

Your very devoted K. Baedeker, Coblenz 12th Aug. 1845.

The next letter is the strangest in the whole collection, and surely one of especial interest to the student of Austrian and German history. Things were happening on the religious/political front (the two factions being inextricably linked), and presumably some kind of ferment was in progress which would blow off its lid in the year of revolutions in Europe, 1848. Could the "cages" referred to have contained heretics? Or were they simply used to carrry religious relics in procession?

My dear Mr Murray,

You cannot imagine how sorry I am that your wishes have received such dilatory treatment here. But you will realise that I am entirely blameless in this matter.

Even today, I can only send you the… "relics", [tr. note: the word seems to be either "Wiedertäufer", i.e. Anabaptists, or "Wiederläufer", which no dictionary has a word for, lit. "those who run again" – reprints, reruns?]. The cages were noted down, as my correspondent tells me, by using a telescope.

I have received the enclosed hopeless answer from Vienna. I do not think that anything else is to be achieved there, unless it is done through the Legation. Gerold's answer incidentally matches the whole state of things in Austria. The "aristos" have access to everything, the other people nothing.

I had offered 4 groats 5 thalers for the drawing in Aachen. My correspondent writes to me that nobody would take on the task for that sum. I asked again what they were demanding, to do it, but have received no answer. We can expect nothing from Aachen until 4 weeks have elapsed, they are too busy there with the “Heiligthumsfahrt” [pilgrimage to the relics]. The ultra-Catholic party is playing a dangerous game to let this follow immediately after the successful Trier pilgrimage. I think they will find they are mistaken. The bow was stretched too taut, it is hardly likely that weariness will not set in. The success of the Trier pilgrimage is due in no small part to the opposition of Rhenish Catholicism to Prussian Protestantism or, rather, to the liberal opposition in politics which cloaked itself in legal church garb, against the present system of the Prussian ministers, devout Protestants, to whom one offered “check” in this fashion.

The eyes of the liberal Catholics are beginning to open, though. They are already beginning to feel the pressure from the Jesuit party, and starting to oppose the latter’s efforts.

Please excuse these digressions, but I cannot talk to you only about business.

I am bound to thank you most warmly for the much too good opinion of me which you have printed in your new edition of Northern Germany. The book has gained a great deal in this new edition. Unfortunately, though, it is purchased far less often than previously, so that I still have over 50 copies in stock. It must be selling just as well as formerly in other places, however, for I never see an Englishman with any other guide than yours.

Coghlan’s is very rarely seen, but there are some German and Belgian booksellers who seem to be particularly concerned to circulate it.

I imagine that Switzerland will now be ready. I should like to have:

25 copies of same, and
10 North. Italy,

along with those which your Mr Neck will hand over on receipt of the enclosed. Please despatch them via Ostende, through the Prussian Consul, Herr Back, as soon as possible, also:

6 Byron’s works in one vol.

to be included.

When will the new edition of Southern Germany be appearing?

Fare you well, dear Mr. Murray, and keep your
hitherto good opinion of me, with continued esteem,
Your most devoted Baedeker, Coblenz.

My expenses for the drawings and postage come to 5 thalers 12sg., which I have charged to you at 16s.2d. Do you need any Traveller's Manuals this year?

Baedeker's brother has now moved to Cologne (perhaps for reasons of political discretion). Baedeker is still cross about being charged extortionate amounts for freight. Amid the amicable sentiments, he sounds out Murray, to see if unsold books can be sent back – the beginnings of "sale or return"?

Through the agency of our friend Jordan I am sending you, dear Mr. Murray, herewith the balance of £18.19s.3d. less 17s.2d. which I had spent out on drawings. The auction items have not been delivered to me, despite many reminders. Herr Mayer has not kept properly to his promise. If you still need the drawings, please tell me, and I shall then turn to another for help.

In my order for Southern Italy I had asked you not to send this on its own. My request was ignored by your shop and I was charged £1 for freight quite unnecessarily. Because of the expenses from London I had the honour to write to you on the 7th of August. It is inconceivable to me that a parcel from Albemarle Street to Blackwall should cost as much (5s.) as it does from Ostende to here.

May I commend to you the wishes of my brother in Cologne, which are contained in the enclosure?

Last year's travel season was so favourable to sales of the book about Germany, that I am now busy setting up a new printing of the 3rd edition. I will send you a copy in the Spring, with all the places marked, where changes and corrections have been made. I shall be preparing the new edition of Switzerland in 6 weeks' time, and am looking forward to being able to incorporate more thoroughly the many corrections of your own books.

With my continuing high regard,
Your grateful servant, Baedeker, 12.1.1847

You have put me to shame by the kindly way in which you mention me in your book. The 12 copies of France sent in 1845 are unfortunately still in my stock, with no prospect of disposing of them. Could you… arrange… to Brussels?

Ten days later, encouraged by Mr Murray's magnanimous agreement to accept back the 2-year-old copies of "France", Baedeker proposes to send some of "Switzerland" too. The guidebook-writer comes to the fore in the footnote about the Schams valley in Switzerland.

My dear Mr Murray,

I am grateful to you for your readiness to take back the 12 copies of France which I still have in stock and, as soon as I receive your answer to these lines, shall send them immediately via Herr Bach at Ostende. I can pay the postage as far as there. Please be so good as to charge me for carriage from Ostende to London.

The purpose of these lines is to ask if the new edition of Switzerland will be ready before the beginning of July. If so, I would ask you to take back also a dozen copies of the 3rd edition of that title, which I have in stock. If the new edition will not be coming out till August, I shall dispose of my residue by then. If ever a book has earned good fortune, it is your Switzerland. In my opinion, it is, in many individual ways, even better than your Germany.

As soon as the new edition of Switzerland is ready, I ask you to send me 50 copies via the good offices of Herr Bach at Ostende.

I should be glad if you would have a packet with Flügel's dictionary, which is at Mr Charles Deinhard's waiting for me, collected and packed.

If the new edition does not come out until August, it is too late for my debit for this book, and I would then ask you not to send the copies this year.

The enclosed comments result from my own observations, and I can vouch for their reliability.

You did not send me a copy of the 3rd edition of Switzerland for my own use. Shall I keep one of the ones which I am sending back?

Fare you well, my dear sir, With undying esteem,

Baedeker. Coblenz, 22, Jan. 1847.

Enclosure: the entire Schams valley is Protestant. The Hotel des Bains or Krone at Andeer is expensive for a country inn; I paid 3fr. for a simple lunch with wine. It is the best hotel between Chur and Chiavenna.

The next letter describes one of the sad moments in the history of missed opportunity. Elizabeth I never met Mary, Queen of Scots, Bach never met Handel, and it appears that Baedeker missed meeting Murray by a whisker. The problems of pirating pop up, which so afflicted both publishers. Baedeker, still a model of rectitude, continues to demand his pound of flesh!

> My dear sir and friend,
>
> How much I regret having had to forgo the pleasure of seeing you. I was on your tracks in Basle, but you had departed the same day that I arrived. We were also quite close to one another in Belgium later on, but it just was not possible to get hold of you. You will by now have collected a rich store of material for future editions of your excellent Handbooks which, despite all competition, have the upper hand. You will doubtless know that your rival Coghlan has had to flee from Belgium because of debts.
>
> In Germany alone, in this year, five new guides have appeared, which have copied and used mine to a large degree, including Forster. Despite his impractical verbosity, the latter will be hard to defeat, because he is published by Cotta. After a few years, though, the rest will be forgotten.
>
> When are the new editions to appear? In Spring, I hope, so that I can order again. Unfortunately I do not have the latest edition of Southern Germany here, otherwise I could give you many a tip. I spent four weeks in Bohemia and Austria last summer, and have gathered a wealth of material. I can also give you details about Venice, Padua, Verona and Milan, for I was there also.
>
> Mr Deinhard will settle my outstanding debt for £11.19s. You forgot, in your bill, to credit me with the 17s.2d. for the drawings. I must also complain to you that I never received my free copy, while everybody else here gets one free with every 25 from you. Please draw the despatchers' attention to this, if you would be so kind, so that these deficiencies may be rectified.
>
> Fare you well, dear sir, your most devoted Baedeker, as always.
>
> Instructions enclosed.

A gap of four years now occurs in the correspondence. Let us 'take a break', to study the comparative table of Baedeker and Murray guides on the next page.

The following table shows only those titles covered by both publishers.

Title	*Murray*	*Baedeker* German	French	English
Rhine	1836	1835	1846	1861
N. Germany	1836	1842	1860	1873
Holland, Belgium	1836	1839	1859	1869
S. Germany	1837	1842	1860	1868
Switzerland	1838	1844	1852	1863
Norway, Sweden, Denmark	1839	1879	1886	1879
Russia	1839	1883	1893	1914
Greece	1840	1883	1910	1889
Constantinople etc.	1840	1905	--	--
N. Italy	1842	1861	1861	1868
Central Italy	1843	1866	1867	1867
France	1843	1867	1884	1889-91
Spain	1845	1897	1900	1898
Egypt	1847	1877	1898	1878
S. Italy	1853	1866	1867	1869
Portugal (see also Spain)	1855			
Syria & Palestine	1858	1875	1882	1876
India	1858	1914	--	--
Paris	1864	1855	1865	1865
Algeria (see Mediterranean)	1873			
Mediterranean	1881	--	--	1911
Great Britain	1850-99*	1889	--	1887
London	1849	1862	1866	1878

*Murray brought out England and Wales from 1878. Unlike Baedeker, he did not issue anything for the American continent.

It is clear from this table that, until 1863, Murray published in English only, and Baedeker published later, sometimes after a long gap, in German and French only.

Back to the letters: the year is 1852, and Baedeker's tone to Murray is rather more straight from the shoulder than in the past. Judge for yourself…

> My dear Mr Murray,
>
> The enclosed gives me the opportunity, after a long interruption in our relations, to commend myself again to your memory. On the back of the letter you will find my answer, which went off today.
>
> I must however take this opportunity to tell you that there are loud complaints and expressions of regret from many quarters, that Mr Murray does not himself work at the new editions of his excellent books. I believe that these complaints are not entirely untrue. The books contain much that is out of date, and much that takes up unnecessary space. I know of course from my own experience that it is much easier to add new things than to delete old ones, that it is less toilsome to write a fat book than a good, handy, slim one; for instance, in the new (4th) edition of my Schweiz [Switzerland] which is ready from the press in the next few days, I had to choose a smaller type face, to keep down the number of pages and preserve the book's coat-pocket format. If that had not however been possible, I should have resolved to sacrifice the good to the better.
>
> It now seems to me that it would be greatly to the advantage of those who use your books, if you could find the time and enthusiasm, amongst your other numerous tasks, to cut as much text as possible with a critical and merciful pen. This is perhaps not such a necessity for your countrymen as for Germans; in England one is glad to pay an appropriate price for a good book, while in Germany, because of the considerable competition, everything has to be as cheap as possible. Nonetheless I believe that English readers would in time come to accept a briefer and cheaper good travel guide. It would not be possible for another hand to do this, if you see to the edition yourself, that is to say if you can bring down the price of your books to 10s. again, by making cuts. I repeat, it is very hard to sacrifice good material, but your books will gain

in practical useability by this means, which is a great advantage in a guide.

Last summer I was asked many times in Switzerland to produce an English version, but I resolutely declined, even to the Reverend gentleman in Stuttgart. Your Switzerland contains a lot of outdated material, even in its latest edition. If a new edition is being prepared this year, then I am quite happy to send you at once the new edition of mine which is currently at the printer's. This will happen later in any case, as soon as the book is quite ready. I will mark what is new and the results of my own observations. Only such amendments are of any value to me. I can get very little for my purpose out of books. I recently felt this again, when I picked up Ercher's latest edition. The book is excellent in parts, especially the southern valleys of the Valais, but the overall picture is not reliable and likewise contains a good deal of out-of-date facts, which is in fact unpardonable for a book on Switzerland. This can only be excused by the circumstance that the book must have been at least two years at the printer's.

I wanted to correct the list of booksellers – there are in fact names in your list which have no longer existed for 10 years, or which have recently gone bankrupt. I am however convinced that it is better to draw up an entirely new one. I enclose one here for you to use as you please. I have named those towns and booksellers where one can expect to sell, and where English tourists usually go.

Please be so good as to tell me which of my titles are appearing with you and when these will be ready, so that I can place my order later on.

I think that the year 1852 will be a good one for travel. Jordan sends his greetings. I commend myself to you as your grateful and devoted K. Baedeker (6.1.1852).

One can conjecture that Murray was in a huff about this, for Baedeker's next letter, written three and a half months later, complains that he had had no answer. There is a sidelong reference to the ravages which the year 1848 (revolts in most parts of Europe) caused to the tourist scene and, in so many words, a statement that the Baedeker-Murray connection was first and foremost a business one.

A long time ago I asked you, my dear Mr Murray, to let me know which of your travel guides will appear in new editions this year, but have received no answer. I therefore permit myself to repeat the questions with, at the same time, a request to send me your answer very soon to Coblenz, whither I shall be returning in 14 days. I am in fact on an exploratory journey for the North German section of my book, which I must reprint in the course of next month. I can give you very up-to-date information about Hamburg, Lübeck, Schwerin, Rostock, Stralsund, Rügen, Stettin, Posen, Danzig and Königsberg. I will do my utmost to send you the new edition of this part, also Schweiz [Switzerland] and Rhein [Rhine] after my return.

I must thank you profusely for the new edition of your unsurpassed Southern Germany. Herr Ehrmann will receive my copy. I wanted to wait until I could send it with my own new editions.

Concerning your new edition, I now wish to order direct from you again. Since my needs were small in the sad years of 1848 and afterwards, I managed by ordering these from Weigel, Eisen, Kornecker and others, but hope to have success from the imminent travel season and therefore wish to take up the business connection with you again.

With high esteem, your most devoted K.Baedeker, Coblence
Berlin, 25th April 1852.

Now it is Murray's turn to write, and the topic is again the old one of piracy. Between the lines, it appears that the realm of guidebooks was then, as now, a shark-infested sea, where the interests of men of integrity, such as Murray and Baedeker, could easily be com-promised by other editors who saw no need to go out in search of their own material. "Pirated" editions of Murray's works were produced in France and, before the Berne Copyright Agreement, publishers had to resort to court injunctions, to restrain their more predatory rivals.

My dear sir,

I have been compelled to apply for an injunction in our Court of Chancery to stop the sale of Mr Brogue's guide to Switzerland – a large part of it having been pirated from my Handbook. He tries to excuse himself for some of his thefts by stating that he borrowed them from Baedeker. Now as my book forms the "Grundlage" [basis] of yours, I wish you would write me a letter, which I may show if required what parts of my book were adapted by you in your first edition of your Schweiz. I do not refer to the later editions in which you have altered much, deriving information from your own experience in travelling.

I do not wish to deprive you of any merit of your work – but merely ask you to state the extent of your obligation to my book – pointing out the routes and number of pages which you incorporated – when you first commenced the enterprize of publishing a Swiss guide for the Germans. I beg you to answer this by return of post. I hope you received my letter about red cloth, enclosing specimen. I am, my dear sir,

Yours very faithfully,

John Murray.

Chas Baedeker Esq. (15.12.1852)

It is in the German-speaking areas that Baedeker is able to be of most use to Murray. They evidently covered the same terrain at times and, as always, the rattle of sabres is to be heard off-stage. We revert to KB:

Coblenz, 2nd Dec. 1853.

The results of my walking tour this year will soon be communicated to you, my dearest Sir and friend – Odenwald, Black Forest, Switzerland (Weissenstein, Diablerets, Zermatt, Gemmi, Faulhorn, Grimsel, Furka). They consist of three revised signatures (i.e. sets of 16pp.) of Schweiz and of the new edition of Rheinreise. I had not seen the Bernese Oberland for 5 years, but found that it is necessary from time to time to undertake a thorough revision of these much-visited places. I can particularly recommend the upper Lauterbrunnen valley to you. Apart from the 3 new sections mentioned above, I shall not print anything new about Switzerland this year, so that my observations in Valais will not come into their own until the next edition. I will mark for you everything that is new, so that you can gain a quicker impression and find more easily what may suit your own use.

In Solothurn I find the solid old comforts at the Hotel Krone. Herr Brunner had taken to heart your tip about the privies, which I had also drawn his attention to, years ago, and has completely reconstructed this delicate amenity to my total satisfaction. He begged me to tell you about this, which I promised to do.

The Bear at Imst in Tyrol has been well spoken of from various quarters. It is new and far better than all the post-houses. I hope that Prussia and Austria will find their true wellbeing only together with England and France. As far as Prussia is concerned, there is a great leaning in this direction. Then we need not fear that tourists will be scared off next year by the noise of war.

Cordial greetings, Yours, Baedeker.

In my copy of Baedeker's *Central Italy and Rome* (5th ed. 1877), *Spithoever* is still listed (now at Piazza di Spagna, Rome, nos. 84-5). Is it a sad reflection upon our modern book trade that booksellers do not set up shop any more in other people's countries? Perhaps this is just another result of two devastating world wars. At all events, Baedeker's integrity as a collector of information remains supreme:

My dear Mr Murray,

I learn from a message from my countryman Spithöver that his establishment was mentioned only in passing and given scant attention in the new edition of your book on Rome. This strikes me as unfair towards such a business as his, conducted as it is on the most honourable of principles. For almost 4 weeks I have daily been able to observe how this business is run, because I rented the rooms which had just fallen vacant next to the Reading Room, and thus have been daily to the bookshop. One finds a large number of English papers and magazines in the Reading Room, and the book business is run entirely on German lines, with fixed prices. I have encountered many Englishmen here, who have only praise for the way the shop is run.

I therefore regard it my duty to put a good word in with you on behalf of my thoroughly honest countryman. He feels that a favourable or less favourable judgment in your book is a matter of great importance to him. You have already been told that Spithöver has likewise taken over Monsaldini's business at 79-80, Piazza di Spagna.

With cordial regards, Yours, K. Baedeker,
Rome. (30.4.1856).

And now, just three years before his death at the age of 58, here is Karl Baedeker commending his son Ernst, who is being groomed to manage the retail bookshop (which he in fact stepped into in January 1859).

My dear friend,

May I introduce to you the bearer, my son Ernst, who has entered Mr Williams's business as an assistant. If he may be accorded the same goodwill that his father has always enjoyed from you, then both father and son will owe you a debt of constant gratitude. He is gradually becoming part of our brotherly guild. After studying for a year at Heidelberg, he was briefly in Paris, to revise and prepare my book on that city, for the printing of a new edition, and he discharged his task very well. He is also conversant with the western part of Germany and part of Switzerland, and can perhaps give you the occasional snippet for a new edition of your books. Everything is constantly changing so.

Fare you well, my dear Murray, and keep me in good remembrance,

Ever your grateful and devoted K. Baedeker. (16.10.1856)

That a member of the Baedeker dynasty and the Murray family at last had personal contact is borne out by Ernst's warm words of gratitude. We must admire his command of English (as shown in the next letter) and French.

One can only presume that the disastrous French lawsuit was to do with the infringement of copyright. 1858 was the year when the firm began its move from Coblence to Leipzig, though the editorial side was to stay put for some 14 years after that.

(Ernst Baedeker to John Murray, in English, September 1858):

Dear Sir,

I suppose the enclosed letter will be of any interest for you; my father expressed his intention of publishing an English translation of his guide-books, to Mr Groves, or what's his name? But, of course, he never thinks on it of doing so; it is to prevent any other person of translating it, as Mr Groves seems to be inclined to do so. Our books are not registered at London, but they will be at once. Most likely you have read our verdict in the papers, it seemed to be impossible to everybody, but it is a fact we had to pay 1000 francs damages and the costs amounted to 800 francs! Our advocate was not at all the right man, he was not experienced enough for Mr Viollet's advocate. I suppose you have read part of the transactions in the Publishers' Circular? For instance, when he says M. Baedeker fils parut vivement désappointé lorsque M. Viollet lui présentait la carte à payer [i.e.Baedeker junior appeared acutely disappointed when M. Viollet presented him with the bill to pay], was a fine advocate's trick, and it convinced the French judges for the right of his client.

By the by, I saw in your new edition of Northern Germany that you still put the former number of our establishement [sic] here in

Coblenz: it is not 459, but Rheinstrasse 19. When is your new Edition of Central Italy and Rome coming out?

I hope, Sir, you and your family are in perfect health, you may be convinced that I always feel the greatest sympathy for you. I owe you many thanks, dear Sir, for your kind and affectionate reception in England. I will never forget your welcome house and if I can be of any use to you, I will be at your service any time.

I hope I shall have the pleasure of seeing you some day here in Coblenz. I am going to marry next year, in May, so I will be able of seeing you in my own family. I suppose I have sent you my Verlobungskarte [announcement of engagement]. My future wife is the daughter of Mr Hirzel, publisher in Leipzig. My respects to Mrs Murray if you please.

I am, dear Sir,
ever truly yours,
Ernst Baedeker.

Exactly a year before his death, on the 4th of October 1859, Karl Baedeker is again charging Murray with being out of date. It seems clear that Baedeker is working himself into a premature grave.

Coblenz, 6.10.58.

My dear old friend,

For a long time I have been meaning to tell you that it is time to subject the Handbooks to a thorough revision and to cleanse them of many outdated notions, many mistakes and, especially, many errors with regard to hotels. I am really pained to see how the Handbooks are losing the trust of their readers, and to hear that newer, but unworthy, guidebooks are to be seen in the hands of many English visitors. I was recently in Switzerland, where most English tourists had "Gregory's Practical Swiss Guide", and the Swiss booksellers told me that they sold 50 Gregorys before anyone asked for a Murray. The author is an English priest. I am told that he journeys to the various landlords and offers to produce comments full of praise for 30fr., with the sly addition that his acceptance of an entry occurs only with the provision that what the landlords promise is faithfully carried out.

If I had the time, I should pick up my pen myself. Unfortunately, I have difficulty in getting my own books ready. I have no other option, than to refer the latest editions of the same.

I have sent Deutschland 8th ed. to Mr Williams for you, (I will despatch to you the completely remodelled 8th ed. of Schweiz in February by the same route), which are reasonably reliable as regards the inns, and also quite trustworthy. Our viewpoint admittedly differs, when it comes to judging hotels, but what suits the English view can soon be deduced. In the 12th ed. of Northern Germany, (my warm thanks for having sent me this), even in the much-frequented resorts, hotels are still being mentioned, e.g. the Rheinischer Hof at Neuwied, which disappeared 8 years ago (cf. Baedeker's Rhein, 7th, 8th, 9th or 10th ed., by comparison with which such errors could easily have been avoided). Only today, an Englishman complained that, in the Weilburg tunnel, which Murray describes as "lighted by gas" (North. Germ. p.503), he had almost been drowned, for the tunnel was not even lit with oil, like the town of Weilburg.

In brief, I repeat that the trust which your countrymen bestow upon your books makes it your duty to undertake a really thorough revision. For the most part we are talking about small details, but details which a hungry and thirsty man, in expectation of a good "dinner" or "supper", and then disappointed, will take very badly. Nine-tenths of the letters of appreciation and correction which come to me in great numbers, especially in September and October, concern hotels and similar establishments. I get English letters, too, demands to print an "English Baedeker". I have rendered these attempts harmless by taking precautions, for I have the same notion myself. I am however not at all certain whether, in another publishing house, a compilation might be in the making, with here an extract from Murray, there a few snippets from Baedeker, ready to come to light as a "new Guidebook" – which would be very annoying. To prevent this with all my might, I shall in future state on the title-page that all rights of translation are reserved by me.

I gladly take this opportunity to add to my old debt of gratitude the new one, for the kindness which you have always so cordially shown to my son.

In memory of ancient friendship,
ever yours,
K. Baedeker.

Ernst, who had taken over the bookshop, inherited also the burden of the publishing side (involving many titles that were not guidebooks) upon his father's death. Alas, he too was summoned after only two years but, in that precious time, he journeyed about and issued some 14 guides, of which six were new titles.

The uncle referred to in the next letter is presumably the bookseller Adolph, now in Cologne.

(Ernst Baedeker to John Murray, 4.12.1860):

Dear Sir,

My uncle says that he certainly sent you a parcel containing the Index and estimate of printing expenses. As it never reached you, it must therefore have been lost by some unfortunate accident, which I very much regret.

I have been repeatedly asked to have my guidebooks translated into English but, knowing that in many cases your works served my late father as models for his own, I have, at least with regard to Germany and Switzerland, positively declined to do so, and shall never sanction any translation of these works. The case however is somewhat different with respect to the "Rhine" and "Paris". These two guidebooks were compiled solely by my late father's unaided exertions, and it would be very much to my interest to have them translated. Do you think that such a step would prove prejudicial to the sale of your "France" and "Northern Germany"? If so, I pledge myself to abide by your decisions.

With the copy of your "Northern Germany" I shall do as-you-wish and shall return it to you as soon as possible.

Requesting the favour of an answer at your earliest convenience, I remain, Dear Sir, Very Truly Yrs.,

Ernst Baedeker. [Written in English].

In his letter which follows, Murray describes the great debt which Baedeker owed him in the early days. The carving-up of Europe between the two firms is reasonably logical, but "Paris" becomes the object of possible negotiation:

My dear Baedeker,

I have read with the attention it deserves your obliging letter of Dec. 4.

I am not at all surprised at your declaration that you will neither countenance nor allow any attempt to publish an English translation of your Handbooks of Germany and Switzerland. Such a declaration is worthy of the honourable character which you have and which you derive from your good Father.

There can be no doubt that his Handbooks were in the first instance very nearly direct translations from mine and although in the course of time they have diverged from my model, they still retain so much of the plan, and in some instances the very words of my books, that I should be compelled to resist any attempt to transfer them to English.

The Case is different however with your Guides to the Rhine and of Paris. Here you are on original ground, and I can have no just pretence to oppose your design to publish an english [sic] translation of them. – On the contrary, I should be very happy to second your wishes by becoming the publisher and taking a share in Works and in the risk of their publication, provided you have no other arrangement in view. Let me have your views on this proposal.

You are probably aware that I have for some time past been preparing a Handbook for Paris, it is not actually in type and I have incurred a considerable expense in the editing of it and in the engraving of a map. Perhaps it might be better for you to aid me in making this guide as perfect as possible, taking a share in it, than to start a rival publication. I think my name attached to such a guide would carry weight with it among English travellers.

Turn this over in your mind and let me have a speedy answer,

I am, my dear Baedeker,
Yours faithfully,
John Murray.

Ernst Baedeker Esqr.
Coblentz, Rhine, Prussia. (8.12.1860).

Could it be that the two houses would have begun to collaborate on the production of guidebooks? Unfortunately, Ernst's untimely death put paid to any further discussion along those lines. His speedy answer to Murray was also his last. He died on 23rd July 1861 at the age of only 28. His magnanimous offer to abandon his Paris project is truly in the best tradition of his late father:

Dear Sir!

I was not aware that you are preparing a Handbook for Paris, but as it is so, I renounce my project. If I can do anything to second your Guide, I will be at your service.

Concerning the Rhine, I will carry on my intention to publish an English edition. I am obliged to you by offering me your aid in becoming the publisher of it.

I have put down my proposition, and I think you will find it a reasonable composition. To be quite correct, I have written it in German. I shall be glad to learn that you agree with it.

To lose no time, I have charged Mr Kirkpatrick, an instructed English traveller leaving [sic] in Coblenz, to begin the work, not a literary translation, [he means 'literal', of course! tr.] he must remodel it for Englishmen.

Mr Kirkpatrick hopes to have finished it before the 15th of March, so copies may be had in June or July, the very time to begin the sale of a Guidebook.

Will you kindly favour me with an early answer, and believe me, dear Sir,

Yrs. Very truly,
Ernst Baedeker. (14.12.1860, in English)

With Karl Baedeker I and Ernst now dead, the running of the firm fell to Karl Baedeker II, who lived until 1911. Four years younger than Ernst, his first task was to bring out *London* (June 1862), for which Ernst had written most of the text [German ed.].

As Alex Hinrichsen tells us, 1862 "was the end of the collaboration with John Murray", the agency being taken on by Williams & Norgate (with whom Ernst had worked). Tourism was increasing in Switzerland, and KB II was anxious to corner the market, proposing, in the next letter, to bring out *Switzerland* in English also. He writes in French:

Coblence, 20th October 1862.

Dear Sir,

During the course of last summer, a certain Berlepsch, refugee and writer, well-known in Germany and Switzerland, and living in the latter country, published a guide to Switzerland which, based on the guide by my late father, was so successful, that I shall have difficulty in making the point to him.

In Switzerland, where I spent several weeks this autumn with the sole aim of correcting this book, I learnt that Berlepsch is preparing an English translation of his guide. This publication may not do you any harm, sir, but if anyone should suffer, it will be me. The cause is a simple one. You must be aware, sir, that the number of tourists is increasing by the year. Not only rich people set out as soon as the weather improves, the lower classes vie with them in this respect. Students and others belonging to the latter class, wish to know in advance more or less what their journey is going to cost them, what they will have to pay at hotels, tips etc. etc. It is the case that England provides its contingent of travellers just as much as do France and Germany, and I would venture to say that the small print-run of the French edition of my late father's Swiss guide is taken up largely by the English. If, as a result, Berlepsch publishes an English version of his book, the English public will show its preference for him, naturally preferring this English edition to my French one.

To avoid this drawback, I have to ask you, sir, if you believe that an English edition of Baedeker's Switzerland would be capable of doing you as much mischief, so that I may the better judge, having regard to the amicable relationship which always existed between you and my late father, whether or not to undertake such a publication. In my opinion, the public who purchases your "Switzerland" and the one who equips itself with my late father's simple guide, are two very different classes of buyer. The publication which I am planning would therefore be in no position to harm your book; should such an occasion arise, it would harm only Bradshaw and other publications of the same kind; as for me, I should be the one to stand up against Berlepsch. I should not have otherwise dreamed of bringing out such a publication if I had not, as it were, been compelled to do so by the facts mentioned above.

Dare I ask you in conclusion, sir, to let me have your reply as soon as possible. You will oblige me by so doing.

Your very devoted servant,
Ch. Baedeker.
To Mr J. Murray, London.

Murray was astute enough to read between the lines: despite his politeness and assurances, Baedeker is clearly engaged on a more aggressive business drive than his late brother and father, and this evokes an outburst from Murray, who finds himself dealing with a very different animal now:

Dear Mr Baedeker,

Your letter of Oct. 30th reached me at a time when I was particularly busy, and various engagements have prevented my answering it until now.

I have no hesitation in stating that it has filled me with a little surprise. If the German Swiss Guide of Berlepsch be, as you state, copied from your guide, you have just cause of complaint against him, and you have, I suppose, a remedy – your law-courts – by prohibiting the sale of it in any part of Germany. But I am quite at a loss to understand how an English Swiss Guide by Berlepsch can injure you or even affect you at all. Your father published his guide in German for Germans. It was founded and in part translated from my Swiss Guide, which was written in English for the English. If I had published a German translation of it, do you mean to say that you would have looked upon it as no encroachment on your interests? Then how can you possibly suppose that an English version of your Swiss Handbook would do no injury to me? You might be content as it seems to me with the very large sale of your German & French versions to English travellers. At this I cannot complain, but I shall have just cause of complaint if you should go out of your way to prepare an English Guide for them. It is quite a new idea, never contemplated, I am sure, by your late Father, who never lost sight of the fact that my English Continental Guides gave him the idea, plans and materials in the first instance for his German handbooks.

The very last quarter from which I should expect such an invasion of my rights, as you appear to threaten, is your house, which in various ways, I must assert, is under obligation to me for the recommendation which I have voluntarily published of it and of your Guides. So strongly do I feel on the subject that if you persist in the scheme, I shall publish a cheap Swiss Guide – French & English – which I will take the utmost pains to circulate on the Rhine and in Switzerland.

If I write strongly, it is because I feel strongly on this subject, that if you execute your project it will be an innovation in your Father's plans, an invasion of my works.

I am utterly at a loss to understand how you can suppose that such an English Guide as you hint at could be circulated abroad without injury to me!

I remain, dear sir,
Yours very faithfully,
(signed) John Murray.

P.S. Let me add a Postscript that I do you the justice to believe that when you see the matter in the light in which I put it – you will not persist in your design.

The first edition of Baedeker's *Switzerland* in English appeared in the following year, 1863. Murray's guide to that country spanned the period 1838-1904.

So, although they never foundered in the law courts, the cordial relations came to an end. A lively correspondence in the Pall Mall Gazette in the late 1880s culminated in a letter from the English editor of Baedeker's Handbooks at that time, James F. Muirhead, who defends his masters against John Murray's charges of self-indulgent plagiarism:

> DEAR SIR, - Since it was you who set the ball a-rolling, perhaps you will allow me to direct your attention and that of your readers to Herr (Fritz) Baedeker's recent letter in the Times answering the charges brought by Mr Murray in the recent article in Murray's Magazine?
>
> As Mr Murray has accused me personally of ignoring him and his books in my interview with you, I should like to disclaim any intention of doing so from malice prépensé. I was asked to tell how a "Baedeker" is made now, and I no more thought of going back to the origin of guidebooks than (say) the manager of the London and North Western Railway would think of going back to the invention of the steam-engine in giving an account of one of the famous Scottish expresses. My acquaintance with Baedeker and guidebook-making has been confined to the last ten or twelve years, and I can safely say that in that time Baedeker's guidebooks have been absolutely independent of Mr Murray's publications. In fact, I scarcely see how it could be otherwise, seeing that I believe I am right in stating that from two to four new editions of Baedeker, thoroughly revised on the spot, generally appear to one of Murray's. The only one of Mr Murray's publications that I have found of any great use in my own work is his "Handbook to the Cathedrals of England", and that I have cordially praised in the bibliography of my "Handbook to Great Britain". I do not mean that I copied from that work, but I found it a most interesting companion in visiting the cathedrals, and I dare say it often led me to observe features of interest that I might otherwise have passed over. My account of the only English cathedral I did not myself visit was mainly furnished by a personal friend, and was revised by the Dean.
>
> Towards the end of his article, Mr Murray seems to blame Herr Baedeker for publishing guidebooks to the countries he himself had already annexed; but I do not see how this could

have been otherwise unless poor Herr Baedeker had either invented brand-new countries for himself, or had undertaken to personally conduct the natives of New Guinea or the Arabs of the Sahara, abandoning the tourist-overrun lands of Europe as the private preserves of his English competitor.

I am, Sir, yours, &c.,

JAMES F. MUIRHEAD,

English Editor of Baedeker's Handbooks. (30.11.1889).

(Text, from *Baedekeriana* nos. 13/14, 1990, by Michael Wild and Bill Lister; letters translated by MW; photocopies of originals of letters supplied by WBCL.) Our grateful thanks are due to Mrs Virginia Murray for kindly allowing us to use this archive material.

Origin and History of Murray's Handbooks for Travellers

By John Murray

(From *Baedekeriana* no. 13, Spring 1990)

Arriving at a city like Berlin, I had to find out what was really worth seeing there, to make a selection of such objects, and to tell how best to see them, avoiding the ordinary practice of local Guide-books, which, in inflated language, cram in everything that can possibly be said – not bewildering my readers by describing all that *might* be seen – and using the most condensed and simplest style in description of special objects. I made it my aim to point out things *peculiar* to the spot, or which might be better seen there than elsewhere. Having drawn up my Routes, and having had them roughly set in type, I proceeded to test them by lending them to friends about to travel, in order that they might be verified or criticised on the spot, I did not begin to publish until after several successive journeys and temporary residences on Continental cities, and after I had not only traversed beaten Routes, but explored various districts into which my countrymen had not yet penetrated.

I began my travels not only before a single railway had been begun, but while North Germany was yet ignorant of Macadam. The high road from Hamburg to Berlin, except the first 16 miles, which had been engineered and macadamised by an uncle of mine by way of example to the departments of Ponts et Chaussées, was a mere wheel track in the deep sand of Brandenburg. The postillion who drove the mis-called Schnell-post [express post] had to choose for himself a devious course amidst the multitude of ruts and big boulders of which the sand was full, and he consumed two days and nights on the dreary journey. In those days the carriage of that country (the *Stuhlwagen*) was literally a pliable basket on wheels, seated across, which bent in conformity with the ruts and stones it had to pass over.

On reaching Weimar, having been favoured with an introduction to Goethe, the great poet and philosopher of the time, I had the honour and pleasure of a personal interview with the hale old man, who received me in his studio - decorated with casts of the Elgin Marbles and other works of Greek art, - attired in a brown dressing-gown, beneath which shone the brilliant whiteness of a clean shirt; a refinement not usual among German philosophers. On this occasion I had the honour of presenting to Goethe the MS. of Byron's unpublished dedication of Werner to him…

The first of my Handbooks to the Continent, published 1836, included Holland, Belgium and North Germany, and was followed at short intervals by South Germany, Switzerland – in which I was assisted by my good friend and fellow-traveller William Brockedon, the artist – and France. These were all written by me; but, as the series proceeded, I was fortunate enough to secure such able colleagues as Richard Ford for Spain, Sir Gardner Wilkinson for Egypt, Sir Francis Palgrave for North Italy, Dr Porter for Palestine, Sir George Bowen for Greece, Sir Lambert Playfair for Algiers and the Mediterranean, Mr George Dennis for Sicily &c. In 1839 appeared the first of Baedeker's long series of Guides, that for Holland and Belgium, written in German. The Preface contained an acknowledgment of the compiler's obligation to "the most distinguished (*augezeichnetste*) Guide-book ever published, 'Murray's Handbook for Travellers', which has served as the foundation of Baedeker's little book." * He began his Guide to Germany, published in 1842, by again referring to Murray's Red Book as having "given him the idea of his own, though as his work progressed, he found he could retain only the frame of his original." No doubt, with my book ready made to hand, he was enabled to use the plan and arrangement, to correct, enlarge, and fill in with such information as he thought useful to Germans, as for instance by sedulously pointing out where the best *Bierstuben* [beer parlours] were to be found.

---

* I give a few extracts taken from one or two of Baedeker's Guides:-

"The basis for this little book was provided by the most distinguished Guide-book ever published, 'Murray's Handbook for Travellers on the Continent.'" – Baedeker's 'Little Handbook: Holland,' 1839.

"The usefulness of the travel Guide-books issued by the bookseller *Murray* in London is so well known to the English, that you scarcely ever see one wandering about without the so-called 'red book'. It gave the editor of the present Handbook the idea some time ago, to describe two countries which, despite their proximity, are little known in Germany, using Murray's Handbook as basis and, in similar fashion, to rework a well-known guide to the Rhine." – Baedeker's *Handbuch für Reisende durch Deutschland*, 1842.

Murray writes: "My copy of this work contains the following inscription in Herr Baedeker's own writing:- 'This book is sent to Herr Murray in grateful recognition of the great help his excellent Handbooks 'Northern and Southern Germany' have provided in its compilation, with the plea for the Editor's continued goodwill,
K. BÄDEKER. Coblence, Aug. 1841."

From Baedeker's *Holland* 1851: "The present little volume, based upon the famous Murray's 'Handbook for Travellers on the Continent', first appeared ten years ago."

Karl Baedeker (I) died 4th October 1859. There are many anecdotes about the Baedekers, but the best is undoubtedly the reference from *Gartenlaube* of 1861 in an obituary that, on the day of the funeral – 7th October 1859 – a traveller followed the cortege with the red book in his hand. A citizen of Coblence, August Gertner, who had acquired the 9th edition of *Rheinlande 1856* on the 11th April 1857, immortalised this reference for posterity in his copy.

(From the History of the Firm in the *Baedeker-Katalog* published by Alex Hinrichsen in 1989).

Baedeker in the Making

by

James F. Muirhead (1905)

To John Murray of London belongs the honour of publishing the first true guidebook in the modern sense. On this point I cannot do better than quote from a letter written by Herr Fritz Baedeker to the London *Times* in 1889:

> "I wish to acknowledge, in the frankest manner, that Mr Murray was the first publisher of guidebooks on a large scale. After the terrible wars which devastated the Continent at the beginning of this century. Great Britain was, indeed, the only country in Europe where wealth enough remained to allow of any large section of the public indulging freely in foreign travel.
>
> My father, Karl Baedeker (born 1801, died 1859) had, it is true, on his settlement at Coblenz in 1827, purchased and published a handbook to the Rhine in German and French *(Rheinreise von Mainz bis Köln)*, von Professor S. [sic] A. Klein, Coblenz 1828, and *Voyage du Rhin, de Mayence à Cologne*, Coblenz 1829) which possessed many of the features of a modern guidebook; but it was the sight of the numerous English travellers following the footsteps of Childe Harold, with Murray's handbook under their arms, that suggested to him the desirability of providing his German countrymen with similar books for other parts of Europe. The German handbooks which he then successively published *(Belgien und Holland, Deutschland, Schweiz)* certainly owed a great deal to Mr Murray's books, but included many descriptions of his own, and in the important practical points (recommendations of hotels, information as to means of communication, etc.) were completely independent.

> The later handbooks published by my father and those published by my elder brothers and myself are perfectly independent works, produced with the aid of able helpers, many of whom are eminent scholars and specialists."

Someone has asserted that Baedeker is the most widely read of living authors; and perhaps this is not so far from the truth when we reflect that he has issued upwards of seventy handbooks, all of which are in constant use. Of these 27 are in German, 24 in English and 22 in French. The earliest, as already noted, was the *Rheinreise,* published in 1828; the very latest is the *Handbook to Constantinople and Asia Minor,* issued just the other day, and not yet translated into English. [But see the extracts entitled "Baedeker on the Baghdad Railway and "Troy" later in this book. MW]

Among the most obvious, the most elementary requirements for the equipment of an ideal editor of guidebooks are a knowledge of geography, history, mythology, botany, geology, languages (ancient and modern), painting, sculpture, art, architecture and archaeology; an acute and discriminating taste; a clear head in foreseeing and explaining the complications of travel; and a sympathetic insight into the needs and desires of the average tourist. The mere enumeration shows how impossible it is for one small head to carry all this load; but it is almost necessary to have at least so much knowledge in all these branches as will insure sound discrimination among competing authorities.

Baedeker must be at once scholar and sportsman, bon-vivant and botanist, archaeologist and theatre-goer. He must at one time shiver with the novice on the brink of the most insignificant precipice; at another he must stand steady-headed on the loftiest peaks along with the fearsome race of "adepts" who stalk through his *Switzerland* and *Eastern Alps.* In a book intended for the seafaring Briton he must not be overawed by the fact that there are sixty-eight steamers in the merchant fleet of Belgium, nor must he expect a resident of the Rocky Mountains to grow dizzy at the sight of the sandhills of Vrouwenheide, the highest point in Holland. The German professor must not be allowed to stumble on a sentence mentioning Noah Porter of Yale in the same breath with Kant or Hegel; and a chastening memory of Lincoln and Chartres must control the description of the cathedral of Albany, New York. The ideal Baedeker must never mistake geese, - scenic, historical, literary or otherwise – for swans. He must be at once a student of nature, of art and of man.

It is, of course, well known that the term Baedeker, as generally used, covers the work of a number of different editors and contributors, whose names are not always mentioned. That this is an inevitable and perfectly just arrangement – a fair application of the dictum "qui facit per alium facit per se" (who does for others does for himself also) – seems clear to me, mainly on these grounds: (1) the whole scheme of the books, the framework which the various editors have to fill in, was the invention and device of the elder Baedeker; (2) the head of the firm continues to take a personal and intelligent interest in the preparation of every handbook in the series; and (3) the share played by the publisher's capital, in facilitating travel and investigation, furnishes the actual writer with a large proportion of his material. Half the work is really done before the editors touch their pens. The various individual editors have a chance to exercise a good deal of art in conforming to the uniform style of the handbooks; and that this is not, perhaps, so easy as it looks has been borne witness to by the perennial difficulty of getting usable matter from outsiders, even of wide cultivation and considerable literary gift. I do not believe any editor has more trouble in recasting his "copy" than the editor of a really carefully prepared guidebook. There is no field in which the need of *le mot juste* is more imperatively indicated.

The composite photograph labelled "Baedeker", however, takes in more than the editorial staff, - it also includes many of the travellers who use the handbooks; the reader of today becomes one of the authors of tomorrow. The data sent to Baedeker vary from recommendations of some particularly plump headwaiter up to corrections on important points of scholarship and fact, and highly valuable suggestions for improvement. One laborious gentleman, I remember, not content with our already voluminous index of four or five thousand entries, sent us a complete new index with more than twice as many. On the whole, however, the help offered by travellers is as satisfactory in quality as it is bulky in quantity; and almost the first thing to be done in preparing a new edition is a careful examination of the letters in the pigeonhole of the particular handbook under treatment. Actual cases of misinformation from this source are rare; but the editor must be on his guard against the unintentional bias of letters due to the exceptionally good or bad treatment of the writer, and he must be still more careful to detect bogus or interested letters, and to discount the self-praise of hotel-keepers and the like. The pessimist should take note that we receive at least as many letters of praise as blame; the chronic grumbler is not more in evidence than the traveller of content.

After the letters of travellers comes an equally careful study of newspaper cuttings, census bulletins, railway literature, annual reports of all kinds, magazine articles, and topographical works that have appeared since the last edition of the handbook. This done, the editor is ready to take to the road and collect his own material on the spot. It is, of course, impracticable for him to travel over a whole country for each new issue, though this is indispensable in preparing a first edition; but he can at least visit that section which seems to have undergone most change, and so manage to go over the whole ground again in the course of a few years. For the parts he does not visit he receives his information by deputy or from local residents; and it is an unusually easy job that does not involve in this way the writing of hundreds of letters, and the asking of thousands of questions.

All the mechanical work of the Baedeker handbooks, including the printing, map-making and binding, is done in Germany, most of it in Leipsic, where the firm has been established since 1872. Before that its seat was at Coblenz. The connection of the Baedeker family with the book-trade goes back to Diederich Baedeker, who died at Bielefeld in 1716 as *königlich-preussischer priviligierter Buch-drucker* [printer by appointment to the King of Prussia]. Since his day there has been an unbroken line of printing or publishing Baedekers, forming a good example of that honourable commercial heredity so difficult to parallel, out of Germany.

Some years ago a sapient tribunal in Berlin decided that "Baedeker" meant "guidebook", and that consequently we had no redress against a rival publisher who annually issued what he chose to call a *Berliner Baedeker*. This robbery of one's good name was the more vexatious, inasmuch as it also involved a considerable encroachment on what the high-minded dramatist dismissed as "trash".

The drawing of Baedeker into the realm of humour seems at first sight just a little incongruous; and doubtless most of the humour of his guidebooks is of the unintentional order. Thus one reviewer congratulated us on our felicity of phrase in describing a statue of

Venus as consisting of "undressed stone". The laughable element in the description of the American chicken as a fowl of any age was also, I fear, entirely unpremeditated, as the reference was mainly to such terms as chicken-coop and chicken-farm, where the English say hen-coop and poultry-farm, and was in no degree intended as a slur on the table qualities of the youthful American hen.

Many commentators find food for humour in the absolute confidence shown by certain travellers in Baedeker's guidance, and in their refusal to admire anything unmarked by a Baedekerian asterisk. The *Münchener Fliegende Blätter* represents an English paterfamilias as exclaiming to his flock, "This scenery is all wrong" ("Diese Gegend ist falsch"), when he finds the picturesque castle to the right and the foaming waterfall to the left, instead of vice versa, as asserted by his infallible guide. A writer has hazarded the theory that the average German's love for nature is explained by the fact that it contains so many restaurants; and the frequent collocation of "beer and a fine view" in the German editions of Baedeker might seem to lend colour to the hypothesis.

The unconscious humours of the English editions of Baedeker are often due to the vagaries of an inexperienced translator or the struggles of a German compositor with a manuscript in an unknown tongue. Fortunately most of this humour is reserved for the editorial eye alone; and if any of it has managed to escape into the published volumes, wild horses would not extort from me a confession of the fact. I once found myself wondering whether the most converted of Benedicts would be willing to face the creature strangely described in my proof as a "five-arched bride". On another occasion, I wrote of a room "full of plaster casts", which was returned to me in proof as a room "full of blasted cats"!

Baedeker – how it came to be a synonym for guide-book

(From *The Publisher's Weekly,* January 28th, 1911)

The publishing of a "Baedeker" is a Sisyphean task. Scarcely is it ended when it begins again. Each guide book in the series is cast into the melting pot every three or four years and is thoroughly overhauled at more frequent intervals. During a recent visit to the publishing offices in Leipzig I saw a bundle of pages that had been "corrected" for a new edition, in preparation, of the *Northern Italy* guide. There was scarcely a single line without some important alteration. That new edition will be a new work. I saw also the material which is being collected for a "Baedeker" to *India, Ceylon and the Far East.* The idea of bringing out this guide book was suggested to Messrs. Baedeker by the steady increase which they noticed in the annual statistics of tourist travel to the Far East.

Naturally, the labour involved in this system is enormous and the outlay formidable. All the type is set by hand, there being such a variety of "founts" in a single sentence that the linotype or monotype would be useless.

The maps alone cost vast sums, and the work of bringing them up to date for each revision or new edition is a heavy source of expense. This work is done in the building where the Baedeker publishing offices are situated. But it is done by an independent firm, Wagner & Debes, after the Perthes firm, of Gotha, the most famous map engravers in the world. The engraving is done directly on the stone; thence the map is transferred to the lithographic stone. The result is far more satisfactory and artistic than could be obtained by the photographic reduction of big maps.

Lithographic stone of the requisite fineness of grain is found in its perfect state mainly in Germany. A slab big enough for only four or five very small maps costs $200. More than a thousand of these slabs engraved for the Baedeker guide books are stored in the basement of the publishing offices.

The late Karl Friedrich Baedeker reported that he managed to visit war-torn Leipzig after the end of hostilities. He found the firm's offices flattened by a bomb. While moving (cautiously) around in what was left of the basement level, he came across one of the lithographic stones which had been used for the preparation of maps. He picked it up, but it instantly crumbled to dust in his hand...

Mention has been made in the past few pages of Baedeker's *Indien* (India, 1914) and *Konstantinopel und Kleinasien* (Constantinople and Asia Minor). Both appeared only in German. You will find extracts from both (in my own translation) elsewhere in this book.

Lenin wrote to his mother from Lausanne in July 1904:

> We ourselves will put our rucksacks on at 4 a.m. and go off into the mountains for about two weeks. Our way will take us to Interlaken and thence to Lucerne; we will read up our Baedeker and carefully work out our walking-tour.

(Vladimir Ilyitch Lenin: works, vol. 37 of the Dietz Verlag Berlin ed. of 1962)

The Baedeker Badekur

(or, taking the cure with Baedeker)

[from *Baedekeriana* no. 12, Autumn 1989]

The year is 1929 and the place is Mariánské Lázně (better known to us as **Marienbad**), in the newly-created country (1918) of Czechoslovakia. We have arrived by air ('The aerodrome is in the Neue Bahnhof-Str., a little N. of the station; motor-cars convey passengers hither from the "Čedok" travel bureau, Hauptstr. 45, ½hr. before the start of the aeroplane.' From *Austria*, 12th rev. ed. 1929). Most of the hotels, Baedeker tells us, are closed in winter, but a couple of dozen of them cater for all pockets in the season, ranging from the '**Esplanade*, 160 beds (90 bathrooms), first-class,' to the '*Walhalla*, Jewish, 50R.'

Here, the Visitors' Tax includes a music tax, to support the 'Band, 7-8.30 a.m. and 6-7 p.m. at the Kreuz-Brunnen [fountain], and 11.30 a.m. – 12.30 p.m. at the Wald-Quelle [spring] (in wet weather in the Colonnade)'. One wonders what spa visitors made of the sound of trombones and drums in the early morning! Marienbad, we are told, attracted 40,000 patients in 1928 to its 40 cold springs (containing Glauber's salts, carbonic acid, chalybeate and saline waters) and peat baths. ('The peat is cut every autumn in the *Peat Bogs*'). 'The North Bohemian spas,' says Baedeker, 'are thronged with patients of every nationality.'

Even better known, in 1929, is **Karlsbad** (Karlovy Vary), which sports two railway stations, though the aerodrome is 'under construction'. Its largest hotel (**Pupp)* has 400 beds. There are restaurants and cafés and wine parlours, and you can enjoy the Karlsbad Wafers ('Oblaten'), 'a kind of thin waffle baked in iron moulds. "Brunnenkuchen", eaten by patients, is a simple variety of ginger-bread without spices.'

One might be tempted to believe that the cure is just a front for seekers of pleasure and lionisers of high society. My dictionary gives 'der Kurschatten' as 'romance from/at the spa'. The Visitors' Tax includes a grade 'for children under fourteen and servants, 10 Kč.' You do not have to pay extra for the town band at Karlsbad. There is Horse Racing, a 9-hole Golf Course and a Theatre ('operettas, dramas, comedies'). However, at some stage you will have to become closely acquainted with one or more of the sixteen Karlsbad Springs (radio-active alkaline, for drinking and bathing – for 'complaints of the stomach, liver, gall-bladder, intestines etc… The oldest and most copious of the springs (440 gall. per minute) is the *Sprudel* (162° F), from which the natural Karlsbad Sprudel salt is extracted.'

Indeed, you can take home a souvenir from the Art Shop in the form of 'Sprudelstein wares… and Karlsbad incrustations (objects incrusted with lime by the mineral waters).'

Goethe must have felt the need to take the cure more than most, for he came to Karlsbad 13 times between 1785 and 1823. Or was he here just to socialise and be seen? Baedeker remains silent about his symptoms, and about those of Peter the Great (here in 1711 and 1712, presumably picking up some 'western ideas'). At all events, Baedeker describes Marienbad and Karlsbad as elegant resorts for the upper echelons of polite society, and does not touch at all here upon the daily routines of draughts of water, mud baths etc. (It seems that not all spa doctors were genuine: a 'Kurpfuscher', for instance, was the name given to a quack).

Perhaps things medical are taken more seriously at **Spa** itself, a small Belgian town of 8500 inhab. in 1897, and 8100 in 1910, with its 15 or so hotels, its three physicians (incl. Dr Cafferata of Liverpool) and its three kinds of carriage: 'those with one horse and seats for two persons; those with one horse and seats for three; and others with two horses.' (One wonders if the latter were seatless). There are also ponies called 'Bidets', 'of a peculiar variety.'

Gaming having been suppressed at Spa, one must resort to Golf and the Race Course. Baedeker says: 'Like other watering-places it consists chiefly of hotels and lodging-houses, while numerous shops and bazaars with tempting souvenirs and trinkets, a pleasure-seeking throng in the promenades, and numbers of importunate valets-de-place and persons of similar class, all combine to indicate that character which occasioned the introduction of its name into the English language as a generic term. This the original and genuine "Spa", the oldest European watering-place of any importance, has flourished since the 16th cent., though it attained its zenith in the 18th century. Peter the Great was a visitor here in 1717, Gustavus III of Sweden in 1780, the Emp. Joseph II and Prince Henry of Prussia in 1781, and the Emp. Paul, when crown-prince, in 1782. After the French Revolution its prosperity began to decline, but it has of late regained much of its popularity, and many new buildings have sprung up. It is now (1910) frequented by upwards of 12,000 visitors annually, a large proportion of whom are English. The Season lasts from May to October, and is at its height in August. The pretty painted and varnished woodwares offered for sale everywhere are a speciality of Spa ("Bois de Spa"). The "Elixir de Spa" is a fine liqueur.'

Peter the Great *must* have been making his social rounds. Evidently the spa was also the arena for diplomatic and cultural exchange (and, doubtless, intrigue). After all, if you wanted to drink the water for its medical properties, you did not need to leave home. The same is true today, as your supermarket shelves testify. The water of the spring POUHON 'which is perfectly clear and strongly impregnated with iron and carbonic acid gas, is largely exported.' One walked the picturesque paths if one could, though (burping as privately as possible at every turn), admired the views, gambled (when it was still allowed) and, for the sake of form, took the waters – even Peter the Great condescended thus with the *Géronstère Spring*, 'formerly the most celebrated. Its properties were tested by Peter the Great, whose physician extols them in a document still preserved at Spa.'

In 1958, Spa still had only 9000 inhabitants, despite its valiant efforts to become a winter-sports centre. But those who suffer from anaemia, gout or rheumatism can still follow in the footsteps of 'Peter the Great, the emperor Joseph II and many other celebrities.'

The above-named almost certainly did not take the waters at Clerkenwell, much nearer home for us. 'Among the spas and more or less disreputable places of amusement for which Clerkenwell was noted in the 17-18th cent. were *Bagnigge Wells,* in King's Cross Road; the ***London Spa,*** at the corner of Rosoman St. and Exmouth St., the assembly room of which became in 1779 the first chapel of the Countess of Huntingdon's Connexion (now the Spa Fields Church in Lloyd Square); *Hockley-in-the-Hole*, a bear-garden to the N.W. of Clerkenwell Green; and *Sadler's Wells*, later a theatre (in

Rosebery Avenue; still in existence). The *Spa Fields* (now built over) are remembered for the Reform Riot of 1816.'

If Clerkenwell was hardly a spa in the normal sense of the word, one could resort to Buxton, Harrogate or Bath, which very definitely were. 'At the **Buxton** hotels,' said Baedeker in 1887, 'the prevailing custom is to have table-d'hote [sic] meals and pay a fixed price per day.' At the PALACE, you could get room and attendance from 5s.6d., dinner 5s., breakfast 2s.6d. and "pens" [pension] 14s.6d.' [In 1981, the Palace at Buxton offered B & B and evening meal for £112 weekly].

'*Buxton*, one of the three chief inland watering-places in England and the highest town in the country (1000ft. above the sea), contains a resident population of about 6000, which is doubled or trebled during the summer-season. It has a fine bracing climate, apt at time to be rather cold. The *Hot Springs* for which it is famous (Bath having the only other hot springs in England) seem to have been known to the Romans, and were several times visited by Mary Stuart when in the custody of the Earl of Shrewsbury. They rise in fissures in the limestone rock at a constant temperature of 82° Fahr., and are efficacious in rheumatism and other ailments. The *Tepid Baths* are at the W. end of the Crescent, the most prominent building in the town, and they are adjoined by the *Chalybeate Wells*. At the other end of the Crescent are the *Hot Baths.* In front of the Crescent is a grassy knoll known as the *Slopes,* and to the W. are the *Pleasure Gardens* (adm. 4d. or 6d.; music daily). The S. side of the Gardens is skirted by the BROAD WALK, with its well-built villas. The large domed building, near the Palace Hotel, is the *Devonshire Hospital.*

The Environs of Buxton are rather bleak, but afford opportunities for a few delightful excursions.'

At **Harrogate**, 'the custom of dressing for dinner prevails at some of the more fashionable hotels… *Harrogate* (450ft. above the sea), in a high and bracing situation among the Yorkshire moors, ranks with Bath and Buxton… It consists of two parts, High and Low Harrogate, the former to the left (E.) of the station, the latter to the right. It is perhaps the most aristocratic of all the great English spas, and the one least exposed to the inroads of excursionists… The Wells for which Harrogate is visited are in the lower part of the town, and have been known for nearly 300 years.

'They include the chief sulphur-springs of England, and also chalybeate springs not unlike those of Kissingen and Homburg, though less pleasant to drink owing to the absence of carbonic acid. The *Sulphur Springs*, of which there are two (*Old* and *Montpellier*) strong, and seventeen mild, are efficacious in most affections of the liver, jaundice, gout, rheumatism, and diseases of the skin. The six *Chalybeate Springs* are tonic and stimulant. The so-called *Bog Springs*, 16 in number, rise in a small piece of boggy ground… Near the springs are various *Pump Rooms, Baths* and other adjuncts of a fashionable spa.'

Bath receives much more coverage than Buxton or Harrogate. 'Hotel omnibuses meet the chief trains.' Bath's pedigree is outstanding and it attracted the cream of society from the Romans to Beau Nash and co.

'HOTELS. *GRAND PUMP ROOM, a large establishment adjoining the baths; YORK HOUSE, quiet; WHITE LION, High St.; CASTLE, Northgate St.; *CHRISTOPHER, near the Abbey, commercial, R. & A. [room and attendance] 3s.6d; ROYAL, opposite the G.W.R. station; FERNLEY'S TEMPERANCE, near the Abbey.

Cabs. For 2 pers., with 2 horses, 1s.6d. per mile, 3s. per hr.; with 1 horse or 2 ponies or mules 1s. or 2s.; with 1 pony or mule or 2 donkeys 6d. or 1s.6d… - *Bath Chairs*, 1s. per mile or per hr.

Music. Band twice daily in the *Victoria Park, Sydney Gardens* or *Institution Gardens* (subscrip. for the season 7s.); thrice a week in the *Pump Room,* where vocal concerts are also given (season-ticket 5s.). – High-class concerts take place in the *Assembly Rooms.*

'*Bath,* the *Aquae Solis* or *Sulis* of the Romans, and the chief place in Somerset, is a handsome town of 53,761 inhab., beautifully situated in the valley of the *Avon* and on the slopes of the surrounding hills… Handsomeness and uniformity are the characteristics of Bath architecture, the best examples of which are the Royal, Lansdown and Camden Crescents, the Circus and Pulteney Street, all of which recall more or less similar streets in Edinburgh.' (The writer of Baedeker's *Great Britain* 1st ed. was Mr J.F.Muirhead, M.A, who receives mention elsewhere in this book.)

'Tradition ascribes the discovery of the springs of Bath to an ancient British prince named *Bladud,* who was afflicted with leprosy and observed their beneficial effects on a herd of swine suffering from a similar disease. The therapeutic value of the waters did not escape the keen eyes of the bath-loving Romans, who built here a large city, with extensive baths and temples, of which numerous remains have been discovered…

'The beginning of its modern reputation as a watering-place may be placed about 1650, but it did not reach the zenith of its prosperity till the following cent., when it became for a time the most fashionable watering-place in England. This was mainly due to the indefatigable exertions of the famous master of the ceremonies, *Beau Nash* (d.1761), who introduced order and method into the amusements and customs of the place, and gave at least a "veneering of respectability to the coarse and vulgar material" he found there… It would almost be easier to give a list of the eminent Englishmen of the 18th and early 19th cent. who did not frequent the Parades and Pump Room of Bath than those who did…

'The competition of the Continental Spas and other causes afterwards diverted a great part of the stream of guests, and the "Queen of all the Spas" subsided into a quiet and aristocratic-looking place, patronised as a residence by retired officers and visited by numerous invalids…

'The hot MINERAL SPRINGS to which Bath owes its name contain a small quantity of sulphate of lime, and are efficacious in rheumatism, gout, dyspepsia, biliary and liver complaints, and skin-diseases. The daily yield of the springs is upwards of half-a-million gallons. The water, used both for bathing and drinking, rises at a temperature of from 116 to 120° Fahr., which is reduced, when required, by means of cooled mineral water. The Pump Room, close to the W. end of the Abbey Church, is a large edifice in the classical style… Visitors are admitted free to the Pump Room, as well as to inspect the various baths, etc. The charge for a single glass of the mineral water is 2d.; weekly ticket 1s.6d. A placard hung up in the Pump Room gives a list of the concerts and other amusements for the week.'

The baths tended to be divided into First and Second class, and there was a *Hot Bath* (120°), Bath st., 'for the poor.'

The sad decline of the English spa forces us abroad again, also, for further examples. If there is a correlation between the ancient Romans, hot springs and areas of volcanic activity, then we would expect the volcanic regions of France (Auvergne, dormant) and Italy/Sicily (Naples, Etna region, active) to be rich in spa development.

In the Auvergne we have **Le Mont Dore** and **La Bourboule**, cheek-by-jowl and doing very good trade today in cures of various kinds. In 1914, La Bourboule mostly had 'new and comfortable' hotels open from 25th May to 30th Sept., 'but it is advisable to ask charges beforehand.' Le Mont Dore's season was a month shorter. Here, carriages were 'generally dear, about 20fr. per day (bargain advisable).' Both had Etablissements Thermaux, offering bath or douche and buvette. Le Mont Dore also offered (and still does so today), 'inhalation'. Both establishments provided porters (to carry you in a litter), the rates being per 300 metres (which is presumably the point at which the porters stop to mop their brows).

La Bourboule 'organised its waters' in 1876, and has three springs whose properties are claimed to cure 'anaemia, rheumatism, lymphatic affections, diseases of the skin and the respiratory organs, diabetes and intermittent fevers, and are especially strengthening for delicate children… The waters are highly arsenical and charged with bicarbonate of soda, and possess great radio-activity. La Bourboule is fashionable and expensive.'

Le Mont Dore attracted 8000 invalids annually in 1914, when its population was 2125. In 1961, the pop. had risen to 2500. 'The Mont-Dore cure is world-famous for asthma' and you can see, today, *curistes* of all ages walking around in mufflers and nose-protectors even in high summer. The Romans discovered the place, and the 'Etablissement Thermal, partly rebuilt in 1893, contains a few fragments of Roman architecture and sculpture…

'The treatments consist chiefly in very hot baths (104-113°), douches, vapour-baths, inhalation and hot foot-baths for the reaction. Many of the patients are carried to and from the bath-house in litters, wearing a special flannel costume.'

Much further SE., across the Alps into Italy, we come across **Bormio** ('the chalybeate baths of *Santa Caterina*'). In 1877: 'The *Bagni Vecchi,* or Old Baths of Bormio, perched on the rocks below the road. The handsome *New Bath-house (*Bagni Nuovi,* 4397ft.) situated on a terrace commanding a fine survey of the valley of Bormio, and the surrounding mountains, is much frequented in July and August, but is closed about the end of September. The mineral water (containing salt and sulphur, 93-100° Fahr.) is conducted hither by pipes from the springs at the old bath, 1M. higher up.'

By 1930, Bormio had blossomed: '*The New Baths* (*Grand-Hôtel Bagni Nuovi, open June-Sept., 250 beds) on a terrace commanding a fine survey, draw their water-supply (radio-active, with a small proportion of lime; 92-106° Fahr., beneficial for rheumatism and similar complaints) from the springs rising near the *Old Baths.* The seven springs, mentioned by Pliny and Cassiodorus, rise in the dolomite cliffs above the profound ravine of the Adda. The old *Roman Baths* (piscine) hewn in the rock are interesting.'

The Touring Guide *Italy* of 1962 describes the waters as 91-105° Fahrenheit, 'radio-active and containing a small amount of gypsum… used by rheumatic and other patients.'

From the Dolomites, let us move further south to the environs of Naples. On the island of Ischia, the town of **Casamicciola** is also a spa: '*Casamicciola*, rebuilt under government superintendence since the terrible earthquake of 28th July 1883, in which over 1700 lives were lost, now consists of groups of houses scattered on the slopes of the Epomeo, with a population of 3730. The higher points command beautiful views over the Gulf of Naples to Vesuvius etc. The little town is frequented from May to August by numerous visitors, on account of its cool and healthy situation and warm alkaline and saline springs; and it is a pleasant resort even in spring and autumn. The *Gurgitello,* the principal spring, rises in the *Vallone Ombrasco*, 154ft. above the sea-level, with a temperature of 147° Fahr., and its water is used for baths, douches, inhalation etc., in the extensive bath-establishments of *Manzi* and *Belliazzi* (100-115ft.). The baths for the poor *(Monte della Misericordia)*, on the Marina, with an accommodation for 400 bathers, occupy the site of a building erected in 1604.

'Lacco Ameno, where the earthquake was much less disastrous… At the beginning of the village, to the left, is the *School of Straw-Plaiting* (tasteful specimens for sale)… Near the former monastery and in the garden attached to it rise hot springs which are used for vapour-baths…

'The *Epomeo (2588ft.) falls away on the N. side almost perpendicularly. A little below the top is the convent of *San Nicola* (2576ft.), hewn in the volcanic tufa, from which the mountain is also called *Monte San Nicola.* Wine and bread (bargaining necessary) may be obtained from the hermit, now the sole occupant of the convent, and in any case a trifling donation is expected.'

As the Naples area is less well endowed with spas than one might have expected, we will move south again, to the environs of

Etna in Sicily. Messina had a hydropathic establishment in 1903, offering 'warm, vapour and other baths, managed by Dr Genovese.'

At Acireale, on the way to **Catania,** 'a large *Bath House* called the *Terme di Santa Venera* (open in summer only; mineral bath 2fr., vapour bath 2½fr.), has been erected to the left of the station for patients using the tepid mineral water, which contains sulphur, salt and iodine.'

Catania boasted (also in 1903) warm baths at the *Stabilimento Idroterapico* (Prof. Ughetti), but the town was 'not attractive to tourists,' the theatre being covered in lava.

One has a strong impression that the Romans enjoyed their baths to the full, even if many of their resorts dwindled away later on. Nowadays, in certain countries, the "cure" seems to be a kind of perk, a holiday ordained by an indulgent medical profession for its overworked and stressed-out clientele. Germany has its "air spas" (i.e. climatic health resorts), quiet and pleasant little towns where, presumably, you can breathe your way back to good health. Socialising on the grand scale seems to have lost its attraction. The titled, royalty and so on, have abandoned the spa as a meeting-place. Peter the Great would doubtless view the decline of the watering-place as a symptom of decadence. It seems, though, that he did not introduce the notion into his own country. Even in 1914, the only "baths" at **St Petersburg** were the '*Central, Tzelibyeyev* and *Voronin* (warm bath 1rb.). - RIVER BATHS (very primitive)... Bath 5-10, sheet 10, towel 5 cop.' He might have done better to patronise some of the Polish spas.

The Polish uplands are rich in curative springs, which are mainly salt or sulphur (though some are acidulous), there being just one thermal spring, near Zakopane. From Baedeker's *Das Generalgouvernement* I choose Busko and Krynica:

'**Busko** (280m.), 1½km. S. of the little town, at the end of an attractive avenue (Badstrasse), in a valley basin surrounded by hills, is the *State Spa Busko,* the most important rheumatic spa in the Generalgouvernement, since its discovery in 1776, with its 13 sulphur and saline springs and its sulphur mud-baths (4000 visitors in 1942). It is also suitable as a centre for recuperation, by virtue of its mild climate and low precipitation. (Cure season, May-October). In a fine park, the cure-and bath-house is to be found, an imposing structure of 1836, with a pillared hall and ballroom.'

Bad Krynica sported three hotels in 1943, numerous guest-houses and sanatoria. Its spa amenities included the Bath Houses, Drinking Hall, several German doctors, two chemists and a hospital.

'The state spa *Krynica* (station 573m., town up to 741m.), a municipality of 5000 souls, in a beautiful situation in the SE. corner of the locality Neu-Sandez (part of Cracow district), not far from the Slovakian border, and lying among the forested Beskid Mts. in the *Kryiczanka* valley, opening up to the south – Krynica is the largest curative spa in the Generalgouvernement, frequented also for its almost sub-alpine climate as a climatic resort, and further for winter-sport. Krynica's position reminds one somewhat of Karlsbad, with which it to some extent shares medicinal indications. The seven springs – the *Zuber* spring (most potent alkaline acidulous water in Europe, with lithium, iodine and bromine), the *Johannes* (hypotonic water, also acidulous), the *Main Spring* (alkaline chalybeate water), the *Slotwinka* (mild alkaline acidulous water), the *Josef* (potent chalybeate), the *Karl* (pleasant-tasting chalybeate table-water) and the *Krynica-sprudel* (alkaline table-water) – are used for bathing and drinking cures for cardiac and nervous diseases, rheumatism, complaints of the stomach, intestine, kidney and gall-bladder, and women's ailments. There are also peat baths.

'The HISTORY of *Krynica Spa* ("Krynica" means "spring"), first mentioned as a village in 1547, began in 1793, when Styx von Saunbergen, the district commissioner of Neu-Sandez, recognised the value of the curative springs, which the local populace had been using for a long time. He had the Main Spring tapped, and a wooden structure erected over it. The spa undertaking then developed rapidly, especially after the building of the railway from Muszyna to Krynica (1902). The spa became a favourite resort of the Russian and Polish aristocracy and attracted about 12,000 visitors annually already before the First World War; up to the end of August 1939, this number had risen to 40,000. Before the outbreak of war, the Poles totally cleared the spa and destroyed its fittings. The damage was however speedily put right, and since 1941 the German spa undertaking has been working to full capacity and is continually being extended.'

Here I must rest my case. Apologies to all other spas not mentioned. You, the reader, can resort to your Baedekers, to fill in some gaps. This modest piece of research does however point to the considerable social and medical importance of the spa, even if it has long since passed out of fashion in the British Isles.

Bibliography

For the above article, I consulted the following:

Encyclopaedia Britannica

Baedeker:

Austria, 12th ed. 1929
Belgium and Holland, 12th ed. 1897; 15th 1910.
Benelux Autoguide, 1958.
London, 18th [English ed.] 1923.
Great Britain, 1st ed. 1887
Southern France, 6th ed. 1914.
France Touring Guide, 1961.
Northern Italy, 4th ed. 1877; 15th ed. 1930
Southern Italy, 14th ed. 1903.
Italy Touring Guide, 1962.
Russia, 1914.
Das Generalgouvernement, 1943.

Baedeker beyond the Curtain

[from *Baedekeriana* nos. 14/15, Autumn 1990 and Spring 1991]

If Baedeker seems very much at home on German soil, that is only to be expected. One might even suggest that he emulates Heineken beer, reaching parts that other handbooks do not. In recent years, for instance, he has led the field in guides about the German Democratic Republic or 'DDR' ['Deutsche Demokratische Republik'] (which, as I write these words on October 2nd, 1990, is about to be consigned to mere historical concept.)

To serve the cause of tourism in a country which has suffered such vicissitudes and changes of frontier in this century alone requires a dedication and vision not possessed by all writers of guidebooks: Baedeker was not afraid to swim against the tide, to describe parts of Europe which people were streaming out of, rather than towards. Refugees hardly make good tourists and, as I have said elsewhere, war and its (often lengthy) aftermath are ruinous to the proper development of tourism.

Baedekeriana does not concern itself more than peripherally with political or economic circumstances, because Baedeker does not either. What follows is therefore intended to be a brief survey of the extent to which Baedeker has been able to throw light on some of the hitherto darker corners of Central and Eastern Europe (not only German), with special reference to those which, until last November or so, still lay beyond the Iron Curtain or the Berlin Wall. It makes sense to breach these two obstacles, and rediscover a world which often did not seem to add up to us in the West, or from which we were virtually excluded.

This summer, I made it my business to pay a brief visit to the German Democratic Republic (hereafter called GDR or DDR), before it ceased to exist as a separate state. The currency union had already taken place in July and so, on Monday, August 13th, my wife and I drove across near Lübeck. The West German customs post at Schlutup was empty. We continued for a few hundred metres between trees, and were suddenly on a different road surface and in open country. At right-angles to our road, the sandy 'death strip' still ran, the fence gone already on our left, but very much in evidence still on our right, where it pursued its chilling, orderly course towards the forest. The East German customs house, a large complex of buildings with many parking lanes and barriers, was also deserted. One drove straight through. Watch towers, set back quite a long way, turned blind eyes upon our progress. Later, where the road ran close along inside the frontier, the watch towers had been turned into roadside snackbars. Ubiquitous were the Trabants ('Trabi') and Wartburgs, East German cars carrying families the other way for a day's outing to Lübeck and Travemünde.

Our first town was Wismar, where Baedekers (new ones) were already on sale in a bookshop, at normal West German prices. (We later learnt that, after the currency union took place, it was deemed that nobody would want East German books any more, so they all went to the tip, and the world is poorer, for a great many fine books were produced in the GDR.) We were the only British vehicle parked in the cobbled market square. Wismar was dowdy but, in its way, delightful, very 1920ish. I took a picture of St Mary's church tower (all that remains, from the Sargmachergasse (Coffin-makers' Alley).

> "Wismar, a Mecklenburg town with 15,518 inhab., possesses an excellent harbour and several fine churches. In the architecture of *St Mary's* (Marienkirche, choir consecrated 1353), the influence of the Marienkirche in Lübeck is distinctly traceable. The *Fürstenhof,* formerly a ducal palace, and now the seat of the municipal authorities, is a good specimen of German Renaissance. The *Thormann'sche Haus* contains handsome old furniture, oil-paintings, etc. (strangers admitted)."
>
> [From Baedeker's *North Germany,* 9th ed. 1886, p.186].

And now, in stark contrast:

> "Wismar: Rostock District, alt. 5 metres above sea-level, 57,800 inhab. The second most important port in the GDR. Next to the harbour, the shipyard, the industries and the new social and cultural amenities, it is chiefly the sights of the old town, a jewel of medieval architecture, that determine its particular

quality. 70% of the Inner Town was destroyed by severe air-raids during the Second World War. The restored old part of the town, together with the market-place, forms a conservation area. **Market Place,*(10,000 sq.m.) This is one of the largest in the N. part of the DDR. **Marienkirche* [St Mary's]. Close to the Market Place on a piece of open ground remains the huge tower of the Marienkirche, almost totally destroyed in 1945 (1339; substructure 1260-1280).
Fürstenhof. To the E. of St George's Church stands the architecturally important Fürstenhof (1553/54), a 3-storeyed Renaissance building, used today by the Kulturbund [Cultural Federation]."
[From Baedeker's *DDR*, 5th ed. 1990, updated after the 'latest events of October/November 1989'. Extract tr. MW]

Baedeker was surely at his bravest when he brought out (under special licence from the Allied occupying powers) his guide to Leipzig – home of the Baedeker firm – in 1948, being a "collaboration with the Bibiographisches Institut" which produced Meyer's guides. The mayor of Leipzig welcomed "this little handbook, which will be of less use to foreigners who will hardly be coming here in the foreseeable future". It will, he adds, be more of interest to Germans, who will "enjoy and tend all the better our much-reduced collection of cultural objects." Those who live on in Leipzig are urged to make a new home out of their city.

Karl Baedeker's own introduction is equally glum. His historical sketch makes no reference at all to Nazism, but does refer to the bombing raid on 4th December 1943, when 400 English planes demolished a great deal of the inner town and the entire bookshop quarter. "On 17th April 1945 the town was occupied by the Americans after a brief, pointless period of resistance, and the Soviet army replaced them on 2nd July."

Reciting a list of Leipzig's publishers down the ages, Baedeker modestly tacks himself on at the end, after Tauchnitz, Teubner and the Insel Verlag. His second edition of *Leipzig*, issued in 1973 (9 plans and 28 drawings, the plans by Lahr of Switzerland) mentions the "first post-war product by *Hans Baedeker* (1874-1959) who had run the publishing house since 1925."

"Not far to the W. of the Market," [1948 ed.] rises the city's main church, the late Gothic Thomaskirche, where the great musician *Johann Sebastian Bach* worked, whose bronze statue, by Carl Seffner, has stood on the S. side since 1908, the lifelike head shaped, with the help of the anatomist Wilhelm His, according to measurements of the skull... The oldest part is doubtless the S. tower vestibule, XIVth c.; the choir and sacristies were erected around 1477, the triple-arched nave with its huge saddle roof in 1482-94 by Claus Roder. The entire building was renovated in 1885-89 by Constantin Lipsius in a methodical but not entirely faithful manner, in Gothic style: extension of the W. front, which used to lie by the city's moat, to the main porch, and painting of the vaulting. The slender helm tower of 1702, which fell victim to an air-raid in 1944, has been replaced by a temporary roof."

[From *Leipzig,* 1948, 73pp. and 3 maps, from one of which the Soviet Kommandantur had to be laboriously erased by hand.]

The 1973 2nd edition runs to 101pp., and embodies a good deal of its predecessor's text. An in-text drawing shows the helm tower duly restored, there is a carefully-drawn plan of the interior, and we are told that, in 1962, the inside walls were painted white, the ribs of the arches being picked out in red. (Remember that, in the Communist GDR, churches were generally woefully neglected).

The Allianz-Baedeker of the *DDR* (5th ed. 1990, as mentioned above) cannot allow itself the space to dwell for too long even on the Thomaskirche, but it does give the church a star and a colour photograph, and informs us that Bach's grave has been located inside it since 1950. All this goes to prove that a guidebook has to be every bit as resilient as its subject-matter: Hans Baedeker was hard put to it, in *his Leipzig*, to write a page that did not contain some reference to war damage. Although much was left unrestored in the GDR (viz. Wismar), the succeeding guides portray a Leipzig where the trade fairs and book fairs are booming again.

For factual accuracy, I must say here that my wife and I did not get to Leipzig. In a day's brief tour, we were pleased enough to see, after Wismar, the beautiful town of Schwerin with its castle and its lakes and, further south, the imposing castle at Ludwigslust. If we got lost now and then, people kindly helped us out. We were intrigued to see here and there a Lenin-strasse or Karl-Marx-Platz (with statues) – but for how much longer, I wonder?

I should like to have had the chance to press on to Weimar, which, quite apart from the political overtones of the Republic that took its name, is the town most associated with Goethe and Schiller. These, like Bach, were able, through the genius of their art, to transcend ages and frontiers. Baedeker (as we know) does not emote over the great men who people his pages. He, perhaps wisely, leaves that to us. His handbooks grow in stature for their lack of sentiment.

> "Schiller's house in the Schiller-Strasse, which has been purchased by the town, contains a few reminiscences of the poet (shown daily, 8-12 and 2-6; fee).
>
> In front of the *Theatre* rises the *Goethe-Schiller Monument, erected in 1857, in bronze, designed by Rietschel. The illustrious pair are united in a happily-conceived group.
>
> Goethe's house in the Goethe-Platz, in the S. quarter of the town, opposite the fountain, was acquired by the town on the death of the poet's last grandson in 1883. At present the collections are shown on Fridays in summer, 9-12 o' clock."
>
> [From Baedeker's *Northern Germany,* 9th ed. 1886].

By 1936 (when Weimar is sporting the obligatory Adolf-Hitler-Strasse), the descriptions of the writers' houses is already considerably fuller:

> "Here, on the E. side, stands *Goethes Wohnhaus, a comfortable-looking house built in 1709, rented by Goethe in 1782-89 and presented to him by the Duke Karl August in 1794… The plain study; and, to the left of the last, the bedroom in which he died peacefully, seated in an armchair, on 22nd March 1832." [Baedeker's *Germany,* 1936.]

In 1990, Baedeker's *DDR* gives Weimar 11 pages of coverage with an excellent map (clearer than in the 1886 ed.!), and good quality colour photos of Goethe's house. A page is devoted to the 'Roman House' (Römisches Haus) by the river Ilm, and the park laid out by Goethe, with the simple 'garden house' where he did some of his writing. Weimar seems to have been relatively unscathed by the war, though there is also a page given over to the nearby concentration camp Buchenwald, where the President of the (then) German Communist Party, Ernst Thälmann, met his end during the "national-socialist regime of force, in crass contrast to Weimar's humanistic traditions."

In the end, all roads seem to lead to Berlin, until last year an enclave of West Germany in the middle of the GDR, and now one city and capital again. Baedeker did his best, but even he was taken by surprise. From the mid sixties onwards (7th ed. 1965), there have been many Baedeker guides to Berlin, some of them (German) devoted to specific parts of the city. All have had in common the fact that the city was physically divided by the Wall, from August 1961 onwards. The most recent, the *DDR* guide of 1990, had to issue a 10pp. coloured Beilage [supplement] bearing the title "Special Extra, DDR 1989" with, on the front and back cover, a colour photo of people on the Wall, pulling others up. *DDR* runs to 704pp. It was impossible to alter all of it, but the Preface mentions "recent events", and p.49 (at the end of the Historical Survey) starts on 7th October 1989, taking us to 6th May 1990, keeping manfully abreast of the almost daily developments. Congratulations to all concerned! It was not possible to excise Walter Ulbricht from the gallery of celebrities, but the next edition (presumably just *Deutschland*) will be able to get even him into perspective.

Here, on p,174 (facing a fine panoramic coloured photograph), we have "Berlin (Ost) – Hauptstadt der DDR", whose map shows the Wall near the Brandenburg Gate and at 'Checkpoint Charlie', but only on the very edge. There is a fine coloured drawing of Unter den Linden, and a description of Europe's possibly most famous monument (after the Eiffel Tower):

> "***Brandenburg Gate*. The avenue Unter den Linden is blocked at the Pariser Platz end by the Brandenburg Gate (1788-1791, C.G.Langhans; no access), based on motifs in the Propylaea in Athens, with a 6-metre tall Quadriga of Victory (in copper, 1793, to a model by Schadow). After the defeat by France the Quadriga was taken to Paris in 1806 on Napoleon's orders. After the Wars of Liberation it returned to Berlin and, amid great rejoicing by the Berliners, was set up again in its former place. The lateral colonnades were added by Strack in 1866. In the Second World War, the Gate was severely damaged. After renovation the new Quadriga (cast in W. Berlin) was set up again in 1958 (one of the original horse's heads is in the Märkisches Musem.)" [Baedeker's *DDR*, pp. 185-6, tr. MW]

In his *Städteführer Deutschland* (city guide to Germany) of 1988, Karl Baedeker gives the Brandenburg Gate only one star. But then he is looking at "the most impressive hallmark of the divided city" from the west: the Quadriga faces east.

The Baedeker-'AA' guide to *Berlin* (1984) has a photo of the Gate from the west, but gives it *two* stars:

> "There are six Doric columns on each side. The wider central passage was reserved for the carriages of the Court… Originally the goddess (of Victory) was naked, but this gave rise to so much moral indignation on the one hand and so many ribald jokes on the other, that Schadow felt compelled to clothe her in a decent garment of sheet-copper."

The second English edition (1975) of Berlin (small city guide) also gives two stars to the Gate:

> "Since 1961, it has been blocked up and is inaccessible, even for pedestrians, who are not allowed to go beyond Otto-Grotewohl-Strasse (the former Wilhelmstrasse). The Prussian eagle and the Iron Cross, formerly borne by the goddess as symbols of victory, were removed by East Berlin before the group was replaced."

Baedeker's 7th English edition of *Berlin* of 1965 (always one of the favourites in my collection) runs to 316pp., with a supplement of strip maps in the old tradition:

> "The fateful *Brandenburg Gate is situated on East Berlin soil and since 1961 has been blocked by the Wall… The rise of Prussia found its most striking expression in the Gate."

The 1886 edition of *Northern Germany* (already quoted here), portrays a Berlin very different from now:

> "The *Brandenburg Gate, at the W. end of the Linden, forms the entrance to the town from the Thiergarten. The material is sandstone. Adjoining the gate on the side next the town are two wings resembling Grecian temples, of which that on the right or N. side contains a *Telegraph Office* and a *Pneumatic Post Office,* while that on the left (S.) is the *Guard House."*

If this article seems preoccupied with cities, that is hardly surprising: it is they that have shown the greatest change in the course of the years, and a good deal of the northern swathe of Germany possesses "uninteresting scenery", as even Baedeker is prepared to admit. 37 miles SE. of Berlin, in the direction of Görlitz, however, is the Spreewald, which he dwells upon:

> "The Spreewald is a wooded and marshy district, about 28M. in length and 1-5M. in width, intersected by a network of upwards of two hundred branches of the Spree. Most of it has been drained, but the wilder parts are only accessible by boat in summer or on skates in winter. The inhabitants are a Wendish race, who still retain their Slavonic dialect, costumes, and manners. Their villages consist of small groups of log-houses surrounded with water, an arm of the Spree generally serving as the street."

Baedeker's *DDR* devotes 6 densely-packed pages to the Sorbs, who are an officially recognised "national minority group" in the GDR. Of Slavic origin, they were subjected to attempts to "Germanise" them after the First World War, and their culture was virtually extinguished during the Third Reich. In 1948, when the two separate Germanies came into being, laws were passed in the GDR to protect the Sorbs, their language and their culture.

The Slavonic connection naturally carries us further eastwards from Berlin. In 1886, the frontier with Poland (then reduced by partition to being a Russian province) lay far to the east of the present one, on the Oder-Neisse line, and Königsberg, Danzig, Posen and Breslau were all very much German towns. There is a reference to "Bohemian territory" at one point. Baedeker, in his *Russia* (1914), devotes some 16pp. to Warsaw and its immediate environs, reminding us that "the NAMES OF STREETS are given at the street-corners, both in Polish and in Russian." In 1914, Warsaw was the capital of the "General Government of Warsaw or Poland" – "It is the intellectual centre of Poland, and its appearance is far more like that of West Europe than of Russia. The river is crossed by three bridges. The streets teem with activity."

There is a remark about the Jewish population so derogatory that I shall not repeat it here, but one wonders whether it was made an excuse for the later maltreatment of those in the Warsaw Ghetto.

"On the E. side of Palace Square, near the Vistula, stands the **Royal Palace** (Королéвскій Зáмокъ), founded by the Masovian dukes, rebuilt and fitted up as a royal residence by Sigismund III, and Wladislaus IV... Most of the older works of art and objects of value were removed to St Petersburg and Moscow in 1831, but the palace still contains several portraits of Polish kings, views of Warsaw by Canaletto etc.

"The small imperial château of *Łazienki (i.e. 'Baths'; Лазенкóвскій дворéцъ) makes a most attractive impression, especially when viewed from the artificial water, and its light colouring contrasts very effectively with the verdure of the park... On the walls of the 'Green Cabinet' hang the portraits of numerous beauties of Warsaw in the reign of Stanislaus..."

The beautiful *Park contains several small villas; a Chinese palace; a *Rotunda,* with marble busts of Polish kings.

"To the W. of the Łazienki Park is the château of Belvedere, the beautiful garden of which, laid out in the English style, extends to the *Belvedere Barrier* (Бельведéрская застáва). The château, now the summer-residence of the Governor General, was rebuilt in 1822 and occupied by Grand-Duke Constantine Pávlovitch (d. 1831). The rooms used by the Grand-Duke and his wife, Princess Łowicz, are still in very much the same condition as during their lifetime...

"We pass between the forts of *Alexéi* and *Vladímir*, cross the railway, and reach the Alexander Citadel (Александровская цитадéль), situated on the Vistula, at the N. end of Warsaw. It was built in 1832-35, at the cost of the city, as a punishment for the revolution of 1830. In the interior (adm. only by permission of the Commandant) a barracks, a prison for political offenders, and the Alexander Nevski Church...

"The Alexander Bridge, an iron girder-bridge, is 560 yds. long. Smoking on the bridge is forbidden. The bridge offers a pretty view of Warsaw. To the N. we see the Citadel, commanding the Vistula, the railway-bridge, and the buildings of the Old and New Towns, extending down to the brink of the river. In front of us, on the hill, lies the Royal Palace, forming a charming group with its terraced garden and the church of St Anne. Above the bridge are the streets skirting the Vistula and the promenades and gardens surrounding the imperial château of Łazienki." [Baedeker's *Russia,* 1914].

I have dealt elsewhere with the Baedeker to occupied Poland (*Das Generalgouvernement*, 1943). The difference here was that Poland was a 'General Government' not under the Russians but the Germans. By 1943, Warsaw had been reduced to a shadow of its former self (like Leipzig and Dresden in 1945), and again it had been forced to relinquish its status of capital to Cracow. Again, too, it is given 16 pages of description, virtually all of which refer to buildings damaged or destroyed during the Second World War:

> "During the Polish era from 1919 to 1939, in which Germanity was preserved by various cultural and political associations (Deutscher Club Warsaw, Jungdeutsche Partei [German Youth Party] etc.), Warsaw, as the capital, underwent a powerful but uncoordinated spurt of building development until, in the *Polish Campaign,* the pointless defence of the city (which was neither equipped to defend itself, nor evacuated) led to a bombardment and weapon assault, to which numerous buildings and sections of streets fell victim. On 27th Sept. 1939, the city surrendered to the German troops... and is once again undergoing a reconstruction programme with German direction.
>
> "Warsaw's URBAN SCENE lacks any impression of unity. Because of its position on the high bank of the *Vistula,* the town did not spread out uniformly in all directions from its medieval nucleus, but stretched for some 12km. along the l. bank of the river."

The old Market Square was reduced virtually to rubble, but, in these pages, it is described as though it were still intact:

> "The nucleus of the old town is the *Alter Markt [Old Market], a typically German rectangular square (in the middle of which a town-hall stood until 1817), framed all around by fine patrician houses, originally Gothic but mostly rebuilt in Renaissance and Baroque style after the great fire of 1607. Worthy of special mention are no. 1, with three courtyards, formerly owned by the Giese family which settled here from Franconia in 1511, and honoured for its part in the development of Warsaw; no. 19, the former jury house; no. 25, built in 1466, and in possession of the Fugger family since 1566; no. 27, the *Fugger House,* built by the wine-merchant Korb at the beginning of the XVIth c., and property of the Fuggers only since 1810,

with a fine balcony, notable hallway and yard, and old wine-cellar; no. 31, the house of the dukes of Masovia; no. 32, the house of the Baryczka councillors, one of the oldest buildings in the Market; no. 34, the house of the Schlichting family (XVIIth c.); finally no. 40, a house which contained Michael Gröll's German printing-press at the end of the XVIIIth c. At the N. corner of the Market begins the 'Stone Staircase', a medieval little street like a flight of steps.

"At the SE. edge of the Old Town, where Krakauer Strasse begins, is the Schlossplatz [Palace Sq.], at whose centre rises the 20m.-tall *Sigismund Monument*, erected in 1644 to King Sigismund III (Wasa) by his son Ladislas IV, to designs by the Italians Tencalla and Clemens Molli: on a column 9.6m, high, rises the 2.6m. statue of the king, cast in bronze by Daniel Thym (Thiem) of Danzig. – On the E. side of the square stands the former Royal Palace (partly burnt down in 1939), founded in 1280 by the Masovian dukes (the courtyard wing still has a Gothic façade in the manner of the castles of the Teutonic Order, and Gothic vaulted cellars) under Sigismund III and his son (see above) in the XVI & XVIIth c., and restyled in early German Baroque in 1598-1619 by Andreas Hegner (SW. side; with cour d'honneur and gate-tower). It was altered again during the Saxon period by J. Chr. Knöffel (E. side; a grand design by M. D. Pöppelmann in 1713 was not carried out). On the S. side, the palace abuts on to the *Blechernes Palais* [lit. 'Tin Palace', on account of its earlier tin roof], lying rather lower and dating from the Saxon period (1720), and displaying a heavier style in the manner of the Dresden master-builder G. Bähr."

The Belvedere, referred to above, was the seat of the German governor-general von Beseler during the First World War. It then reverted to Marshal Pilsudski, who died there in 1935. It was altered in 1941, and now (at the time of writing of *Das General-gouvernement*, from which the above extracts are taken – tr. MW) serves as the Governor General's official seat, when he is visiting Warsaw. (No access to visitors).

If you travelled east from Warsaw to St Petersburg in 1914, you would pay (for the 18½hr. rail journey of 1046 versts or 693 miles), 27 roubles and 90 kopeks in 1st class, and 18rb. 90kop. in 2nd (reserved seat, 2rb. 10k.). If it was winter you could pick up the Nice to St Petersburg express.

At first, "the train runs NE. through the ancient duchy of *Masovia* and traverses extensive forests." [This, and subsequent quotes are taken from Baedeker's *Russia.*]

At Malkinia, one may pursue the branch-line to Ostrołeka (35mi., in 2hrs.)

> "The French defeated the Russians here in 1807, and the Russians gained a victory over the Poles on almost the same field in 1831.
>
> 107mi. from Warsaw, the train reaches Białystok. The RAILWAY STATION (*Restaurant*) lies to the NW. of the town. – HOTELS. *Nyemetzkaya* [i.e. 'German'], Bazárnaya, with restaurant, R. 1-4 rb. – IZVOSHTCHK [cab] from the station to the town 40-50, per drive 15-20 kop. – TRAMWAY from the station to the town, 5 kop."

Białystok, a strong garrison containing 86,200 inhab., of which about three-quarters were Jews, was…

> …the centre of an important woollen-manufacturing district. We proceed to the Town Park, passing on the right the Tzar Nicholas Institute for Girls, in a converted château, formerly belonging to the Counts Branicki. A little to the E. is the new Lutheran Church, the tower of which commands a view of the town and of the well-wooded and hilly surroundings."

Not quite 30 years later, Baedeker writes very differently of the same town. [Extract from *Das Generalgouvernement]:*

> "184km. (from Warsaw) Białystok (134m.). chief town of the German district Białystok, set on the *Biala* and numbering 100,000 inhab. is a town founded by Germans, with important textile industries. The town already belonged to Prussia in 1795-1807, to Russia in 1807-1919, and then was occupied by German troops in 1915-18; it became Polish again in 1919, was occupied once more by German troops in 1939, then, however, ceded to the Soviets, becoming a German possession again on 1st August 1941. – In the middle of the town is the extensive market-place with *town-hall* (XVIIIth c.), crowned by a tower; to the E., the R.C. *parish church* (1908) and, nearby, the small, older Baroque church of 1617; further on, the former *Palace* of the Counts Branicki, built by Saxon master-builders (XVIIIth c.), in which

the kings August II and III resided (now seat of the German authorities); to the S. of the town, a fine large *Park* and the German Military Cemetery."

One is almost as concerned for the welfare of the girls of the former Institute as for the Tzar himself. Back to *Russia,* 1914:

> At *Bialowieża*, a prettily situated shooting-lodge of the Tsar… The Byelovyézh Forest, 396 sq.mi. in area and attaining a height of 645ft., is a bleak hilly district in the government of Grodno, overgrown with firs and pines. The auroch or bison (Bison bonasus L.) occurs here as in the Caucasus. There are believed to be about 600 head, which may not be shot or hunted without the permission of the Tzar…
>
> 78V. *Grajewo*, the Russian frontier and customs station. The German frontier station is *Prostken*, whence a railway runs to (121mi.) *Königsberg* (see Baed. *N. Germany*).
>
> The train enters the government of Vilna. – 315V. *Oráni* (Rail. Restaurant). A branch-railway runs hence to (133V. or 88M.) Suwatki, passing *Artilleriskaya,* with artillery ranges and a summer camp for sappers and infantry… Beyond a tunnel we reach - *Vilna."*

In our day and age, we know it as Vilnius, the capital of Lithuania, one of the three 'Baltics' (another formerly Germanised eastern province). In Baedeker's *Russia,* it is "Vilna, Вилна, Polish *Wilno,"* sporting six named hotels and two restaurants (including the *"Railway Restaurant,* D. 1rb., fair"). The tourist is invited to devote 3hrs. to the "CHIEF ATTRACTIONS:

> Ostra Brama chapel; cathedral of St Stanislaus; Castle Hill… Those who leave their compartment during the long wait here should hire a porter to guard their belongings… The station clocks keep St Petersburg time (61min. in advance of Central European and 2hrs.1min. in advance of Greenwich time) and occasionally local time as well. [The difference between Greenwich and St Petersburg time now stands at 3hrs!]
>
> *Vilna* enjoys a pleasant position on a group of sand and clay hills. It was formerly the capital of Lithuania, an important railway and commercial centre, with a trade in timber and ca. 192,700 Jewish, Lithuanian and Polish

inhabitants... The streets in the older parts are narrow and badly paved, but contain many quaint old churches."

Sacked many times (by Swedes, Russians and Cossacks) since it was first made the capital in 1323, Vilna has the dubious distinction of having been chosen by Napoleon for his strategic centre, until he slipped away, disguised, "on the night of Nov. 24th (Dec. 6th) 1812." Not only the clocks are wrong, but the calendar also.

The first-named 'attraction', the chapel of Ostra Brama, was famous for its miracle-working statue of the Madonna, visible however only during services, a fact which did not deter pilgrims of Greek and Latin Catholic persuasion from kneeling in some numbers in the street outside. It would be interesting to know if this practice continues. The Cathedral is in the square of the same name:

> "...a building in the form of a Greek temple, founded in 1387 on the site of a sanctuary of Perkunas, a pagan god of light... A baroque marble chapel to the right of the high-altar contains the silver coffin of St Casimir and eight silver statues of Polish kings and queens... There are also numerous monuments of scions of distinguished Polish and Lithuanian families."

Enjoying all this Baedekerian thoroughness, one can understand why *Russia* is so sought after as a guidebook, still, as well as a collector's item. (It was rated at DM 600 in 1988). The Baltic states of Lithuania, Latvia and Esthonia are dealt with in some detail (46pp.) before we even get to St Petersburg (the final destinations being Vladivostok and Peking!) The story of the compiling of *Russia* has never been told in detail – perhaps the facts are lost – but one marvels at the fulness of the material, gathered, after all, in Tsarist Russia, with censorship and the secret police to contend with. It has been rumoured that many copies of this book found their way into the libraries and collections of Russians themselves. In the Preface, Baedeker says, uncharacteristically, "absolute accuracy is unobtainable, and changes are constantly taking place." The writers of the modern Baedekers to Eastern Europe will nod sagely at this!

I have already alluded to the monotony of the landscape of the great North European Plain (Baedeker's *Das Generalgouvernement* would make an entry in the German version of the Guinness Book of Records for the number of times he uses the phrase "undulating arable land"). On p.40 of *Russia* (route 8), he says: "The railway traverses the government of Vitebsk, the scenery of which offers little variety."

There is a moment of excitement later on, though: " – On passing the boundary of the government of Pskov, we enter Great Russia proper."

Pskov manages to wrest an asterisk out of Baedeker (who gets more tight-fisted, the further he goes east) for the …

> "*CATHEDRAL OF THE HOLY TRINITY, founded about 1138 but dating in its present form from 1691-99… It is 236ft. high (to the top of the cross)."

He is however unimpressed by the Latin inscription on the sword of St Gabriel, the first prince of Pskov (d.1138) which says "honorem meum nemino [sic] dabo". He will, it seems, give his honour to no-one, but the grammatical case is wrong. Princes were crowned in this cathedral, wearing Prince Dovmont's sword (d.1299), which hangs in a side chapel. There is a touching story about Ivan the Terrible who spared Pskov from destruction "by the representations of the monk Nicholas Salos, who feigned madness to effect his end."

Those with an interest in Russian opera can take a steam-launch up the river Velikaya as far as the village of *Libutino*…

> "… said to have been the birthplace of St Olga (d.969), wife of Igor, Prince of Kiev.
>
> The train now describes a wide curve; to the left, in the distance, is a range of hills, skirting the Gulf of Finland from this point to St Petersburg.
>
> 837V. (555M). *St Petersburg* (Warsaw Station)."

Although very scarce, Baedeker's *Russia* can be found (either in the original or in David & Charles' reprint of 1971) much more easily than the volumes devoted exclusively, in the pre-Revolution years, to St Petersburg. For the record, here is a complete list of the original titles, with Hinrichsen numbers (and comparative auction-room prices in DM from his *Baedeker-Katalog,* 1988):

Russia	E244	1st and only ed. 1914	(600)
La Russie	F210	1st ed. 1893	(500)
	F211	2nd ed. 1897	(280)

Russland	D457	1st ed. 1883 (W. & Central Russia)	(700)
	D458	2nd ed. 1888	(480)
	D459	3rd ed. 1892	(380)
	D460	4th ed. 1897	"
	D461	5th ed. 1901	"
	D462	6th ed. 1904	(450)
	D463	7th ed. 1912	(500)

St Petersburg (German only, but really just an abstract from *Russia*):

D464	1st ed. 1901	(900)
D465	2nd ed. 1913	(800)

Before we allow ourselves to arrive in St Petersburg, though, it is necessary (as pre-Revolution travellers) to do some homework on Mother Russia. I will spare you the language, though Baedeker obligingly provided help with this, in the form of:

S14	Manual of the Russian Language 1914	(200)
S12	Kurzer Leitfaden der russ. Sprache, (5 eds., 1883-1912)	"
S13	Manuel de langue russe, (3 eds., 1893-1903)	"

Instead, let us begin with his suggestions regarding apparel:

> "CLOTHING should not be too light, for even in summer the nights are often chilly, and changes of temperature are frequent and extreme. Woollen underwear is recommended. The traveller should be provided with a pillow or air-cushion, linen sheets (useful on long railway journeys and in provincial hotels), towels, a coverlet or rug, a small india-rubber bath, and some insect-powder. Visitors to S. Russia should have a light summer suit; the Russians themselves often wear suits of linen. – For winter-journeys warm furs and well-lined rubber boots (best obtained in Russia) are indispensable. In spring a spell of warm weather is often succeeded by a sudden frost; it is therefore safer not to discard winter clothing until summer has actually arrived. – *Unboiled Water* should be avoided. Tea is a good substitute."

Customs regulations were quite stringent at that time:

> "For the introduction of firearms a special permit is necessary, for which application must be made some months beforehand to the ambassador at St Petersburg. This permit is valid for six months, and the traveller may be required to deposit the amount of duty leviable, which is refunded only after considerable delay. After the expiration of six months full duty must be paid. – Books in large quantities are submitted to a censor. Travellers should avoid works of a political, social or historical nature; bound books are subject to duty. – Luggage booked through to Eastern Asia, China or Japan is not examined in Russia."

Even road travel was beset with hazard and inconvenience:

> "*Posting.* There are no diligences or stage-coaches in Russia, but travellers by road can obtain carriages and horses at a regular tariff at the various posting-stations. The horses are always good, but the carriages leave much to be desired. In winter sleighs (kibika) with hoods are provided.
>
> The *Telega* or mail cart is a four-wheeled conveyance without springs and somewhat resembling a rude edition of the American buckboard. As a rule no seats are provided except for the driver, the passengers sitting on their trunks or on the hay or straw with which the bottom of the cart is littered. As the roads are bad, travelling is very rough and often painful. The so-called *Mail Telega* is somewhat better. Where procurable, as it is in most towns, the *Tarantass* is to be preferred. It is somewhat like a hooded victoria, the body swung by leathers on the wooden frame, or furnished with springs."

Once you arrived, accommodation had to be found:

> "The hotels in provincial towns, especially the older ones, satisfy as a rule only the most moderate demands, and they often leave much to be desired in point of cleanliness. In spite of these failings they frequently have high-sounding names, such as Grand-Hôtel, etc. The traveller is thrown back upon Russian, as no other language is understood. He should at once ask the charge for his room in case there is no card of rates shown on the wall. The washing arrangements are generally unsatisfactory, usually consisting of a tiny wash-basin communicating with a

small tank, from which the water trickles in a feeble stream. Bed-linen and towels are often charged for separately. Every candle used appears in the bill (10-15 kop.)."

Amateur photographers were given an unequivocal warning:

"The taking of photographs near fortresses is naturally forbidden; and even in less important places the guardians of the law are apt to be over-vigilant. In order to escape molestation the photographer should join the Russian Photographic Society… Imperial chateaux and the like may not be photographed without the permission of the majordomo."

Before we tackle St Petersburg proper, a few choice remarks:

"Those who do not shrink from an expensive supper and somewhat Bohemian society should make a point of hearing one of the Russian or Gipsy Choirs… No notice should be taken if the izvoshtchik – i.e. carriage driver – declares there is no room in the hotel he has been told to drive to… The shooting of the aurochs or bison is forbidden under a penalty of 500rb. The same rule applies to the elk-cow, the hind and the doe… Russians generally roll their own cigarettes… The Russians have no taste for pedestrian exercise… The *Police (Gorodovoi),* at least in the larger towns, are helpful and obliging… In spite of their name the White Clergy wear robes of a brown or blue colour… Women are not allowed to enter the sanctuary, and men must lay aside hat and umbrella before doing so… In winter an electric tramway runs over the frozen surface of the Neva from the Winter Palace to the Muitninskaya Naberezhnaya, fare 3kop."

In 1914, St Petersburg was blessed with a profusion of tramways, (electric, steam and horse), with steamboats on the Neva, and seven railway stations. It was, and still is, endowed with a huge number of fine buildings, worthy of the former capital city.

"*Winter Palace,* open daily, 11-3, during the absence of the imperial family…

Chief sights. At least a week is necessary to see the chief objects of interest in St Petersburg and its environs. As the distances are often considerable, a liberal use of cabs will be found an economy of time. It should be noted that most of the collections are closed on Mon., and open only from 10 or 11 a.m. to 3 p.m. on other days."

He recommends a drive through the town to begin with, then visits to the following: Alexander Nevski Monastery, Hermitage, Pavlovsk, Kazan Cathedral, Carriage Museum, Church of the Resurrection, Russian Museum of Emperor Alexander III, St Isaac's Cathedral (with ascent of the dome), Peter the Great Monument, Winter Palace, Imperial Library, Tzarskoye Selo, various museums and the Cathedral of SS Peter & Paul.

I have to say that I find Baedeker a touch superior when he is writing about this city:

> "Except for the imperial palaces and some of the public offices, the buildings in the chief thoroughfares are wholly modern and of large (sometimes huge) proportions. They are, however, somewhat monotonous in style, and their only unusual characteristic is the bright colours with which they are painted. The rows of secular edifices are interrupted by numerous churches. Both private and public buildings usually stand on piles, necessitated by the sumpy nature of the ground.
>
> The Streets of St Petersburg are much less animated than those of other European capitals, though they are a little less dull on Sun. and holidays. The horses are generally good, especially those of the private carriages; and the drivers, in their heavy wadded gowns, usually urge them through the streets at great speed. The scarlet liveries of the royal carriages are conspicuous. Nearly one-tenth of the male population of St Petersburg wear some kind of uniform, including not only the numerous military officers, but civil officials, and even students, schoolboys and others. Characteristic street figures, which are, however, fast disappearing, are the vendors of ices (morozhenoye) and kvass (a cooling drink brewed from rye-bread or fruit), who carry their pails and glass jugs on their heads.
>
> The wet nurses, dressed in bright and rich national costume (blue, when their charges are boys, and pink for girls) are a conspicuous feature. They generally wear a white mantle richly ornamented with silver tassels; their becoming headgear (kokoshnik) is of the same colour, shaped like a diadem, and adorned with imitation pearls and silver."

If one wants to be really disparaging (Communism not yet having made its appearance), one can always resort to an unbiased account of climate!

> "The CLIMATE of St Petersburg is raw, damp, and very unsettled; woollen underclothing is the best protection against chills. *Unboiled water should on no account be drunk.* – July is the warmest month (64° Fahr.) and January the coldest (15° Fahr.), the annual mean being 40° Fahr. Rain or snow falls on about 200 days in the year. Winter lasts for six months, and snow often falls as late as May. June, July, and (often) August are pleasant summer months, but sometimes the second half of August is raw and inclement. In September and the first half of October the weather is generally more settled. – In summer, owing to the long light nights, most people go late to bed; the more important shops do not open until 9 a.m."

Let us now leave Baedeker to admire virtually every other nation's art in the Hermitage, and instead go off on an excursion to Peterhof (now known as Petrodvorets) on the Gulf of Finland. He recommended the traveller to drive to Peterhof along the coast road, preferably on a Sunday in June or July, and return by railway, the distance being 27 versts or 18 miles. (Today the tourist can go there from St Petersburg by hydrofoil).

Built in the 18th c., Petrodvorets was destroyed by the German forces during the Second World War, and painstakingly restored in the ensuing years to its former magnificence. The following extract is taken from *The Environs of Leningrad*, Progress Publishers, Moscow, 1981):

> "Founded in 1710 as a summer residence of the tsar. Original designer unknown. The further building involved architects J-B.Leblond, P.Yeropkin, M.Zemtsov, B.Rastrelli and A.Voronikhin among others. Since the October Revolution, it has been a place of recreation and a museum complex. Situated 29km. west of Leningrad, it was occupied by the Hitlerite forces from September 1941 to January 1944 and nearly razed to the ground.
>
> As the fascist invaders drew nearer to Leningrad the palaces and parks of Peterhof were the scene of tremendous activity as the treasures and masterpieces of the estate were hastily evacuated. Under constant artillery and air attack the staff of the

Peterhof museums worked to evacuate all they could of the estate's priceless collection. 7,363 *objets d'art* were in all evacuated together with 49 statues from the Great Cascade (the central fountain ensemble) and the gardens of Monplaisir Palace. But such was the difficulty of the situation at the time when neither transport nor manpower sufficed for the work in hand, that not all of the articles of value could be hidden in time. When on September 23, 1941 the fascists reached Peterhof 34,214 museum pieces including paintings, statues and other *objets d'art* and 11,700 valuable books from the palace libraries had to be left behind.

On January 19, 1944, Peterhof was liberated by the Soviet Army. It presented a terrible picture of desolation to the troops as they entered. The beautiful palaces were in ruins and the lovely parks were marred with dugouts and trenches. The fascists had cut down 14,000 trees that were centuries-old, destroyed the fountains and put the whole plumbing system and locks on the canal out of action. At the same time they had carried off statues, bas-reliefs, vases, chalices, mascarons and even bronze door-handles."

Today, thanks to the many years of patient restoration, Petrodvorets is again pretty much the same as when Baedeker described it in his *Russia* in 1914:

"The *Imperial Palace of Peterhof was built by Peter the Great in 1720 from the plans of *Leblond,* and, though it was enlarged in 1746-51 by *Rastrelli* for Empress Elizabeth Petrovna, it has retained its original character of an imitation of Versailles. The main building is in three stories and is connected with the wings by galleries. Its red and white colouring harmonizes with the iron roof and the richly gilded domes. The *Terrace,* which is about 40ft. in height, is formed by the natural slope of the ground towards the Neva Bay, and commands a distant view of the Finnish coast. When the fountains are playing (in June and July daily, 3-5 & 7-9 p.m., in Aug. & Sept., 4-6 p.m.), the spectacle here is very imposing. A huge cascade rushes down in two arms over six wide steps of coloured marble into a large basin, in the centre of which stands the **Samson Fountain.* This consists of a bronze-gilt figure of Samson, by Kozlovski, forcing open the jaws of a lion, from which a jet of water as thick as a man's arm shoots up to a height of 65ft. The cascade is flanked with about 45 gilded statues, vases and the like. The space between the palace and the beach, 330yds. in width, is laid out as a park. The paths skirting the canal are enclosed by lofty pine-trees interspersed with 22 fountains (11 on each side).

Interior (fee to the attendant who shows the rooms, 50 kop., for a party more in proportion). On the FIRST FLOOR are the state rooms, the first of which is known as the *Portrait Room,* from the 328 portraits of girls and young women from all parts of Russia, painted by Count C.Rotari during a journey of Catherine II. We then pass to the right into the *First Chinese Room,* the walls and furniture of which are lacquered in black and gilt. The *Reception Hall* contains four portraits (by Levitzki) of girls who received the first prize at the Institute of the Noblesse in the reign of Catherine II [1762-96]. In the *Divan Room* are portraits of the Empresses Elizabeth Petrovna and Catherine II. The *Boudoir of Empress Elizabeth Petrovna* contains a beautiful tortoise-shell and bronze-gilt cabinet (Italian work of the 16th cent.) and the adjoining *Cabinet* has a portrait of the Empress Elizabeth Petrovna by Rotari. The *Standard Room* is upholstered in yellow silk. On the left side of the *Cavalier Room,* in red silk, is a portrait of Peter the Great by Balerini, while to the right is a portrait of Peter the Great on the Gulf of Finland by Dobrovolski. The predominant feature in the decoration of the *Dining Room* is the monogram of Empress Elizabeth Petrovna. The *Blue Guest Chamber* contains an oil-painting by Saltzmann, representing the reception of the Emperor William II at Kronstadt in 1888. We next reach the suite of eleven elaborately fitted-up *Rooms occupied by Queen Olga of Wurtemberg* (d.1892), daughter of Emperor Nicholas I, and three *Rooms of Princes.* The *Cabinet of Nicholas I,* in carved oak, contains a mosaic portrait of Peter the Great by Yunevitch (1855), a portrait of Nicholas I by Borthmann after Krüger, a picture of a parade of the Horse Guards under Nicholas I (by Sauerweid), and models of three ironclads.

We now return to the Portrait Room and proceed to the left into the *Second Chinese Room,* resembling the one above described. In the *White Room,* so called from its stucco decorations, are five beautiful chandeliers of rock-crystal. The *Room of the Maids of Honour* is decorated in white and gilt. The *Room of Peter the Great* contains a piece of tapestry after Steuben, representing Peter the Great on Lake Ladoga (comp. below), and also four full-length portraits (by Buchholts) of Peter the Great and the Empresses Catherine I, Anna, and Elizabeth.

> Opposite the tapestry are four scenes from the naval battle of Tchesmé (1770), by Erich. The *Saloon of the Guards* is decorated with twelve scenes from the battles of Tchesmé and Sinope, two of which are by Erich, while ten were painted by J.Ph.Hackert at Rome in 1772. The *Merchants' Room,* which we next reach, is fitted up in the rococo style, and is the largest of all. In the *Anteroom of Peter the Great* are an oil-painting by Tanneur ('Storm') and the model of a group by Ustryalov (1864), representing Peter the Great saving the lives of some fishermen on Lake Ladoga (May 26th, 1690).
>
> On the GROUND FLOOR are the *Prussian Rooms,* so named because occupied from time to time by Prussian princes. They contain paintings by Lancret, Robert, Kügelgen, and others.
>
> At the E. corner of the palace is the *Church,* with its five gilt cupolas, built in 1751 by Rastrelli. Below the palace is the shell grotto (no admission). The palace is surrounded by the houses of various court-officials. Adjacent is the small *Winter Chapel,* built in 1832."

Of all these portraits and items of furniture, a good many are back in their original places in the palace. The following extract is taken from *The Environs of Leningrad*, Progress, 1981:

> "The Portrait Gallery is one of the most luxuriously appointed rooms in the whole palace. The walls are hung with pictures of young women, which are all the work of Pietro Rotari. The whole collection was acquired by Catherine the Great from the painter's widow and hung here on the walls of this room. During the war these 368 pictures were preserved and after the restoration of the palace put back in their original places."

You will find the descriptions in the above book somewhat lacking in reference to the Russian Revolution and the fate of the last Tsar and his family, so vehement is it in its attack on the invading German armies during the last war. The reader is advised to compare and contrast the material, allow for bias, and so come to his or her own judgment about these events.

Baedeker, like a true German, sticks a "T" on the front of words which we begin with "ch" (there being no German "ch"-sound as in "cheek", the phonetic approximation has to be used). Consequently, even in his English version of *Russia,* he refers to the battle of "Tchesmé" (see above). The modern (English-language) guide to the environs of Leningrad uses a slightly different spelling, and recounts the following anecdote:

> "Hackert was commissioned to paint the pictures in honour of the Battle of Chesma in 1771. However Count Alexei Orlov (who had commanded the Russian squadron in the battle), on examining the sketches for the paintings, was critical of one canvas which depicted a ship exploding. Hackert replied that he had never seen an exploding ship, upon which Orlov immediately decided to show the artist what a real explosion looked like. With the sanction of the Russian empress and the Duke of Tuscany a sixty-cannon Russian frigate, the *Svyataya Varvara* was selected as the 'victim'. Seven miles off the coast of Livorno in Italy (where a number of Russian ships at Orlov's command stood at anchor) the *Svyataya Varvara* was packed with gunpowder and exploded. Goethe noted that this was the most expensive model that had ever been used for artistic reproduction."

One only hopes that Hackert did not blink at the vital moment! Now, after the tour of the Palace, we can follow Baedeker (in his *Russia*) through the superbly landscaped gardens of Peterhof:

> "In the W. part of the LOWER PARK are the *Lapidary Works,* established in the reign of Peter the Great. Adjacent is a bronze group by Bernstamm, representing Peter the Great holding the little King Louis XV of France in his arms. A little to the E., surrounded by water, stands *Marly,* a small two-storied white house, built in 1714 by Peter the Great. In this, to the left, are a table made by the Tzar, and his bedroom, containing his bed and dressing-gown." [The Chinese dressing-gown was retrieved from Marly – which was destroyed in the war – and is now in the Bedroom of Monplaisir Palace at Peterhof. MW]
>
> To the right is the kitchen, with Delft tiles. Passing along the Marly Pond, we see on the right the *Marly Cascade,* descending over 20 marble steps, some of which are gilded. To the N., on the shore, is the *Hermitage,* built by Peter the Great. The dining-room, on the first floor, contains 113 paintings by Netherlandish masters." [Today, there are 124 pictures! MW] "Part of the table is so constructed that it can be made to sink to the floor below."

Baedeker's need for conciseness is understandable, given that he is only on page 181 of a 500-page guide, and must keep on thrusting eastwards towards and beyond the Urals. Nonetheless, his readers are bound to be mystified by this last sentence about the sinking table. In 1914, Baedeker's *Russia* offered a large bibliography of other books about Russia in English, and it may well be that one of them contained an explanation of the eccentric Peter's arrangements at the Hermitage. Fortunately, the invaluable *Environs of Leningrad* gives a full account, if you will kindly bear with it:

> "The Hermitage was built by Johann Friedrich Braunstein, but Peter the Great himself participated directly in the design. Thus he directed that the kitchen should be built on the ground floor and the fireplace on the first floor. It was also his idea to cover the walls of the first floor with paintings, build balconies and put wrought-iron grilles on the windows resembling those of his flagship, the *Ingermanlandia,* aboard which in 1716 Peter commanded the joint forces of Russia, England, Holland and Denmark in the Northern War.
>
> As its name implies the Hermitage is situated far from the main paths in the park right by the sea. It is surrounded by a moat for which the only way across is by a drawbridge that could be pulled up, thus isolating the inhabitants from the world outside. Guests invited to a banquet could also be protected inside the palace from the gaze of onlookers. On the ground floor were the vestibule, kitchens and servants' quarters, while the whole of the first floor was taken up by a single room at the centre of which stood a dining table seating 14 people. A special device was built for raising the centre of the table from the ground floor so that food and wine could thereby be delivered to the guests, who were only required to leave a note in the centre and ring a bell for the centre section to be lowered and shortly afterwards raised again with the ordered dishes.
>
> Today an oak staircase runs from the ground to the first floor. This did not exist in Peter's time. Then the guests had to sit in a type of lift-chair which brought them up to the first floor of the Hermitage, but as he was being raised a rope broke leaving the monarch swinging in mid-air. So angry was he that he ordered the lift to be pulled down and a staircase built in its place."

My article "Baedeker Badekur" on p.80 mentions some of the western spas frequented by Peter the Great, and the strong western influences upon the style of architecture and furnishing of the royal palaces in and around St Petersburg indicate the extent to which he was determined to bring that culture home to Mother Russia. Back to Baedeker:

> "Proceeding to the E. from the Marly Cascade along the broad avenue, and passing the *Lion Fountain* and the *Eve Fountain,* we reach the *Harbour Canal.*
>
> In the E. part of the park is the *Adam Fountain.* To the NE. of the Adam Fountain, on the beach, lies –
>
> *Monplaisir*, a villa built by Peter I, in the Dutch style and adorned with numerous paintings. Its terrace commands a fine view of the sea, with the dome of St Isaac's on the E. horizon and Cronstadt on the W. The main building contains the bedroom of Peter the Great, and also a Dutch kitchen in which the Empress Elizabeth Petrovna sometimes prepared a meal for her guests with her own hands. The right wing is fitted up with baths. – To the S. is a *Bronze Statue of Peter the Great* by Antokolski, erected in 1883.
>
> On the E. the Lower Park is adjoined by Alexandria, including the so-called *Ferme,* a favourite resort of Alexander II [1855-81]. Hard by is the imperial *Villa of Alexandria,* originally built in the Gothic style by the Empress Alexandra Feodorovna, and now used as a summer-residence by Emperor Nicholas II. – Near Alexandria are the attractive little *Church of St Alexander Nevski,* built in the Gothic style by Schinkel in 1832, the villa of *Renella,* a Tudor structure by Stavasser, and other buildings.
>
> The *Stables* form an imposing pile of buildings in the Tudor style; the *Riding School* has a fine oaken ceiling."

One might well argue that, in purely western terms, the Tudor stables are the last outpost of what we would recognise as "our" architecture. Thereafter, as Baedeker continues eastwards, other (if anything more fascinating) styles take over, different cultures replace ours. In 1914 it was all very much frontier country, even if the different regions were not demarcated with barbed wire and walls. The disappearance of the physical frontier between "old East Germany" and the west has not really done much more than alert the tourist to things that were already there and clamouring to be visited.

The greatest barrier is perhaps the psychological one: overcome that, and the world truly is your oyster. Baedeker seemed not to be beset by qualms. He seemed even to relish every obstacle that geography and officialdom could throw across his path. Let us leave him on the slopes of Mount Ararat, imperturbable, utterly European, a pioneer of the Old School:

> "About 40V. (26M.) to the S. of Erivan (carriage in 6hrs., 7rb.), and 12V. (8M.) to the S. of Kamarlyu (phaeton 4-5rb.), lies the village of *Araluikh* (2760ft.), the best starting-point for the ascent of Mt. Ararat (Armenian *Massis,* Turkish *Aghri-Dagh*). This volcanic mountain stands completely isolated, at the spot where the boundaries of Russia, Persia and Turkey meet. In front, on the right, rises the icy dome of the *Great Ararat* (17,055ft.; Mt. Blanc 15,780), which falls off steeply toward the W.; on the left is the pointed peak of *Little Ararat* (12,845ft.); between them is the saddle of *Sardar-Bulag* (8335ft.). Old Testament tradition identifies Ararat with the mountain where Noah's ark rested after the flood.
>
> The best season for the ascent is Aug. and September. Rugs, cooking utensils, tea, red wine, rice, and two bags of coal must be carried. Information may be had from the frontier-officer or from the village-chief at Araluikh. Each porter receives 5rb. for the whole excursion. – As the traveller may possibly be molested by the nomadic Kurds, he is advised to take a revolver and procure an escort of Cossacks from the frontier-officer."

The Baedeker Star

[from *Baedekeriana* no. 6, Autumn 1986]

The "Sternchen" or asterisk is used as a sign of commendation for hotels, restaurants, buildings, views etc. The single asterisk is quite common, the double one much scarcer. With regard to the award or withholding of a "star", the following passage is illuminating and amusing. The late Karl Baedeker ('Karl Friedrich'):

> "I remember a difference of opinion I had with my uncle Hans when we were working together on the guidebook to Munich, in 1950. In the field where the Oktoberfest takes place, there is a big bronze statue of the goddess Bavaria. It's been there since 1850 or so. I proposed that the statue be given one star, but Hans disagreed... I thought it deserved a star because it was a famous sight. He saw it purely as a work of art. In the 1950 *Munich,* it didn't get a star but, in the 1972 *Munich* it does. I think that we at Baedeker have always been a little too frugal in awarding stars."
>
> [Acknowledgment to Mr H. W. Wind and the *New Yorker* of 22.9.75]

In the light of that, it is interesting to take down a Baedeker and see what gets asterisks and what does not. Here follows a list of "double-starrings" in *Great Britain,* 8th ed. 1927. You may be surprised that the Tower of London and St Paul's are not found here. They were given only one star, although they get two in Baedeker's *London.* Obviously standards of priority apply here: the visitor to Britain (or the Briton visiting his own country) cannot possibly see everything. The double asterisk indicates things that should not be missed, or sights worth making a detour to see (as M. Michelin would put it). The following items come in the same order as they are to be found in the book:

London, National Gallery, Westminster Abbey, Victoria & Albert Museum, Wallace Collection, British Museum, ditto with Elgin Marbles.

Rochester Cathedral: doorway in S. choir transept;
Canterbury Cathedral
Winchester Cathedral, also stalls and E. window
Avebury Circle
Salisbury Cathedral & spire
Stonehenge
St Mary Redcliffe, Bristol
Wells Cathedral
Gloucester Cathedral Choir & Great Cloister
Tewkesbury Abbey
Windsor Castle; Hampton Court Palace
High Street, Oxford
St Mary's Warwick: Beauchamp Chapel; Warwick Castle
Kenilworth Castle (Blenheim gets only *)
Coventry Cathedral spire ("one of the finest in Europe")
Chester Cathedral, Choir stalls
Lichfield Cathedral, west front
Dovedale (Wharfedale gets only *)
Peterborough Cathedral & West Front
Ely Cathedral & Octagon (Norwich Cathedral gets only * - unfair!)
Cambridge: King's College Chapel & its stained glass
Lincoln Cathedral & Angel Choir
Furness Abbey; Lake District; Windermere: view from Orrest Head
The Keswick-Buttermere road via Borrowdale & Honister Hause
Durham Cathedral & Choir; York Minster & Five Sisters Window
Rievaulx Abbey; Fountains Abbey; Hexham Abbey
Beverley Minster & Percy Shrine
Llandilo: Castell Carreg Cennen
Carnarvon [sic] Castle
Snowdon & View from its summit
Edinburgh: Princes Street
Loch Lomond
Fingal's Cave, Staffa; Iona
Loch Coruisk, Skye; Coolin Mts., Skye
Glencoe
Forth Bridge

It is tempting to mutter "predictable", and equally tempting to make up one's own list. One may go cross-eyed in the process!

Rare and Unpublished Baedekers

By L. Laurence Boyle

[This article appeared in *Baedekeriana* no. 9, Spring 1988]

Why are some titles rarer than others? Apart from the ravages of time and the influence of collectors we have to look at the size of each edition. Thus although *Indien 1914* and *Madeira 1934* were excellent, they served the needs of only an elite section of the travelling public. Others such as *Russia 1914* became out-of-date very quickly and suffered initially from difficulties of distribution in an enemy country during a war. Since this volume was still being sold in Germany in 1943, one suspects it is not very rare anyway, unlike *Madeira 1939* (1st and only Eng. version) which was only on sale in Britain for a few months [Hinrichsen gave its auction-room value as DM 1000! MW].

Some editions, such as *London 1878* or *Spain and Portugal 1898* had to be replaced quickly due to reviewers highlighting their defects, while books such as the *Conversation Dictionary 1889* were just unpopular. Anti-German feelings made all post-World War I French editions scarce, while sales of *Dalmatien 1929* or *Riviera 1931* (Engl. Ed.) were affected by international poverty. Others such as *Athens 1896* or *Weimar und Jena 1932* or even *Rom 1933* were never intended to serve more than a local temporary need.

In Baedeker's heyday the classic series to the East could be produced as a matter of prestige and sheer academic pride without reference to sales potential, but after 1930 financial subsidies for *Schlesien 1938* [Silesia], *Wien und Niederdonau 1943* [Vienna and the Lower Danube] or *Das Generalgouvernement 1943* were necessary prerequisites. The very rare *OT-Führer Italien 1944* [top price today DM 1000] was commissioned for military use with no civilian sales, while the *Autoführer Deutsches Reich 1938* [Motoring Guide to the (Nazi) German Empire] turned out to be a best-seller.

After World War 2, the *Leipzig 1948* and the German *Stuttgart 1949* are the only titles usually sought by collectors, yet the English *Stuttgart 1949* is 20 times rarer, the only Baedeker in broken English, and even an interesting book!

Totally impossible to obtain are the Baedekers which were announced but never appeared. *England 1846* would have bowed out in deference to John Murray, while author Wilhelm Lachmann probably never finished the text of *Ostende 1845.* The fourth German edition of *Holland,* announced in 1857, never appeared as a separate work, while a French translation of the 1927 edition (to accompany *Belgique 1928)* never materialised. We still await the *Ireland* volume always promised to accompany *Great Britain,* the only description of Ireland being in the German *Grossbritannien.* In fact a manuscript was completed in 1968 and was destined to be *Great Britain V (Ireland).* Like *Great Britain IV (Scotland)* this has still not been published. Tourism in Ireland has not been great since 1969. [But see pp.150 et seq. MW]

Hostilities prevented the publication of *Steiermark* [Styria], *Franken und Bayerische Ostmark* [Franconia and Bavarian Austria], *Oberdonau* [Upper Danube], *Ungarn* [Hungary] and a new edition of *Württemberg,* all of which were in preparation in 1942. The publication of *Southern Germany 1939* had already been abandoned: the complete text was then lost in the bombing raid which destroyed the Baedeker concern in 1943. The unpublished manuscript of *Jugoslawien 1944,* is however safe in the Library of Congress.

Todays' speculative collector might do well to buy up those current volumes which are not selling well!

[At the time of writing, Dr Boyle, lecturer at the University of Kent in Canterbury, was processing large quantities of editorial letters and family photographs in preparation for his *Guide to Baedeker*, making him undoubtedly the foremost Baedeker scholar in this country. My gratitude to him for permission to reprint this article, which originally appeared in the American journal *Guidenotes.]*

The Baedekers of Leonard and Virginia Woolf

[from *Baedekeriana* no. 9, Spring 1988]

The volumes listed below formed part of the Woolfs' Library collection, taken from Monks House, Rodmell, Sussex and 24 Victoria Square, London, and now in the possession of Washington State University, Pullman, USA.

Austria,1929
Southern France, 1907
Northern France 1899
Northern Germany 1925
Southern Germany 1929
Greece 1909
Italy from the Alps to Naples 1928
Northern Italy 1930
Norway, Sweden and Denmark 1909
Paris & Environs 1900
Paris and its Environs 1924
Rome and Central Italy 1930
Rhine 1926
Switzerland
1928 Tyrol and the Dolomites 1927

(From the catalogue by Holleyman & Treacher Ltd. of Brighton, printed in 1975).

My American correspondent Harold Otness, who supplied this information, has added, in his own handwriting: "Also Murray's Handbook for France, 1882."

Belgium & Holland

in Baedeker's guides

[from *Baedekeriana* nos. 12 & 16, Autumn '89 & Autumn '91]

Baedeker's *Belgium & Holland,* 14th ed. 1905, must rank as one of the 'commonest' titles but, because it is so easy for the reader to become absorbed with rarities such as *Madeira* and *Russia,* a handbook to the Low Countries (with Luxembourg) tends to suffer from undeserved neglect, as I will now try to demonstrate.

Eighty-four years ago, George V was on the throne of England, Leopold II on that of Belgium and Queen Wilhelmina on that of Holland. The pound sterling was worth 12 Dutch guilders, 25 Belgian francs and 20 Deutschmarks. The crossing from Dover to Ostende (often 'Ostend' in the guide) lasted 3-3½hrs., (3½-4½ today!)

Prices were however rather different: London to Brussels single (1st) cost £1.18s.10d., (2nd) £1.8s.4d., (3rd) 19s.8d. A second-class return from London to Ostende was £1.17s.4d. There were three boat-trains a day: the morning train began at Charing Cross, the afternoon ones from Victoria, Holborn and St Paul's. Night travellers could depart from Charing Cross and Cannon Street (also from Victoria on Fridays).

In addition to steamers from Dover, one could sail from St Katharine's Wharf, London, twice a week to Ostende in 10-12hrs., but there was no connection with trains to Brussels. The Dover-Calais route is also described.

The Guide begins with separate notes on Belgium and Holland. Both the Belgian and Dutch hotels come under attack: Belgium: 'it can hardly be said that hotels of the first class are uniformly of that excellence which the modern tourist expects and finds elsewhere'. Holland: 'In spite of the Dutch reputation for cleanliness, the traveller will often find the sanitary conditions of these hotels far from pleasant.'

In Belgian taverns, 'the arithmetic of the waiters is sometimes faulty.' In Holland, 'the front part of the café, separated by a curtain from the rear half, is generally left unlighted in the evening, so that the guests may the better enjoy the view of life in the street.'

The question of language is a fascinating field, which I can only touch on here. Belgium is not just restricted to Flemish and French in 1905, but also Walloon ('an early French patois').

> 'In spite of the efforts of the Flemish population, FRENCH is still the language of the government, the army, of most of the newspapers of public traffic, of scientific literature and indeed of all the upper classes, as it has been since the time of the crusades.' (p.xiv). In 1905, though, 'Flemish, although rich and expressive, cannot be called a highly-cultivated tongue, being spoken by the uneducated classes only, and possessing but little original literature.'
>
> 'In 1888 a knowledge of Flemish was made obligatory for military officers; but the fact remains unchanged, that a knowledge of French is still considered indipsensable to all but the lowest agricultural and labouring classes.'

Since that period, the Flemish (northern) part of the country has been making great strides, and there is a Flemish government and Flemish universities in Belgium.

Dutch, on the other hand, was classed as 'a lower Frankish dialect'. It was 'expressive and highly cultivated, and free from the somewhat vague and ungrammatical character which stamps Flemish as a mere patois.' Baedeker, as usual, is considerate in giving tips on pronunciation, and a small grammatical guide (including pronouns and paradigms of the verbs 'to be', 'to have' and 'to become' – those three indispensable pillars of any European language worth its salt!). He does however admit that Dutch is more guttural (throaty) than German, 'and therefore more difficult for the English student'.

His short list of Dutch expressions resembles the style and content of the material in the *Manual of Conversation:* 'coachman, drive us to…'; 'wait, I must fetch my luggage. I have forgotten something'; 'bring me roast beef, breast of veal, ham, fish, potatoes, vegetables, bread, butter, fruit, eggs, cheese, wine, beer, coffee, tea, gin.' One wonders if European travel has really changed for the better! [see p.227. MW]

In Belgian churches, one usually has to call upon the services of the sacristan to show pictures, 'as they are often covered with curtains or concealed in side-chapels.' The visitor to Dutch galleries is warned 'to be on his guard against spurious antiquities, which are freely manufactured in Holland.' The section headed "Dutch characteristics" is amusing and fascinating, my favourite comment being:

> 'The Dutch love of cleanliness sometimes amounts almost to a monomania. The scrubbing, washing and polishing (*schoonmaken*) which most houses undergo once a week, externally as well as internally, are occasionally somewhat subversive of comfort.'

This, combined with the rather devastating opinion 'Nature has not bestowed her charms lavishly on Holland', tends to knock the touristic bottom out of that country before the Guide proper has even begun.

In 1905, Belgium had been within the frontiers, which we know today, for only 74 years. In 1903 she had a merchant fleet of 73 ships, and a fishing-fleet of 403. She had no navy. The Dutch merchant fleet was huge by comparison (257 steamers, 436 sailing-ships), and its navy comprised 92 vessels. There was also a colonial army of 36,000 men.

Both countries suffered from the Spanish yoke (16th c.) and Louis XIV (17th). At the time of the French Revolution, Belgium 'was occupied by *French Republicans,* who divided it into nine departments', while Holland was known as the republic of Batavia. In many places in this Baedeker, there are references to the wanton damage, often to churches and abbeys, caused by the *sans-culottes* of 1793 and their Belgian allies. Both countries finally succeeded in ousting the French in 1813/14.

The almost 30 pages taken up by Professor Anton Springer's "Historical Sketch of Art in the Netherlands" are rich in observations which also obtain today. His very first paragraph reminds us how organically the art of the Low Countries springs 'out of the very soil', and how the backgrounds and characters of Dutch paintings are still everywhere to behold.

> 'A Titian is lustrous even in St Petersburg; Dürer's incisive pencil asserts itself in Madrid. Nevertheless the historical significance of Art can be understood by those only who will explore the scenes which witnessed her life's first dawn, particularly when lapse of time has failed materially to alter the character of such scenes.'

When mentioning the churches of the region, Springer is hard on Antwerp Cathedral, 'where a lamentable want of structural harmony must be noted, more particularly in the spire, whose toppling height rather astonishes by its audacity than delights by its beauty.' (The true treasures of this building are to be found inside, as we shall see later on). He also says: 'We do not visit Holland to study ecclesiastical Gothic'.

There is, for us, a poignant quality in the praise heaped upon places such as the Cloth Hall of Ypres, which were to succumb less than a decade later to the ravages of the Great War. Previously, it was still possible to say:

> 'Nothing amid the quiet streets and gabled houses of these towns will prevent the traveller from yielding himself wholly to the memories of the past, or from transporting himself in imagination to the days when the Van Eycks and Memling flourished and Flemish painting attained its first period of bloom.'

The greater part of Springer's essay is devoted to painting, with Rubens and Rembrandt commanding particularly prominent positions, as might be expected. The latter is given a generous introduction: 'Slandered and grossly abused as Rembrandt has been by dilettanti scribes of the 18th century, the enthusiastic eulogium bestowed upon him by the youthful Goethe must be noticed as an exceptional tribute.' [To the young Goethe, Rembrandt was 'a great poet comparable to Shakespeare, and a painter equal to Rubens and Raphael.']

The integrity of the essayist comes out in statements such as: 'Absolutely nothing is known of the course of Hubert (Van Eyck)'s early training, of his school or early works.' He is fairly scathing about the influence of the Renaissance on Flemish art: 'The Italian forms and even colours found no response in the inmost spirit of the Flemish painters, and the result is often mere frigid prettiness or artificial idealization… The 16th century hailed this inroad of the Renaissance upon their native art as a sign of progression!'

Rubens' female nudes are castigated here for their 'flagrant want of taste… We naturally recoil from the spectacle of naked females disfigured by the labours of maternity… coarse unwieldy shapes.' Though, in fairness, the essayist allows even all this to be an indication of 'irrepressible vitality'. More of Rubens later…

Rembrandt, by contrast, is one who 'dazzled as the flash of a meteor'. As was the case with so many Flemish and Dutch painters, a small fraction of his output remains in his native land (estimated at 30 out of 550). Of those thirty the largest and most famous, "The Night Watch", is also regarded as his greatest work, (which will receive detailed mention later in this article).

Frans Hals and Jan Steen, the 'solitary personage', favoured earthier subjects, and are dealt with in fairly humorous fashion, ending on a modest note: 'We conclude these slight observations with the wish that they may induce to a more searching study of Dutch art in a careful examination of the works themselves.'

The Guide proper is organised, in the customary manner, into a series of routes, of which the first 32 refer to Belgium (9 of these being devoted to the major towns and cities); nos. 33-35 deal with the Duchy of Luxembourg, and the remaining 23 with Holland (7 of them describing towns and cities). The Guide is furnished with the usual maps and plans (15 and 30 respectively). The normal 'Baedeker style' obtains as always, e.g. two early pages of Route 1b list châteaux (one of them 'built in imitation of Windsor Castle and belonging to the Marquis de Chasteler'), abbeys, branch-lines, steam tramways etc. For such a small country, Belgium was remarkably well served by railways in 1905.

The usually rather sceptical Baedeker treads warily when referring to religious legends, as that of **Notre Dame* de Hal, where, 'in a recess under the tower, behind a railing, are 33 cannon balls, caught and rendered harmless by the robes of the wonder-working image (of the Virgin) during a siege of the town.'

Route 2 is devoted to OSTENDE and its Environs. A spa guide to Ostende was mooted by the original Karl Baedeker and announced in 1845, but, as Alex Hinrichsen says, in his *History of the Firm,* Part I of his Baedeker-Katalog, Holzminden 1988, pp.9-10 of my own translation), 'the book by the Brunswick professor, Dr Wilhelm Lachmann, cannot have appeared (nor has there been any sign of the ms. to date), since Jügel of Frankfurt brought out, the same year, a similar work by Dr Hartwig, who was recommended by Baedeker as a spa doctor.'

Ostende may not exist as a separate volume, but, in the 14th ed. here under discussion, it merits 9pp., a town-map (1 : 18,500) and a double strip-map of the Belgian coast to each side of Ostende, with the steam tramways to Blankenberghe and Nieuwport faithfully included. (Though very much in Flemish Belgium, the latter is 'Frenchified' to Nieuport-Bains).

Hotels and lodgings abound, the most expensive being naturally those with a sea view. 'At the height of the season a room cannot be obtained under 5-6fr. a day, or 35-42fr. per week, except in the less desirable streets of the old town.'

The description of the bathing-machines is engrossing: the superior machine ('voiture spéciale') was towed by 2 horses. 'A knock with the whip on the top of the vehicle is the signal that the horse is being attached… The manager, the driver of the machine, and the towel-woman each expect a gratuity of 10c… The drinking-water at Ostende is not particularly good.' (Now where have we heard *that* before?) There are dire warnings about 'troublesomely importunate' hawkers and pickpockets.

One can amble along the Digue, 'thronged with fashionable loungers', or attend the (Dutch) fish auction with its backward counting system. Then we may move inland to Bruges, where, in the Musée Communal ('no catalogue'), some scorn is reserved for 'the Madonna… the ugliest ever painted by Van Eyck, the Child, with its aged expression (meant to indicate the presence of the Deity?), is lean and unattractive, and St George, in spite of his brilliant armour, has much the appearance of a rude common soldier.'

The eye is caught by the occasional name in small type: *Passchendaele* is here still only a station on a branch-line from Bruges to Ypres. On the same page we find that, at *Sotteghem* ('boot and shoe manufactories'), Count Egmont (executed by beheading, along with Count Hoorn, in the Grande Place at Brussels in 1568 by the Spanish Duke of Alba, allegedly for treason) is buried here with his family. The history of Ghent (about 3 times the population of Bruges at the turn of the century) makes enthralling reading. One admires the courage of its inhabitants in medieval times:

> 'When (their) princes attempted to levy a tax that was unpopular with the citizens, the latter sounded their alarm bell, flew to arms, and expelled the obnoxious officials appointed to exact payment. During the 13-15th centuries revolutions seem almost to have been the order of the day at Ghent.'

Only Baedekerian thoroughness would give us such details as 'Cow Drinking' (painting by W. Maris in Room B of the Musée des Beaux Arts at Ghent), or the Dutch name of a horticultural society: *Maatschappij van Kruidkunde* or, indeed, make references to Ghent's prisons. We learn on p.70 that John of Gaunt was in fact John of Ghent (Gand in French), and born here at the Abbey of St Bavon in 1340, the son of Edward I and Queen Philippa. (Perkin Warbeck, the Pretender, was born in Tournai).

(The Belgian) Tournai Cathedral rightly receives two stars. To those who are interested in the Merovingian Dynasty, Tournai was in the 5th century the seat of the Merovingian kings.

> 'Next to the church of *St Brice,* the tomb of *Childeric* (d.481; father of Clovis), the King of the Franks, was discovered in 1653. Childeric's sword and most of the other curiosities found in the tomb were carried off to Paris in 1664, but many of them were stolen from the National Library in 1831. Among them were upwards of 300 small figures in gold, resembling bees, with which the royal robes are said to have been decorated.'

Napoleon is said to have admired the gold bees, (of which there is a photo in *The Holy Blood & The Holy Grail* by Baigent, Leigh and Lincoln). There is also a reference to Pepin's daughter St Gertrude, and to Pepin, 'the Frankish major-domo' – born at Herstal; Pepinster, whose name is said to be derived from Pepin, is the junction for Spa and Luxembourg.

BRUSSELS: the Belgian capital receives over 50pp. of text, with a large fold-out map of the city. In 1905, the Central Station (underground) had not yet been built, so trains terminated at the Gare du Nord or Gare du Midi. Foremost among the hotels was: '*BELLEVUE, Place Royale 9, frequented by royalty and noblesse, expensive (may soon be taken down).' As the Hôtel Bellevue et de Flandre, it is still there in the 15th ed., 5 years later, though now at Place Royale 7.

The Gallery in the Palace of the Duc d'Arenberg can sport a couple of gloomy companions for our drinking cow: *A. Cuyp,* Gray horse; *D. Teniers the Younger,* Dead calf. Paintings seem to vie with one another for which can have the longest title: *A. de Vrient's* 'Excommunication of Bouchard d'Avesnes on account of his interdicted marriage with Margaret of Flanders' jockeys for position with *E. Wauters*' 'The Prior of the Augustine monastery to which Hugo van der Goes had retired in 1842 tries to cure the painter's madness by means of music.'

Shoppers make for the '**Galerie St. Hubert,** constructed from a plan by *Cluysenaar* in 1847, a spacious and attractive arcade with tempting shops…'

The most touristic place in the city is of course the Grande Place [Grote Markt], containing a sumptuous array of ancient guild houses, and also…

> 'The ***Hotel de Ville** *(Stadhuis*), by far the most interesting edifice in Brussels, and one of the noblest and most beautiful buildings of the kind in the Netherlands… The principal façade towards the market place is in the Gothic style, the E. half having been begun in 1402, the W. in 1444. The graceful *Tower, 370ft. in height, which was originally intended to form the NW. angle of the building, was completed in 1454… Probably some of the niches in the façade were intended to be purely decorative; at all events, the original sculptures having been ruined by the French Sansculottes of 1793 and their Belgian allies, the façade now seems somewhat overladen by the multitude of modern statues of the Dukes of Brabant and other celebrities with which it has been adorned, though smoke and the weather have contributed to soften this effect. The open spire terminates in a gilded metal figure of the Archangel Michael, 16ft. in height, which serves as a vane…
>
> The old ***Guild Houses** *(Maisons des Corporations)* in the Grand'Place date mainly from the period after the bombardment by the French under Villeroi in 1695, and they were carefully restored in 1889-1902. The Grand'Place owes much of its quaint and characteristic appearance to the picturesque gables of these houses, to their pilasters, balustrades, and carved decorations, and to their rich adornment with gilding…
>
> At the back of the Hôtel de Ville, about 200yds. to the SW., at the corner of the Rue du Chêne (Eikstraat) and the Rue de l'Étuve (Stoofstraat) [Étuve is a steam-room, whereas Stoof is

> merely a foot-warmer!] stands a diminutive and, it must be confessed, somewhat naïve figure, one of the curiosities of Brussels, known as the **Mannikin Fountain**, cast in bronze after *Duquesnoy's* model in 1619. He is a great favourite with the lower classes, who regard him as 'le plus ancien bourgeois de Bruxelles' [Brussels' oldest citizen, and known on the spot as the Manneke-pis, because the statue depicts a small boy perpetually relieving himself]. A similar statue in stone formerly stood here, to which Charles V., among others, presented a gala suit of clothes. When Louis XV took the city in 1747 the mannikin wore the white cockade, in 1789 he was decked in the colours of the Brabant Revolution, under the French régime he adopted the tricolour, next the Orange colours, and in 1830 the blouse of the Revolutionists. Louis XV, indeed, is said to have invested him with the cross of St Louis. The figure is not without considerable artistic excellence.

Those wishing to read up the Battle of Waterloo may first note this curious comment:

> 'Rue des Cendres, where (at no. 7, now a convent) the Duchess of Richmond gave her well-known ball on the eve of the Battle... The actual dancing took place in the adjoining building.'

Waterloo's battlefield is dealt with in detail (with a plan of the monuments). As is usual with major tourist attractions (even battlefields), one has to 'escape the importunity of beggars and guides.' As if that were not bad enough, 'the garden of a peasant contains an absurd monument to the leg of the Marquis of Anglesea (d.1854), the Lord Uxbridge, the commander of the British cavalry, who underwent the amputation immediately after the battle'.

Baedeker's long description of the Battle of Waterloo is both stirring and evenhanded. All parties come out of it with glory, but the carnage is enormous. Barely has the 'morne plaine' of Waterloo swallowed up its sacrifice of blood and bone, than the Franco-Prussian war erupts (1870-71) and then, just a century after Waterloo, on territory barely a day's drive away, the First World War. Germany can claim consistency: she always fights against France (it was the 73-year-old Marshal Blücher's rallying to Wellington's side that won us the battle against Napoleon). The reader must make up his or her own mind. But... in Waterloo,

Sedan, Passchendaele, the Ardennes – there must be some lesson for us, or the human losses were in vain. See also the récit of the Battle of Ligny, pp.238-9.

Leaving Brussels, our northward-bound train soon reaches Vilvoorde, where William Tyndale, 'the zealous English Reformer and translator of the Bible' was burned as a heretic in 1536. About half an hour after that, our train pulls into a grand terminus:

> 'Near the Central Station are several houses, such as *The Falstaff*, the *Royal* and *Worthington Taverns* (Bass & Co.), where pale ale and stout may be obtained on draught, with bread and cheese etc.'

You might think that this comes from Baedeker's *Great Britain*, but we are in fact in **ANTWERP**, a city strongly fortified still in 1905 and…

> 'the principal arsenal of the kingdom of Belgium… It is intended to serve as the rendezvous of the Belgian army, should it be compelled, in case of violation of the neutrality of the country, to retire before an enemy of superior forces.'

Antwerp ('Anvers' in French) might well earn the title of 'Rubens's town', since he lived and died here, and the *Cathedral is home to his 'far-famed masterpiece, the **Descent from the Cross', and several other works by him. His family vault is in the Church of St Jacques. [As Sint Jacobs-Kerk, it gets a star in the *Benelux* Autoguide of 1958.]

There is a rather coy reference to Matsys, 'originally a blacksmith from Louvain who, according to the legend, became enamoured of the daughter of a painter and, to propitiate the father, exchanged the anvil for the palette'.

Everywhere, it seems, one finds testimony to the unwelcome presence of the Duke of Alba (or Alva) and his Spanish soldiers, sent here by Philip II of (Catholic) Spain to subdue the heretical Low Countries – which they did with extreme cruelty. In 1635, 'metal of a statue formerly erected in the citadel by the Duke of Alva himself' was recast in the form of a crucifix, now in Antwerp Cathedral. Louis XIV caused no less havoc to the Netherlands.

The church of St Andrew contains 'a small medallion-portrait of Mary, Queen of Scots (by *Pourbus*), with an inscription in memory of that unfortunate sovereign, and of two of her ladies-in-waiting who are interred in this church.

The Rubens Collection (2000 reproductions of most of the extant works of the artist) is in the *Royal Museum of Fine Arts, whose **PICTURE GALLERY contains a superb collection of paintings, crowned by Rubens's '**297, Christ crucified between the two thieves, a very celebrated picture, considered by many to be his *chef d'oeuvre.*'

LOUVAIN 'is a dull place with 42,100 inhabitants.' Having thus fired his shot below the waterline, Baedeker tries to make up for it by giving a derivation of the name: '*Loo,* signifying a wooded height, and *Veen*, a marsh, words which are also combined in *Venlo.*' Louvain/Leuven was not always so dull:

> 'Here, as in other Flemish towns, the weavers were a very turbulent class. During an insurrection in 1378, thirteen magistrates of noble family were thrown from the windows of the Hôtel de Ville, and received by the populace below on the points of their spears.'

In common with a great many of Belgium's major buildings, the Town-hall (**) was restored during the 19th century.

LIÈGE (or, as the map has it, 'Liége' – the acute accent was finally changed to the grave in 1946, according to Baedeker's *Benelux*, but no reason is given) was famous, and still is, for the manufacture of weapons.

> 'It contains depôts of arms, for the pieces are made and mounted by the workmen in their own houses. These mechanics, 40,000 in number, work at their own risk, as a piece containing the slightest flaw is at once rejected.'

The equestrian *statue of Charlemagne* by Jehotte, 1868 (in the Parc d'Avroy), has a pedestal portraying various Merovingian rulers. W. Geefs, another sculptor, was responsible for a great many of the public pieces of statuary all over Belgium, mentioned in this Baedeker. He made the wooden pulpit for Liège Cathedral in 1844.

It is doubtless the German admiration of industry which causes Baedeker to recommend the steamboat trip ('picturesque') to Seraing. 'After passing under the handsome railway-bridge, we notice on both banks numerous iron-foundries and steel-factories of all kinds.'

The pages beyond Liège (routes 27 & 28) give us glimpses of the beautiful rocky and wooded scenery of the Ardennes, as traversed by train. The PETERSBERG caves (just over the border in Holland) can be visited, but one should go with a guide:

> 'The bodies of foolhardy explorers were formerly not unfrequently [sic] found in the more remote recesses, preserved from decay by the properties of the tufa. If any guide remains more than 3hrs. in the quarries another is sent in search of him.' – [with a ball of string, one hopes!]

Baedeker's (enforced) adherence to the railway system brings its disadvantages. On the stretch between Liège and Namur (route 30) he had to admit: 'Many of the prettiest points escape the railway-traveller.' However, there is a bonus for those who travel from Liège to Aix-la-Chapelle (Aachen):

> 'for the country traversed to the Prussian frontier is remarkable for its picturesque scenery, while the engineering skill displayed in the construction of the line is another object of interest… This is the most beautiful part of the journey between England and Germany, and should if possible be performed by daylight.'

The above part of this article having dealt with some of the finer points of Belgium, we will shortly move north of Antwerp and over the border into Holland. But first, you are going to be put through something of an assault course, concerning the different Baedekers of the Low Countries and Luxembourg, in all their editions – a bit of a minefield, even. Ready?

The first Baedeker (German) guide to Holland was issued in 1839 in two different bindings: (i) a brown unadorned binding and (ii) a 'Biedermeier' paper binding. It ran to three editions, Holland being brought together with Belgium for the first time in 1858 (6th German ed. of *Belgien*). Thereafter, until the 25th (German) ed. of 1914, they remained together. Luxembourg (for the record) was first mentioned as 'through routes' in the 15th ed. of 1880, but then appeared in its own right with its larger neighbours in the 18th ed. of 1888. An extract entitled 'Holland', from the 25th main ed., appeared in 1914. The next, 26th ed. (1927) was devoted only to Holland, and the last ("26th ed." of 1930) dealt with Belgium and Luxembourg, but not Holland.

Nowhere is the term 'Netherlands' used, and the seven editions of the Autoguide *Benelux* (1957-78, German), 1958 (French, one ed.) and 1958 (English, one ed.) are as close as one gets to that name.

The first English version of 'Holland' was included in *Belgium and Holland*, 1st ed. 1869, which ran to 16 editions (up to 1931, this latter one offering Belgium & Luxembourg but not Holland), and introducing Luxembourg in the 11th ed. of 1894 onwards.

The first French edition appeared in 1859 as *La Hollande et la Belgique*, but became *Belgique et Hollande* in subsequent versions, running to 20 editions (up to 1928, *Belgique et Luxembourg*) and introducing Luxembourg in the 13th ed. (1888) onwards.

The 15th English ed. of 1910 was reprinted in 1919, the 19th French ed. likewise. The German ed. was not reprinted in this way. Collectors are interested in the 15th English ed. of 1910 containing the Supplement to the Brussels International Exhibition of that year – not issued in the German and French editions.

If you are still with me at this point, I offer you my congratulations, with an assurance that the going will now become somewhat easier. It is a cliché to regard Holland as a flat country of dykes, flowers, windmills and prominent church towers, and Baedeker certainly strove in all his guides, to counteract such simplistic impressions by offering something meaty, readable, amusing but, above all, deeply edifying. (I refer mainly, here, to my own copy of Baedeker's *Belgium & Holland*, 15th ed. 1910).

First of all, the English traveller has to get there – very easy and quick today, maybe, but not always like that. Forget hovercraft, hydrofoil, or even Eurostar, and instead get the steamer from London, Tilbury or Queenborough. Or, if you live in the Midlands or the North, you can embark at Hull for Rotterdam, Amsterdam or Harlingen (15s. single, 20s. return); or Goole, Grimsby, Newcastle, Leith, Grangemouth or Dundee will furnish a steamer to Rotterdam. New York to Rotterdam takes about 12 days, 'saloon from 105 dollars'. Needless to say the Harwich-Hook of Holland crossing was also well established.

For my money, it would have been Queenborough to **FLUSHING** [Dutch 'Vlissingen'], starting, say, with a train from Holborn

Viaduct, then steamer (6-7hrs.), with a ticket on to Amsterdam, for 38s.7d. At Flushing I would have stopped off at the 'GRAND-HOTEL DES BAINS, 80R. from 2½, B.¾, D.2½, pens. from 5fl., closed from Nov. to end of Feb.'

If the next day were a Sunday, one could attend the 'Scottish Presbyterium [sic] Service in St Jacobs Kerk at 10 a.m.' Otherwise, the weather being hot, one might try 'The SEA BATHS of Flushing (Grand-Hotel des Bains), patronised also by German families. The air is softer and the surf not so strong as at other bathing resorts on the coast.'

One cannot visit Flushing without acquiring some snippets of its history:

> 'After the "Water Beggars" had taken Briel, Flushing was the first Dutch town to raise the standard of liberty (in 1572). Admiral de Ruyter, the greatest naval hero of the Dutch, was born here in 1607 (d. 1676). He was the son of a rope-maker, but his mother, whose name he assumed, was of noble origin. His greatest exploit was the ascent of the Thames with his fleet in 1667, when he demolished fortifications and vessels of war and threw London into the utmost consternation... During the Napoleonic wars Flushing was bombarded and taken by the English fleet under Lord Chatham in 1809, on which occasion upwards of a hundred houses, the handsome town-hall, and two churches were destroyed. This was the sole and useless result of the English expedition to the island of Walcheren, undertaken by one of the finest British fleets ever equipped, the object of which was the capture of Antwerp.'

Entering the Groote Kerk ('begun in 1412'), Baedeker seems put out that the tower was left unfinished, and also that the interior, 'as in most Dutch churches, is disfigured by the wooden stalls and pews. The organist may be engaged to play for an hour, and show the internal mechanism, for a fee of 10fl.'

Time to move on, using either the normal railway or the 'dense network of light railways, mostly worked by steam *(Stoom Tramwegen)*. Others are worked by horses *(Paarden Tram)'*. Baedeker shows a fondness for the *Stoombooten* or steamers: 'An excellent idea of the character of the country and of the peculiar charms of Dutch scenery is afforded by the steamers on the smaller canals.' Humph. Who was it that wrote *'Nature has not bestowed her charms lavishly on Holland'*?

We arrive in **ROTTERDAM**, where the *Boyman Museum has 25 pictures meriting a star. Here are a few gems chosen from rooms C & D:

> '*56. River-scene by morning-light, *55. Two gray horses, 59. Eating mussels, 58. Cow's head. – *Aelbert Cuyp*, 61. Dish with apples, 287. *Jan Steen,* Stone-operation: a stone being cut out of the head of a credulous peasant by a doctor, to the great amusement of the bystanders ('le malade imaginaire'). *262. *Jabob van Ruysdael,* cornfield in sunshine, a very beautiful landscape, evidently influenced by Rembrandt. *255 *Rembrandt* 'De Eendracht van't land' (union of the country), an allegorical painting executed in 1648, the year of the Peace of Westphalia, which Dutch poets and painters were never tired of celebrating.'

The latter comment implies that Baedeker had already had enough of the Peace which finished the Thirty Years War and left Germany 'ravaged, impoverished and little more than a geographical expression.' [*Times Atlas of World History].*

'A little to the S. of the Geldersche Kade is the Boompjes, a broad quay, which derives its name from the scraggy elm-trees planted upon it.' Many Dutch words are a delight to the untutored English ear!

So far, no mention of windmills or dykes. Instead, we are steeped in Dutch history, which obviously lives and breathes in every brick and stone, wherever we turn. On, then to **DELFT**, for Holland has the charming attribute for the jaded tourist, that nowhere is very far from anywhere else:

> '*Delft,* an old-fashioned town of 34,000 inhab. (one-third Rom. Cath.), with remarkably clean canals bordered with lime-trees, is situated on the *Schie,* which flows into the Meuse [Maas] at Delfshaven. The town was almost totally destroyed by fire in 1536, and in 1654 it was seriously damaged by the explosion of a powder-magazine; but it still possesses numerous interesting buildings of the 16th cent.'

Baedeker, perhaps thinking of Venice, is pleased not to find rubbish or dead dogs floating about here! Though a smallish town in

1910 (it has doubled its population to 70,000 in the *Benelux* Autoguide of 1958), Delft was of considerable historical significance:

> 'A melancholy celebrity attaches to the PRINSENHOF, as the scene of the death of William of Orange, the Silent, founder of Dutch independence, who was assassinated here on 10th July, 1584. The Prinsenhof, previously a monastery, was fitted up in 1575 as a residence for the Princess of Orange and was afterwards used as a barracks… By crossing through the door opposite the tower of the Oude Kerk and crossing the court, we reach the spot where the tragedy took place, on the first floor, to the right by the staircase. It is marked by an inscription. The murderer, a Burgundian named *Balthasar Gerards*, who was prompted by a desire to gain the price set upon the hero's head by Alexander Farnese, took up his position in front of the spot thus indicated, and when he discharged his pistol was quite close to his victim, who was ascending the staircase with his friends… Stepping into the NIEUWE KERK, we see the effigy of the prince in white marble on a black marble sarcophagus, beneath a canopy supported by four clustered pillars and six isolated columns, all likewise of marble… The vault below the monument is the burial-place of nearly all the princes of the House of Orange, down to the present day.'

If, like me, you welcome a little more detail, there is a very good sketch at the front of the *Benelux* Autoguide, explaining that the Prince of Orange mentioned above was a forebear of 'our own' William III of England, (1672-1702), grandson of Charles I.

> 'In the old cemetery near the Watertoren is the grave of *Karl Wilhelm Naundorff* (d.1845), a German impostor who gave himself out as Louis XVII (who had died in 1795 in Paris), son of Louis XVI and Marie Antoinette.'

There is still no mention of windmills, though Baedeker's keen eye descries 'extensive fields of hyacinths and tulips, in bloom in spring.' (He will do the bulb-fields proud when he gets to Haarlem). Not far from the latter, near the delightfully-named village of *Vogelenzang* ('bird-song')…

> 'is situated *Hartenkamp,* a country residence, where Linné (Linnaeus), the celebrated Swedish naturalist, resided in 1736-38 with his wealthy patron George Clifford, who was English ambassador at that time. Linné wrote his "Hortus Cliffordianus" here.

At **THE HAGUE** nearby, one could doubtless acquire Baedeker's guides in one of the many booksellers (*Van Stockum & Son*, Buitenhof 36, for instance) and discover the meaning of the name "Hague":

> 'Fr. *La Haye,* originally a hunting-resort of the counts of Holland, whence its Dutch name *'S Gravenhage, S'Hage* or *den Haag* (i.e. "the count's enclosure" or "hedge")... now the residence of the Queen of Holland [Wilhelmina]... Owing to the jealousy of the towns entitled to vote in the assembly of the states, The Hague was denied a voice in that body, and therefore continued to be "the largest village in Europe", until Louis Bonaparte, when King of Holland, conferred on it the privileges of a town... Many Dutch artists reside at The Hague.'

This latter comment reminds us that the jewel of this town is the Mauritshuis, with the...

> '**Picture Gallery (*Koninklyk Kabinet van Schilderyen*)... The nucleus of the Gallery of the Hague consists of collections made by the princes of the House of Orange. As early as the first half of the 17th cent. Frederick Henry (d.1647) and his consort Amalia... ordered so many pictures from Dutch and Flemish masters that they left no fewer than 250 works to be divided among their four daughters (1675). This collection was scattered...'

It was replenished by various royal successors, for whose extravagant patronage the world is eternally grateful. 'The catalogue now numbers about 500 paintings... Many of the rooms are distinctly overcrowded.'

The Autoguide says this collection 'surpasses all the other galleries in Holland by the high standard of its pictures' and mentions the following as being of especial interest:

> 'Rogier van der Weyden: Descent from the Cross (outstanding).
>
> Hans Holbein the Younger: three brilliant works (itemised in the 1910 ed. as: *276. Portrait of Robert Cheseman, falconer of Henry VIII. *277. Portrait of a man (1542). 278. Portrait of Jane Seymour (original at Vienna).
>
> Rubens: portrait of Bishop Michiel Ophovius et al.
>
> Van Dyck: "three admirable portraits, e.g. *242. The Antwerp painter Quinten Simons, one of the finest portraits painted by the master before he went to England" (1910 ed.)
>
> Franz Hals: "several brilliant portraits".
>
> Rembrandt: 15 works, including the famous "Anatomy Class", self portraits etc.'

The 1910 ed. gives a long description of Rembrant's [sic] '**School of Anatomy", 1632, and similar coverage to the '**Presentation in the Temple'. These, and many of the other artists' works (**92. Jan Vermeer, View of Delft, described on p.325) make a visit to Holland absolutely imperative to anyone interested in Dutch art. To stand before the originals of these very well-known subjects is both enthralling and moving – one feels one is among old friends - and, of course, often humorous as well:

> '170. Jan Steen, The Oyster Feast. This work was formerly styled a "picure of human life", many persons being of the opinion that Steen painted scenes of conviviality with the same moralizing tendency as Hogarth, for the purpose of rebuking human follies and vices. The picture contains about twenty persons. While the elders are enjoying their oysters, the children are playing with a dog and cat. Jan Steen himself plays a merry air, while a young woman is looking towards him, and a portly boor is laughing, glass in hand. In the background are card-players and smokers.' The famous large portrait of Steen and his family contains 'his wife, a corpulent lady in a blue-trimmed velvet jacket, filling a pipe, which one is almost tempted to think is for her own use.'

The Mauritshuis does not have the monopoly of the great: the *Steengracht Gallery (adm. daily, 'in the absence of the owner, Baron Steengracht, ring!') sports Rembrandt's *Bathsheba, Rubens's Heads of SS. Peter and Paul, Infant Christ, Drunken Bacchus, as well as modern pictures ('modern' in 1910, that is). The *Municipal Museum, not to be outdone, possesses 'an interesting picture gallery', including 'four corporation-pieces by *Jan van Ravesteyn* (1572-1657), the favourite painter of the town-council and fashionable society of the Hague.'

Also, '*106 *Jan van Goyen*, View of the Hague (14½ft. by 5½ft.), one of the most important works of this master, who knew so well how to pourtray [sic] the autumnal colouring of a Dutch landscape (1651).'

The name Mesdag crops up everywhere, culminating in the 'Mesdag Museum, containing the art-collections of the painter H.W.Mesdag, the finest modern picture-gallery in the country.' It actually houses 2 windmill paintings, but these are by a Frenchman: '260. G. Michel, Windmills at Montmartre… 259 Windmill.' Corot, Delacroix, Courbet and Alma Tadema are also represented here.

As a change to being cooped up in galleries (however superb their contents), the traveller is invited to make an excursion or two from The Hague:

> 'A steam-tramway runs to the SW. via *Halfweg* (near which is the prettily-situated cemetery of *Eik en Duin* to *Loosduinen* and via *Poeldyk* in one direction to *'S Gravesande* and the *Hook of Holland* and in the other to *Naaldwyk, De Lier* and *Maaslandsche Dam*. This line intersects the fertile *Westland,* noted for its fruit, particularly its excellent grapes. – From Loosduinen a branch runs in summer to the sea-bathing resort of *Kykduin* (Köningin Wilhelmina Hotel, board ¾fl., R. extra; sea-bath 25-40c.)' [Baedeker should not have put that Umlaut on the "o" of Koningin – Dutch does not use it.]

Bathing, as we find when we get to **Scheveningen** ('the most fashionable watering-place in Holland') is organised in almost military fashion:

> 'Bathing is permitted daily from 7 a.m. till sunset (on Sun. not after 2 p.m.), Tickets (valid for the day of issue only) are procured at the office on the Boulevard in front of the Kurhaus: gentlemen's bathing-place (large bathing-coach) and mixed bathing-place, 50c…; small coach at gentlemen's bathing-place 20c.; ladies' bathing-place (large coach) 70c. Children under ten, half price. Two towels are supplied for these charges. Bath-sheet 15, bathing-drawers 5, costume 25c.; services of an attendant 30c. – On purchasing his ticket the bather receives a number, which he will hear called out when there is a vacant coach. –

> *Tent* for the season 30, per month 10, per week 3fl.; *Beach Chair*, an excellent protection against sun and per day 20, for morning, afternoon or evening, 10c…
>
> 'Kurhaus. For the season 22½fl.; for members of families 'cartes secondaires' at 7½fl. are also issued. Day tickets 1fl. (after 5 p.m. ½fl.); book of ten tickets 7½fl. The ticket-holders are admitted without charge to the dancing 'réunions' and to the *Concerts of the Berlin Philharmonic Orchestra (daily at 3 and 7.30 p.m.; soloist-concerts on Wed., symphony concerts on Frid.), while for theatrical performances (in French) and special entertainments they pay reduced prices.'

The ever geographically-minded Baedeker reminds us that we are in the Rhine delta, as we reach nearby **LEYDEN**…

> '…or *Leiden*, in the middle ages *Leithen*, one of the most ancient towns in Holland (although probably not the *Lugdunum Batavorum* of the Romans)… situated on the so-called *Old Rhine,* the sluggish waters of which flow through the town.'

Although Rembrandt, Jan Steen, Gabriel Metsu, Jan van Goyen etc. were all born here, 'it possesses few specimens of their works.' Nevertheless, the gallery of the Municipal Museum would leave most other provincial European galleries standing. It's all relative! Baedeker gets more excited by the *Museum of Antiquities, with its 'Greek, Etruscan and Roman sculptures, Dutch antiquities and an important Egyptian collection.' In the Autoguide, Leyden is still a beautiful old town which actually sports a *hill,* on which stands the *Burcht,* or Castle.

Leyden was besieged often in its time, as was **HAARLEM**, the next town to the N. (just before Amsterdam). Baedeker writes:

> 'The town was taken by the Spaniards under Frederick of Toledo, son of the Duke of Alva. The commandant, the entire garrison, the Protestant clergy, and 2000 of the townspeople were executed.'

On a more peaceful note, about half of p.355 (15th ed.) is devoted to the bulb-growing industry:

> 'About the end of April and the beginning of May whole fields of hyacinths, tulips, crocuses, anemones, lilies, etc.,

grouped in every variety of colour and diffusing the most delicious perfumes, are seen around the town.

In 1636 and 1637 the flower-trade in Holland assumed the form of a mania, and tulips became as important an object of speculation as railway-shares and the public funds at the present day. Capitalists, merchants, and even private individuals entirely ignorant of floriculture, traded extensively in bulbs, and frequently amassed considerable fortunes. The rarer bulbs often realized enormous prices… At length, however, a corresponding reaction set in. Government declared that the contracts made were illegal, and the mania speedily subsided… About a century later a similar phenomenon occurred in the trade of hyacinths and an official list of 1734 prices a “Bleu Passe non plus ultra” at 1600 florins.

‘In front of the Grote Kerk rises a bronze statue of Coster, the alleged inventor of printing… On the strength of a story that came into vogue about 1560, Haarlem claims for *Laurens Janszoon Coster* the honour of being the inventor of printing, though no works printed at Haarlem are known with a date either before or shortly after 1447, the date of Gutenberg’s earliest productions. All that can be said with certainty is that Haarlem possessed the first printing-press in the Netherlands.’

We cannot pass through Haarlem without making a pilgrimage to **Room IV of the *Municipal Museum, which is ‘devoted to *Frans Hals*, represented by ten pictures painted between 1616 and 1664, so that we may trace his development from his thirty-second year onwards. His finest work is no.126, representing an Assembly of the officers of the Arquebusiers of St Andrew, with fourteen lifesize figures’.

On the edge of the town is the ‘Pavilion, a château erected in 1788 by the wealthy banker, Mr Hope of Amsterdam, and afterwards purchased by Louis Bonaparte, King of Holland, who signed his abdication here on July 1st 1810. From 1817 till 1821 it was in the possession of the widowed consort of Prince William V of Orange, whose bedroom is shown unaltered (free).’

At nearby Bloemendaal, ‘roads lead through woods and meadows, passing the grounds of the lunatic asylum of *Meerenburg,* to the red brick ruins of the château of *Brederode,* once the seat of the powerful counts of that name, dating from the 13th cent. but freely restored… The *view from the dunes to the NW. of Meerenburg (200ft.) embraces to the E. the admirably cultivated and partly wooded plains of N. Holland, Haarlem, the Y, Amsterdam, and the innumerable windmills of the Zaanland;

to the W. are the undulating and sterile sand-hills.' (Windmills at last!)

And so to **AMSTERDAM**, to which Baedeker devotes over 40 pages in the 1910 ed., (incl. 5 maps and plans, in colour). He warns us, for starters, that…

> 'In summer Amsterdam suffers from a plague of mosquitoes… The houses are all constructed on foundations of piles, a fact which gave rise to the jest of Erasmus of Rotterdam, that he knew a city whose inhabitants dwelt on the tops of trees like rooks… No permanent building can be erected unless a solid substructure be first formed by driving piles into the firmer sand beneath.'

Various European cities with water flowing through them get dubbed 'the Venice of the North', or whatever, but, from the above description, Amsterdam may well qualifiy. In 1910, the tourist was offered wine rooms, confectioners, baths and money changers. There were also concerts at the world-famous *Concert-Gebouw*, except in Aug, on Sun. 2-4 and 8 p.m. (popular concerts), Thurs. 8 p.m. (symphony cocnerts); adm. 1 fl., symphony concerts dearer.

How did the traveller get around this unusual city?

> '**Electric tramways** *(Gemeentetram)*. The various lines are distinguished by numbers, which hang conspicuously from the collector-bow, and by coloured discs. Fares 2½, 3, 6, 7½ or 10c., according to distance; a payment of 10c. entitles the traveller to a transfer ('overstappen').
>
> **Light Railways**. ELECTRIC RAILWAY from the Spui via Sloterdyk and Halfweg to *Haarlem* every 10min.'

There are also steam tramways and steamboats. The many canals…

> '…are flanked with avenues of elms and present a pleasant and at places a handsome and picturesque appearance. The finest buildings, including many in the peculiar Dutch brick style of the 17th cent., are on the Keizers-Gracht and Heeren-Gracht… Otherwise the tall and narrow houses of the town,

with their gables turned towards the streets, present a somewhat monotonous appearance.

The streets are pleasantly enlivened, especially on Sun. and fête-days, by the picturesque costumes of the children educated at the different *Orphanages.* Those of the Municipal Orphanage wear costumes in which the black and red city colours appear; the girls of the Roman Catholic Orphanage have black dresses with white head-dresses; and those of the Walloon Orphanage wear violet-coloured dresses.'

Those with a genuine interest in art make for the **'Ryks Museum'** [sic], to which Baedeker devotes no fewer than 21 pages, about half his allocation for the entire city:

'... an imposing brick and stone building covering nearly 3 acres of ground, was erected in 1877-85 fom the plans of *P.J.H.Cuypers* in the Dutch Renaissance style of the first half of the 16th century. The PRINCIPAL FAÇADE (N.) is turned towards the Stadhouders-Kade... The central gable, which is flanked by towers, is surmounted by a statue of Victory by Vermeylen. The alto-relief above the archway contains an allegorical figure of the Netherlands, receiving the homage of the Dutch artists. The figures in encaustic painting in the pediment and on the towers symbolize the Dutch towns and provinces. – The Museum is almost exclusively devoted to the illustration of Dutch art and life... - The general director ('Hoofd-Directeur') is Baron B.W.F. van Riemsdyk.'

The Museum is not just given up to paintings, though it has a huge number of these. There are also rooms containing military items, sculpture, works in gold and silver, porcelain, furniture etc. Baedeker sometimes complains that exhibits are 'poorly lit'. It is impossible to see more than a fraction of the collections at any one time, but nobody leaves the Museum without paying homage to the...

'**Rembrandt Rooms**, in which are assembled all the works of the great master belonging to the Museum...

ROOM I. **2016. *Rembrandt's* so-called Night Watch, the master's largest and most celebrated work (11¾ by 14¼ ft.) painted in 1642 for the Kloveniers-Doelen at Amsterdam. It represents Captain Frans Banning Cocq's company of arquebusiers emerging from their guild-house ('doele') on the Singel. The scene is laid in a lofty vaulted hall lighted only by windows above, to the left (not visible to the spectator), an arrangement probably specially adapted to the original position of the painting as it is to its present position.

In the middle, in front, marches the captain in a dark brown, almost black costume, at his side Lieutenant Willem van Ruitenberg in a yellow buffalo jerkin, both figures in the full sunlight, so that the shadow of the captain's hand is distinctly traceable on the jerkin. On the right hand of the captain are an arquebusier loading his weapon and two children, of whom the one in front, a girl, has a dead cock hanging from her girdle (perhaps one of the prizes). On a step behind them is Ensign Jan Visser Cornelissen. The other side of the picture is pervaded with similar life and spirit, from the lieutenant to the drummer Jan van Kamboort at the extreme corner, who energetically beats his drum. In an oval frame on a column in the background are inscribed the names of the members of the guild. The remarkable chiaroscuro that on bright sunny days usually prevails in imperfectly lighted interiors is here reproduced with so much poetic fancy that it was long supposed that Rembrandt intended to depict a nocturnal scene. The peculiar light and spirited action of the picture elevate this group of portraits into a most effective dramatic scene, which ever since its creation has been enthusiastically admired by all connoisseurs of art. – Each guild member represented paid 100fl. for his portrait, so that, as there were originally sixteen in the group, the painter received 1600fl. for his work.'

A former colleague of mine, not usually given to public emotion, confessed to having wept as he stood before Rembrandt's masterpiece.

Before we leave Amsterdam, a note on p.373 reminds us how careful Baedeker was to include, in his English editions, information which that readership would appreciate:

'In the Beguynenhof stands the **English Reformed Church** (service, Scottish Presbyterian at 10.30 a.m.; minister, *Rev. William Thomson*) built ca. 1400, assigned to the English community in 1607, and enlarged in 1665. The brass desk on the pulpit was presented in 1689 by William and Mary, King and Queen of Great Britain. The carved panels of the pulpit are a memorial of the accession of Queen Wilhelmina in 1898. A bronze tablet (1909) in the church commemorates the arrival of the Pilgrim Fathers in Amsterdam in 1609.'

The bronze tablet in question would have been put in place while this edition of *Belgium and Holland* was being 'revised and augmented'. The printer must have been nodding, though, by the time the 10th edition reached p.367. In the brief introduction to Amsterdam, there is a confusion at the beginning of two lines:

> '...granted the town exemption from the imposts of Holland
> and Zeeland, and
> mrced it to acknowledge his suzerainty. In 1368 Amsterdam was a
> foember of the Hanseatic League.'

Leaving the city, we make for the countryside immediately beyond, only to find that...

> '...the neighbourhood of the Dutch commercial capital has little to offer in the shape of picturesque scenery; but most travellers will find much to interest them in the extensive system of canals and sluices that has been constructed since the beginning of the present century to afford to vessels of heavy burden the access denied them by the silting up of the Zuiderzee. Of no less interest is the other system of sluices intended for the purpose of defence and enabling the Dutch to place the entire district under water in case of war. Amsterdam forms the centre of the national system of defence, and plays in Holland the same part as Antwerp does in Belgium...
>
> The HUT OF PETER THE GREAT (*Czaar Peter Huisje*) is the principal curiosity at Zaandam... The hut is situated on the W. side of the Zaan. It is a rude wooden hut, now protected by a substantial brick structure. It was occupied by the Czar Peter for a week in 1697, while he studied the ship-building and paper-making industries of Zaandam. The tradition is that he worked as a ship-carpenter in the building-yard of *Mynheer Kalf* under the name *Peter Michaeloff,* but being incessantly beset by crowds of inquisitive idlers, who penetrated his disguise, he was forced to return to Amsterdam. – The hut now belongs to the Czar of Russia.' [Nicholas II, MW].

En route for Edam, we pass *Broek* 'in the *Waterland,* a village noted for its almost exaggerated cleanliness.'

> 'Edam, which is famous for its cheese and gives its name to the cheese of the whole district, has some interesting brick buildings of the 17th century… Behind the Gothic *Groote Kerk* (Church of St Nicholas), of the 14th cent., restored in 1602-26 (stained glass) is an idyllic cemetery.'

This is not the first time that Baedeker has admired a cemetery! He also writes of the 'quaint costumes of the fisher-folk of Volendam, the seat of a small colony of artists.' The next stop is…

> 'Alkmaar, the centre of the N. Holland cheese trade. On market days (Fridays) the whole of the picturesque Place in front of the Weigh House is covered by huge piles of red and yellow cheeses, while the streets are full of the gaily-painted waggons of the neighbouring peasantry.' [Here, one feels, Baedeker is evoking one of Brueghel's *genre* paintings]. In this area, steam tramways abounded in 1910, one of them running from the town of Helder '(*Hotel Bellevue, 22R. at 2fl. incl. B., D. 2¼fl. incl. wine) to the *Lighthouse,* rising on the dunes 1½M. to the W., whence there is a magnificent view of the sea. An interesting walk may be taken along the *Helder Dyke* (6¼M. long), running round the extreme promontory of N. Holland, which is exposed more than any other part of the coast to the violence of the wind and the encroachments of the sea. The dyke is entirely built of blocks of Norwegian granite and descends into the sea to a depth of 200ft., at an angle of 40°. The highest tide never reaches the summit, while the lowest still covers the foundations.'

The map at the back of the 15th ed. shows that a dyke across the Zuiderzee was already projected, (much to the relief of boat-travellers): "The STEAM FERRY from Enkhuizen across the *Zuiderzee* to *Stavoren* takes 1½-2hrs.; in stormy weather sea-sickness is not unknown.'

The Autoguide shows the dyke in place from Den Oever to Harlingen and even gives it 2 stars! ("Place of unique interest"):

> 'The great PROJECT FOR THE DRAINING OF THE ZUIDER ZEE, the original area of which was 2025 sq.m., was begun by the Netherlands Government in 1920 from the plans of the engineer C. Lely. The first dyke was built in

> 1924, shutting off the *Amsteldiep* and uniting the former island of Wieringen with the mainland. By 1930, S. of this, the *North-west* or *Wieringermeer Polder* (73 sq.m. – 'm' is of course 'mile, not 'metre' in this ed. MW) was created, being intended at first as an experimental polder. In 1932 the great embankment across the mouth of the Zuider Zee, over 18½m. long, was completed; this shut off the Zuider Zee from the North Sea and reconverted it into an inland freshwater lake without tides, renamed the Ijsselmeer.'

Far from the sea, Eastern Holland is another story: the flat lands give way to woods and hills, as Germany ('Prussia' in 1910) is approached. Nymwegen (30ft.) 'occupies a site on an amphitheatre of seven hills' which, for Holland, is an achievement indeed!

It is to the Autoguide that I turn again, for my final look at Holland. Right down in the extreme SE. corner of the country, at the foot of the narrow strip that is the province of Limburg, lies…

> '*Vaals* (453ft.), the Dutch frontier town, with trams to Aachen. The *Vaalser Berg,* ½hr. S., is the highest hill in Holland (1056ft.); it has a view tower and a restaurant. Close by are the 'Drielandenstenen' ('Three Countries Stones') marking the point where Holland, Belgium and Germany meet.'

IRELAND

(from Baedeker's ***Grossbritannien und Irland, 3rd. ed. 1899)***

(The reader need hardly be reminded that the text of this was aimed at the German public, and that Ireland was partitioned as late as 1922/3. My translation appeared originally, in full, in *Baedekeriana* no. 18, Summer 1992. As it runs to over 30pp. I have abridged it slightly here. In the absence of maps and plans, I have omitted grid references from the text.)

Itinerary. A visit to the island of Ireland is to be recommended, and may easily be made from England or Scotland. A journey of 2½-3 weeks could be broken down as follows:

From London to *Dublin*	1 day
Dublin and environs (County Wicklow)	2
Blackwater Tour	1
From Cork to **Glengarriff*	1
From Glengarriff to *Killarney*	1
**Killarney* (Gap of Dunloe, etc.)	2
From Killarney to *Limerick*	1
From Limerick to *Kilkee*	1
From Kilkee via *Miltown Malbay* and *Ennis* to *Galway*	2
From Galway to *Clifden* and *Westport* (Connemara Tour)	2
Via *Athlone* back to Dublin	1
From Dublin to *Belfast* (poss. via Greenore & Newcastle)	1
From Belfast to the **Giant's Causeway*	1
Via *Londonderry* and *Enniskillen* to Dublin	2
	20

Crossing. Of the numerous steamer connections between Great Britain and Ireland, the following are most important to the tourist:

From *Holyhead to Kingstown* (64mi.), twice daily in 2¾hrs., connecting with the express trains of the London & North Western Rly. Large and well-appointed ships of the City of Dublin Steam Packet Co., (fare, Holyhead-Kingstown, 1st cl. 10s., 2nd cl. 7s.; return ticket valid 4 weeks 15s. and 10s.6d.; berth, advisable on night crossings, 2s. extra), with rail connection to Westland Row Station, Dublin. Travelling time from London to Dublin by express rail train, 10¼-10½hrs., fare 1st cl. 53s.2d., 2nd cl. 35s.6d., 2-month returns 93s. and 47s.

From *New Milford to Waterford,* 110mi., daily (except Mon.) in 8½hrs, (5½ on open sea); fares 46s., 35s.6d., 20s., return (valid 2 months in summer) 76s.,. 59s., 33s.6d. Dep. 2 a.m., connecting with the express train of the Great Western Rly., which leaves London (Paddington Sta.) at 5.45 p.m., arriving at New Milford at 1.45 a.m.

From *New Milford to Cork*, 160mi., 3 times weekly (Tues., Thurs., Sat., dep. 10.30), to Passage (Cork Harbour) in 12hrs.; thence by rail to Cork. Fares from London to Cork 48s., 32s., 21s.4d., return 80s., 55s., 37s.10d.

From *Holyhead to Greenore*, 70mi., daily (except Sun.) in 6hrs. (7s.6d., 3s.), connecting with the night express of the London & North Western Railway, 6.30 p.m. from Euston Sq.; the best connection from London to Belfast, the Mourne Mts., etc.

From *Stranraer to Larne,* 39mi., daily (except Sun.) in 2½hrs. (shortest crossing, 2hrs. at sea), connecting with the express trains from Glasgow (Caledonian and St Enoch's Sta.) and London (Euston & St Pancras); connection at Larne for Belfast, the Giant's Causeway, etc. Fare from Glasgow to Belfast 1st cl. 17s.6d., 3rd cl. 8s., return 27s.6d. and 13s.; from London 58s.6d., 45s., 27s.6d., return 100s., 75s., 55s.

From *Glasgow to Belfast*, 129mi., daily (except Sun.) in 7-7½hrs., via *Greenock* or *Ardrossan* (steamer crossing 6-6½hrs.), 1st cl. 12s.6d. (ret. 20s.), 3rd cl. 4s.

Direct steamers (usually good) also ply from *London* to *Dublin, Waterford & Cork;* from *Bristol* to *Dublin, Wexford, Greenore, Belfast* and *Londonderry* etc.

Hotels. In the larger towns and many of the places much visited by tourists, first-class hotels will be found, which cater for all modern tastes. In the smaller towns and remoter districts, there is often very little accommodation, and what there is leaves a lot to be desired regarding cleanliness and service, the prices not being cheap.

Transport. The Irish railway network is well developed. The trains all travel more slowly than in England, and timetabled departure times are not always adhered to, so that connections are often missed. Expresses run only on the main lines (Dublin-Cork-Bantry, Dublin-Galway, Dublin-Belfast). The second class meets all one's requirements.

Where there is no rail connection, passengers are conveyed by *mail cars*, open carriages, on which they sit back to back, with the mail packets between, so that the view is open only to one side. When using a mail car, one should provide oneself with raincoats, travel rugs etc. On some of the more frequented tourist routes, there are *vans* or *long cars* for about 12 people, which are scarcely more comfortable but at least not overloaded with packets.

Tourist coaches of the English variety ply from Glengarriff to Killarney. Private hire cars are cheap (6d., 8d., 10d. and 1s. a mile for 1,2,3 & 4 pers.); the cars are very simple and almost always uncovered.

Geographical notes. The island of Ireland (Irish *Erin*, 'the western isle'), separated from England and Scotland by straits, 13-130mi. wide (the *Irish Sea* or *St George's Channel* and *North Channel*), covers an area of 84,252 sq.km., with 4,704,750 inhab. (1891). The bulk of the island consists of a plateau of carbonifeous limestone with deposits of clay and gravel. Although only slightly jointed on the E. and S. sides, it breaks up, to W. and N., towards the Atlantic Ocean, into numerous promontories and peninsulas, between which deep bays cut into the land. There are also many lakes (*loughs,* Scots loch) in the interior, the largest being *Lough Neagh* in Co. Antrim and *Lough Corrib* in Galway. The chief rivers are the *Shannon* to the W., the *Lee, Blackwater* and *Barrow* in the S., the *Liffey* and *Boyne* in the E., and *Bann* and *Foyle* in the N. The mountains never form into ranges of any size and usually rise near the coast, chiefly in the counties Wicklow and Donegal in the N., Galway in the W., and Kerry to the SW., where *Carrantuohill* attains a height of 1040m. The climate is more mild and equable than in England, the soil fertile overall, though much of the land lies fallow. Snow and ice are rare, and the island is clothed in green even in winter, its vegetation resembling that of S. England. Thus Ireland is also dubbed 'the green island'. It is rich in beautiful landscapes. The lover of antiquity will also find much of interest: numerous ruins of churches and monasteries from early Christian times, the remarkable round towers, of which over 100 still exist (doubtless intended originally as refuges for monks and their treasures in times of war, but at the same time serving as bell towers), the ancient Celtic stone crosses, cromlechs , etc. – The *Irish language* (Celtic or Erse), closely related to Welsh and Gaelic, is still spoken by 680,000 people (1891), but English is spoken and understood almost everywhere, though delivered in a peculiar, hard dialect.

Ireland is divided into four provinces (once kingdoms): *Ulster* in the NE., with the 9 counties of Antrim, Armagh, Gavan, Donegal, Down,

Fermanagh, Londonderry, Monaghan and Tyrone; *Leinster* in the SE., with the 12 counties of Carlow, Dublin, Kildare, Kilkenny, King's County, Longford, Louth, Meath, Queen's County, Westmeath, Wexford, Wicklow; *Connaught* in the W., with the 5 counties Galway, Leitrim, Mayo, Roscommon and Sligo; and *Munster* in the SW., with the 6 counties Clare, Cork, Kerry, Limerick, Tipperary and Waterford. The head of government is a viceroy (Lord Lieutenant), who resides in Dublin and is assisted by a Secretary of State and a Council of State.

Historical notes. The original settlers in Ireland were *Celts* or *Gaels* (also called Scots, in the oldest chronicles). In the Vth c., *St Patrick* brought Christianity to Ireland; numerous monasteries sprang up from which, in the VIIth and VIIIth c., (among others), the first messengers of the faith went out to the mainland. In the IXth c., the Normans conquered the island, but were driven out again in the XIIth. Soon after (1171), the English king Henry II landed, beginning the conquest of Ireland, which was however only completed under *Elizabeth* (1558-1603). In the following century, the Irish Catholics supported the Stuart cause, but were defeated by *Cromwell* (1649) and William III at the Boyne (1690). Already under Elizabeth, but especially under Cromwell and William II, there was confiscation of Irish land on a massive scale, and it is from this that the present circumstances principally arose. In 1800, the Irish Parliament was united with the British one. In 1829, *O'Connell* passed the Emancipation Bill, i.e. allowing the Catholics to become members of parliament and to occupy all public offices. In 1845 and 1846, the land was visited by terrible famine, and hundreds of thousands emigrated to North America. There, where about 5 million Irish now live, the secret society known as the *Fenians* came into being in 1863, whose aim was to tear Ireland away from England. It did not reach its objective, but it brought the Irish question into the open again, which stood for many long years in the forefront of English political interests. The Irish 'Home Rule' party, linked to the 'Land League' since 1880, is striving towards a separate administration and parliamentary self-government for Ireland, to drive out the English landowners and 'hand Ireland back to the Irish'.

The *Irish coat of arms* is a golden harp with silver strings on a blue ground; Ireland's symbol is the clover; its generally revered patron saint is St Patrick.

73. Dublin.

Stations. 1. *Amiens Street Station* (Great Northern Rly., for Belfast, Londonderry etc). – 2. *Broadstone Sta.* (Midland Great Western, for Sligo, Westport, Galway, etc.). – 3. *Kingsbridge* (Great Southern and Western, for Cork, Limerick, Waterford, Killarney, etc.). – 4. *Westland Row*, for Kingstown and Bray. – 5. *Harcourt St.*, for Bray Wicklow & Wexford. – 6. *North Wall*, on the steamer quay, linked to the first three.

Hotels. S. of the Liffey: *Shelbourne, St Stephen's Green, rm. & service 4s.6d.-6s.6d., lunch 5s.; Morrison's, Dawson St. (both 1st class). Powers Royal, Maple's 48 Kildare St; Hibernian, Dawson St.; *Jury's, College Green, well placed, rm. & service 4s.; St Stephen's Park Temperance, St Stephen's Green, rm. & service 3s.6d., lunch 3s.; Nassau Temp., Nassau St.; Grosvenor, opp. Westland Row Sta. – N. of the Liffey: Hôt. Métropole, Imperial, both in Lower Sackville St.; *Gresham, 21 Upper Sackville St., rm. & serv. 4-5s., breakfast 2s.6d., lunch 4s.6d.; Hammam, 11-13 Upper Sackville St.; Northwestern, on the steamer quay near North Wall Sta.; Edinburgh Temperance, U. Sackv. St.

Restaurants. **Mitchell*, 10 Grafton St.; *Hôt. Métropole*, Lower Sackville St.; *Bodega* (Spanish wines), Commercial Buildings, Dame St.; *Franklin's*, Dame St.; *Hyne*, 55 Dame St.; *Sackville Café*, 7 Lower Sackville St.

Theatres. Leinster Hall, Hawkins St.; *Queen's*, Gr. Brunswick St.; *Gaiety*, South King St.

Cabs within town, 1-2 pers. 6d., 3-4 pers. 1s., double rate from 10 p.m. to 9 a.m.; the first hr., 1-4 pers. 1s.6d., every subsequent ½hr. 6d. Larger items of luggage, 2d.

Trams go along all the main streets (1d.-3d.); the main junct. is Nelson Pillar in Sackville St. Connection with the Hadington Road-cars *electric tram* to *Dalkey,* via *Blackrock, Monksdown* and *Kingsdown.*

Post & Telegraph Office, Sackville St., 7 a.m. – 9 p.m., Sun. 8-10 a.m.

German Consul, Mr J. Murphy.

Dublin, the capital of Ireland, with 278,896 inhab., lies in a depression (bordered to the S. by the handsomely shaped *Wicklow Mts.*) on both banks of the *Liffey,* which divides the town into two halves, and flows into Dublin Bay 1½mi. downstream.

Dublin, the old Irish *Ballyath-Cliath* (town on the fording-place of the herds), is an ancient Celtic place, whose inhabitants were apparently converted by St Patrick as early as 448. In 851, under the name *Dubhlin* (black water), it was conquered by the Danes and became the seat of Danish kings, who were repeatedly driven off, but constantly returned and stood their ground. In 1169, it passed to the English through Richard, Earl of Pembroke, known as Strongbow, and it honoured Henry II in 1172. Until the XVth c., it formed a county in its own right, supported the Stuart cause in 1659 and later on (until recently) was the seat of the Irish Opposition. The bishopric of Dublin was founded in 1038, and elevated to archbishopric in 1214.

The town's main thoroughfare is *SACKVILLE STREET with its S. continuations to *St Stephen's Green*. In the middle of the street, at the intersection with Henry St. and Earl St. is the *Nelson Pillar*, a Doric column 40m. high, crowned with a statue (the best view of the town is to be had from the top; entrance 6d.); opposite, the imposing *Post Office*. At the N. end of the street is Rutland Square with the *Rotunda,* a circular room 24m. in diameter; at the S. end, at *O'CONNELL BRIDGE, the *O'Connell Monument*, by Foley.

Fine views up- and downstream from the bridge: below the bridge, on the l., the imposing *Custom House* with its dainty cupola; above, the *Metal or Wellington Bridge* and *Grattan Bridge,* and, beyond, the dome of the *Four Courts* and, to the S. of this, the towers of *Christchurch* and *St Patrick*. S., in Westmoreland St., the *Bank* and *Trinity College,* (see below).

At the S. end of the bridge is the statue to *W.Smith O'Brien* (d. 1864), leader of the Young Irish Party, by Farrell. From here we go down Westmoreland St.., along past the E. side of the *Bank of Ireland,* and the statue of *Thomas Moore* (1779-1852), composer of the "Irish Melody", to *Trinity College,* Dublin's *University,* a splendid building, 90m. long, in Corinthian style.

L. and r. of the entrance, the statues of *Edmund Burke* (1729-97) and *Oliver Goldsmith* (1726-74); inside (entrance free; to visit the rooms, apply to the porter), on the l. side of the large courtyard ("Parliament Square"; 170 X 82m.) are the *Chapel* and the *Dining Hall*; opposite, to the r., the *Examination Theatre* and *Library* (open on weekdays, 9-4), with 250,000 volumes and a valuable collection of Irish mss. (inc. the "Book of Kells", the "Book of Durrow", the "Book of Armagh" etc.; these may be seen only with special permission). Here, there is also an old Irish *harp, supposedly the property of King Brian Borumha, who fell in 1014 at Clontarf when fighting the Danes. The *belltower* was erected in memory of Provost Baldwin. In the New Quadrangle are the Engineering School and the small old *University Press.* In the pretty *College Park,* with games areas for the students, are the richly equipped *Medical School* and *Museum* (open weekdays 10-4, Sun. 10-1), with a large collection of skulls and good zoological collections. To the S. of the Library, in the *Fellows' Garden,* the *Magnetic Observatory.*

On College Green, a fine open area W. of Trinity College, stands a superb statue of the famous orator *Grattan* (1750-1820), by Foley; further W., an equestrian statue of *William III.* On the N. side, the *Bank of Ireland,* the former parliament building (until 1800), with an imposing pillared portico. To the W., Dame St. runs directly to the Castle.

We first make our way along the busy *Grafton St.*, with fine shops, to ST STEPHEN'S GREEN, the town's largest square (above 13 hectares), with attractive parks and statues to *George II,* the Governor *Lord Eglinton* and *Lord Ardilaun* (by Farrell). On the W. side, the *Royal College of Surgeons* with a museum (weekdays 10-4); on the S. side, the *Wesleyan College* and the *Catholic University;* on the E. side, *St Vincent's Hospital* and the *Royal College of Science* with a mineralogical museum (weekdays 10-4); on the N. side, the Palace of the Archbishop of Dublin, and several clubs.

From the NE. corner of Stephen's Green runs Merrion St. (where, in the former *Mornington House*, now the seat of the Irish Land Commission, Arthur Wellesley, future Duke of Wellington, was born in 1769). The street is named after the large, park-like *Merrion Square*. To the W., *Leinster Lawn,* with a *statue of Prince Albert;* on the N. side, the *National Gallery* (Mon. Tues. Wed. Sat. 12-6 free, Thur. Fri. 10-4, 6d.) with sculptures and paintings (incl. numerous works on loan from the National Gallery in London), also an Irish National Portrait Gallery. On the W. side of the square (entrance in Kildare St.) is the noble *Science and Art Museum and Library* (museum daily 11-5, Tue. Thu. till 9, Sun. 2-5; Library weekdays 10-10), with the collections of the *Royal Dublin Society*, founded in 1731. In the large hall, a statue to George IV by Behnes, and numerous busts. There is an interesting collection of photographs (Dunraven's) of Irish monuments and antiquities. The *Natural Hist. Museum* on the S. side of Leinster Lawn contains rich scientific collections, incl. the extremely valuable collection of *Irish antiquities*, formerly housed in the *Royal Irish Academy* (entrance on weekdays 11-5, Tues. until 9, free).

Of especial note are the *Ardagh Chalice*, in gilded and enamelled metal; the *Cong Cross*, wood, with richly gilded and enamelled bronze, made in Roscommon around 1120; *St Patrick's Bell*, a square iron bell with handle,

15cm. high, presented by St Columba to the church in Armagh around 446, with an artistic case (c.1100); a *ms. of the Gospels,* which apparently belonged to St Patrick, a *psalter belonging to St Columba,* etc. Then numerous prehistoric items and fragments of clothing, found in the peat moors; old weapons, jewellery, a replica of Brian Borumha's harp, and another old harp; in the basement, old boats, iron pots, Ogham stones, etc.

Near the Academy, to the S., the *Mansion House,* to the N. *St Ann's Church,* in which the poetess Felicia Hemans (d.1835) is buried. We return to College Green and, going along Dame St. to Cork Hill, reach the main entrance of *Dublin Castle,* (visit to the state-rooms by arrangement with the janitor), a dark building with two courtyards, originally built as a fortress in the XIIIth c., now the Viceroy's official residence. On the S. side of the first courtyard (Upper Castle yard) are the vice-regal state-rooms (St Patrick's Hall, Presence Chamber and the Council Chamber with its life-size portraits of all the viceroys); in Lower Castle yard is the *Round* or *Bermingham Tower* (formerly richly decorated interior) with old stained glass, altar screen of "bog oak", i.e. black oakwood found in the peat; on the walls, the arms of the viceroys; in the decoration, the harp and clover-leaf, the Irish emblems, recur everywhere, along with Celtic crosses). Military music is played daily at the changing of the guard in the inner courtyard.

We continue along Castle St. to *Christchurch Cathedral* (service on weekdays at 11 and 3, Sun. 11.15 and 3.30),originally built in the XIIth c. by Earl Strongbow and Archbishop Laurence O'Toole. It has been almost completely renovated by Street since 1871 at a cost of £220,000 (found by the brandy manufacturer H.Roe), in Early English and Norman transitional style. The Cathedral has now been completely laid bare (the N. side is finest, with its projecting baptismal chapel); on the W. side, linked to the church by a gallery, is the *Synod Hall* of the "Church of Ireland".

From Christchurch Place, Nicholas St. and Patrick St. lead us S. in 8min. to *St Patrick's Cathedral* (service on weekdays 10 and 4, Sun. 11.15 and 3), the more interesting of Dublin's two cathedral churches, on the site of a church which was apparently founded by St Patrick in the Vth c., reconstructed in 1190 in Early English style by Archbishop Comyn, later in ruins, but recently restored by the brewery owner Sir Benj.Lee Guinness at a cost of £140,000. Inside are the banner of the Knights of St Patrick and the tombs of *Jonathan Swift* (d.1745) and his friend *Stella* (Hester Johnson, d.1728), also the monument to *Marshal Schomberg* (Friedrich von Schönburg, 1615-90), who fell at the Boyne. At the S. end, a tasteful *Lady Chapel.*

We continue N. from Christ Church across Richmond Bridge to the *Four Courts* (Law Courts), on the N. bank of the Liffey, a noble domed structure of the late XVIIIth c. The façade is 137m. long; above the central doorway is a huge statue of Moses. In the large *Central Hall,* a number of statues of famous jurists.

We follow the quay W. from here, passing *Whitworth Bridge, Queen's, Victoria* and *King's Bridge*, reaching, in 20min., *Park Gate*, the entrance of *Phoenix Park* which, with an area of more than 700 hectares, is one of the world's largest parks. Immediately to our r., the *Military Hospital* and the *People's Garden*, with attractive grounds; on the l., the *Wellington Testimonial*, an obelisk 62m. high. Then, on the r., the *Zoological Gardens*; admittance on weekdays 9-7, 1s., Sun. 12-7, 2d.), with a good collection of animals of diverse species. 1mi. from Park Gate is the *Viceregal Lodge*, a long building, simple in style. Further on, between the statue to *Lord Gough* (by Foley) and the *Phoenix Pillar*, is the spot where the Irish State Secretary, Lord Frederick Cavendish, and the Under Secretary, Thomas Burke, were assassinated on 6th May 1882. On the S. side of the Park, near Chapelizod Gate, a *cromlech*, discovered in 1838.

In *Glasnevin Cemetery,* on the N. side of the town (tram from Nelson Pillar), stands a 45m.-high round tower in honour of the Irish patriot *Daniel O'Connell* (1775-1847), and the tombs of other Irish notables are to be found here. – Nearby, the *Botanical Gardens,* through which the *Tolka* flows (weekdays 10-6, Sun. 2-6).

Environs. The hills and valleys of *County Wicklow*, to the S. of Dublin, offer a number of pleasant and rewarding excursions. The best centre for these is *Bray,* reached in 35min. from Harcourt Street or Westland Row stations (about 20 trains a day on both lines; fares 2s., 1s.6d., 1s., return 2s.6d., 2s., 1s.6d.). – From Westland row, the line goes via *Merrion,* where it touches the sea (view of the Howth peninsula to the l.), and *Salthill* to (6mi.) *Kingstown (*Royal Marine; Anglesea Arms*), a frequented resort with a good harbour, whence the mail steamers sail for Holyhead. 1mi. S., *Killiney* Hill (about 140m.), with a fine view. We continue via Dalkey (Queen's, poor), an attractively situated place with the rocky *Dalkey Island,* and *Killiney* to

12mi. *Bray* (*Royal Marine; International; Esplanade; Rudd's Temperance*; these on the Esplanade, with sea views; *Bray Head,* 10min. from the sta.; *Royal,* in the town), a frequented seaside resort in a charming position on a beautiful bay between the headlands of Dalkey to the N. and Bray Head to the S. It is worth climbing *Bray Head* (198m.), 1½hrs. return, with fine views. Other pleasant trips may be made to **Dargle Glen*, a richly wooded rocky valley with numerous waterfalls, 1hr. to the W. (the finest points being *Moss House, Lovers' Leap* and *View Rock),* returning via *Enniskerry* (Powerscourt Arms); to *Powerscourt House* and *waterfall,* returning through the *Rocky Valley* and via *Hollybrook* (½hr in all); up the

Great Sugarloaf (505m.), with extensive views, 1½hrs., descending by the *Glen of the Downs* and via *Delgany* (hot.) to (2hrs.) *Greystones sta.;* then back by train.

From Bray to Wicklow and Wexford, 81mi. by rail in 3¼hrs. The line follows the coast via (5mi.) *Greystones* (Grand Hotel), a small watering-place, *Kilcool* and *Newcastle* to (16mi.) *Wicklow (Green Trees; Bridge),* a frequented spa (3300 inhab.), with the nondescript ruins of *Black Castle* (XIVth c.), set on the N. side of *Wicklow Head.* Then our line leaves the sea and turns r. inland. From *Rathnew* (17½mi.), a road runs, r., past the attractively situated (1mi.) *Newrath Bridge Hotel* to (1½mi.) *Ashford (**Ashford Hotel; Glen), a frequented summer resort; 3½mi. to the W. is the romantic **Devil's Glen,* in the gardens of *Ballycurry House* (accessible on weekdays). From Ashford to the Seven Churches, (see below) 12½mi. – 26mi. *Rathdrum* (Royal Fitzwilliam Hotel) is the point of departure for the tour of the *Seven Churches* (8½mi.; coach for 5 or more, 2s.6d. per head). The road runs through *Avonmore Valley* via (3mi.) *Clara Bridge* and (7½mi.) *Laragh,* where it branches l. to the (8½mi.) *Seven Churches of Glendalough (Royal Hotel; inn* by the upper lake), one of Ireland's holy places, where St Kevin lived as a settler and founded a monastery in the VIth c. A few steps from the hotel, within the former ramparts, a round tower, 33m. high, apparently VIIth c. The 'seven churches' of Glendalough (valley of the two lakes), dating from the VIth and VIIth c., lie partly below the smaller lower lake (the so-called *Cathedral, Our Lady's Church, St Kevin's Kitchen, Trinity* and *St Saviour's),* and partly by the larger and more beautiful upper lake, shut in by steep rocky hills (*Reefert Church* and *Teampul-na-Skellig).* Near the latter is *St Kevin's Bed,* the saint's grotto, and, at the lower end, an *inn,* much visited by tourists.

From Rathdrum, the railway runs (r.) past *Avondale* (Mr.C.S.Parnell) to (31mi.) *Ovoca* and (33mi.) *Wooden Bridge (*Wooden Bridge Hotel,* pension or rm. 8s.6d. – 9s.6d.), a charming point where the Ovoca and Aughrim meet (branch line W. to *Shillelagh,* 17mi.). Then SE. through the wooded Ovoca valley to (37mi.) *Arklow* (Kavanagh's Hotel), small town with harbour, and inland again via (58mi.) *Ferns,* (66mi.) *Enniscorthy* (Bennett's) and (71mi.) *Macmine Junct.* (for *Ballywilliam* and *New* Ros, see below) to (81mi.) *Wexford (White's Hot.),* a sea port with 11,500 inhab. and the remains of old fortifications, on *Wexford Harbour,* about 5mi. from the sea. Steamers ply weekly from here to Bristol (15s.) and Liverpool (12s.6d.).

73. ***From Dublin to Limerick and Cork*** *(Killarney)*.

GREAT SOUTHERN AND WEST RAILWAY… Departure from *Kingsbridge Terminus*. The line runs through the *Liffey valley*; monotonous arable land, distant hills on both sides; neglected farmhouses everywhere…

**Kilkenny Castle*, the imposing and well-preserved castle of the Marquis of Ormonde, contains a valuable collection of paintings and other objects of art. *St Canice's Cathedral*, early Gothic, XIth and XIIth c., with a 30m.-high round tower, is richly fitted out inside, and contains tombs of the Ormondes…

Waterford (Adelphi, on the quay; *Imperial*, in the Mall, near the quay; both inexpensive), port with 20,850 inhab. on the S. bank of the broad navigable *Suir.* Apart from the mile-long quay and the *Mall* running up from it, the town consists of narrow dirty streets, above which rises the tall tower of the *Protestant Cathedral*. There is also a Catholic cathedral. A pleasant walk may be taken along the quay and over the bridge, 230m. long. The best view of the town may be had from *Mount Misery* and *Cromwell's Rock*, both on the l. bank of the Suir; a more comprehensive view may be had from *Cheekpoint Hill* (132m.), 2hrs. to the W. on the r. bank, not far from the confluence of the Suir and Barrow. Sea-bathing in *Tramore* (Great Hotel, Marine), 7¼mi. S…

Limerick (Cruise's Royal Hot., Royal George, both in George's St.; **Glentworth,* Glentworth St., closer to the sta.; *Railway*, at the sta.), a considerable town on the *Shannon,* consists of *Newtown Pery* (founded in 1769 by Mr Sexton Pery), with broad, regular streets and imposing buildings, and the older quarters, *Irish Town* and *English Town.* There is a particular trade in corn and ham.

The Danes founded Limerick in the IXth c., and it was later the capital of the kingdom of Munster, until King John conquered it and built a solid fortress here. The main event in the town's later history is its siege and eventual conquest by William III in 1690-91. Limerick was the last place to hold out against James II, and was so courageously defended by the Irish under Sarsfield, that William raised his siege in 1690. When however his general, Ginckle, stormed the fort in 1691, which covered the crossing of Thomond Bridge, the town could hold out no longer, and capitulated on 3rd Oct. 1691, article 9 of the treaty promising the Catholics religious freedom and protection of their property. This promise was not kept, and this is why Limerick is known as 'the city of the violated treaty'. The *Treaty Stone,* on which the document was signed, can still be seen at the W. end of Thomond Bridge.

Limerick possesses few 'sights'. SW. of the sta. is *Pery Square (People's Park*), with a statue of Mr Spring Rice. We go from the SW. corner along Barrington Street to Military Road, then r. across Richmond Place, with a *statue to O'Connell,* at the S. end of GEORGE'S STREET, the town's imposing main street. On the l., in Lower Cecil St., is the *Post Office.* From the N. end of the street, Patrick and Rutland Streets lead past the *Town Hall* and *Customs House* across *New Bridge* to *English Town.* A better route is to go l. by the Royal Hotel along Sarsfield St. to *Sarsfield Bridge* over the Shannon (before the bridge is a statue of *Lord Fitzgibbon,* who fell at the battle of Balaclava in 1854), with a fine view; from here along the r. bank, on North Strand, upstream to *Thomond Bridge* and through the dirty *English Town*, past the impressive Norman *castle* (now a barracks) and the Gothic *St Mary's Cathedral* (founded in the XIIth c.), to *Balls Bridge* over the Abbey River; then through *Irish Town*, with *St John's Church* (Prot.) and the new *St John's Cathedral* (Cath.), back to the sta…

*Cork (*Imperial Hot.,* South Mall, 1st class, rm. & service 4s.6d., dinner 5s.; *Moore's,* Morrison's Quay; *Leech's; Victoria),* the third largest town in Ireland, with 73,345 inhab., occupies an island and the sloping banks of the *Lee,* on both sides. The history of the town goes back to the VIIth c., when St Finbar founded his church on the S. bank, above *Corcach-mór* (the marshy area of Munster, whence its name). The modern parts of the town, with their imposing broad streets (Grand Parade, St Patrick's St., Great George's St., South Wall etc.) contrast strikingly with the narrow dirty streets of the old town.

Leaving *Glanmire Station* of the Great Southern and Western Rly., we follow the l. bank of the Lee, via *Penrose and St Patrick's Quays*, with the steamer landing-stages, to *St Patrick's Bridge.* On the other bank, we turn r. across Lavitt's Quay to Nelson Place with the *theatre* and the *Royal Cork Institution and School of Art*, opened in 1885, with a library and minor collections. – At the beginning of *St Patrick's St.*, which runs S. from St Patrick's Bridge, is a *bronze statue of the well-known apostle of moderation *Father Mathew* (d.1856), by *Foley*; at the end of the picturesque street, on the r., is the Cath. Church of *SS Peter & Paul,* by Welby Pugin. We now turn l. into Grand Parade, then r. along Great George's St. to the *Court House,* with a fine Corinthian pillared portico. From here, passing *Christ Church,* we regain Grand Parade, turning l. at the end of it into *South Mall,* the main street of the town, with a row of imposing banks and clubs.

From the end of the Mall, Lapp's Quay leads to the spacious *Customs House,* on the E. point of the island. Here we turn r. over *Parnell Bridge*, leaving the *Corn Exchange* and *Albert Quay Sta.* on our l., and follow the quays on the r., along the Lee. Opposite, on the other bank, is *Holy Trinity*, Father Mathew's monastery; on the l., in Dunbar St., is the Cath. Church of

St Finbar, with a fine altar. We continue past *Elizabeth Fort* to the Protestant CATHEDRAL OF ST FINBAR, the most outstanding edifice in the town, built in 1862-79 by Burges in French early Gothic style on the lines of Bayeux Cathedral, with a splendidly decorated W. front (side towers 55m., central tower 73m. high). In its richly fitted-out interior are good modern stained-glass windows, sculptures and fine mosaic floors in the apse. – Further to the W. of St Finbar's, in College Rd., is **Queen's College*, founded in 1849, with 300 students and beautiful grounds.

The best view of the town and the Lee valley may be had from *Old Youghal Rd.*, on an eminence on the N. bank of the Lee (8min. from St Patrick's Bridge).

ENVIRONS. Rewarding excursion (by rail from the W. end of Gt. George's St.; also recommended by carriage) to (8¼mi.) *Blarney (inn)* with the *ancient Blarney Castle* (tower 36m. high), in whose walls the legendary 'Blarney Stone' is set (which one must kiss, to acquire the power of oratory), new mansion and pretty park…

*Queenstown (*Queen's,* 1st class; *Royal; European*), busy and heavily fortified sea-port in a splendid position on *Cork Harbour* proper, thus named after the queen's visit in 1849 (earlier *Cove*, or *Cove of Cork*). The new Cath. Cathedral merits a visit. All the postal steamers between Liverpool and New York stop at Queenstown for 1-2hrs. to take on and deliver American mail (several large steamers each week).

**Blackwater Tour* (return ticket from Cork via Youghal to Cappoquin, returning via Mallow, or vice versa, 1st cl. 10s.6d., 2nd cl. 8s.). From Cork to Youghal, 27mi.; by rail (dep. from Summerhill St.) in 1hr.9min. via (6mi.) *Queenstown Junct.* (see above), (12½mi.) *Middleton*, (17½mi.) *Mogeeley* and (20mi.) *Killeagh.* – 27mi. *Youghal (Green Park, Imperial*, both some distance from the sta.; *Strand,* by the sta., for tourists), frequented seaside resort (4300 inhab.), consists of two sharply delineated parts: the *beach*, close to the sta., on the beautiful *Youghal Bay*, preferred by visitors; and the partially walled old town, 1mi. N. of the sta.; on a rise in the *Blackwater* estuary. One should visit *St Mary's Church,* XVth c.; near the cemetery is *Myrtle Grove,* once owned by Sir Walter Raleigh.

It is well worth taking the *steamer trip on the Blackwater to *Cappoquin* (16mi. in 1¾hrs.; 2s., 1s.4d., return 3s., 2s.). The steamer quay is 1¼mi. N. of the sta. (omnibus 6d.). The estuarial bay of the Blackwater extends like a lake, but narrows off after we pass the (2mi.) iron bridge below the mouth of the *Tourig.* To our l., the ruins of Rhincrew Cas.; r., *Ardsallagh House*; then, l., at the mouth of the *Glendine,* the tower of *Temple Michael Castle* (destroyed by Cromwell) and, on an islet on the N. side of the Glendine, the ruins of *Molana Abbey* (apparently VIth c.). Beyond (l.) *Ballynatray House,* the river turns NE. and broadens out (the

'Broad of Cashmore'); r., *D'Loughtane House* and the mouth of the *Licky*. We continue past the picturesque ruins (l.) of ancient *Strancally Cas.* and (3mi. further on) the imposing new castle of the same name, at the mouth of the *Bride*. Above this, l., is *Camphire,* r. *Villierstown;* the river narrows more and more, the banks beautifully wooded. To our r., *Dromana House*, attractively situated, l. *Tourin;* then r. the mouth of the *Finisk* and *Affane Church*, opp. (l.) *Drumroe Cas.*

Cappoquin (Moore's Hot..; Morrisey's,. charmingly sited, is a sta. on the line from Waterford to Mallow. 3½mi. N., the interesting *Mount Melleray Monastery*, founded in 1830 for Trappists driven out of France (strangers are accommodated free of charge).

74. **From Cork to Killarney.**

From Dublin, Cork or Waterford, *Killarney* can most speedily be reached by the Great Southern & Western Rly. via *Mallow* (from Mallow to Killarney, 41mi. in 1¾hrs.) The traveller with time and money at his disposal really should take the railway trip via Cork to *Bantry* and thence do the magnificent carriage trip along the 'Prince of Wales' Route' via *Glengarriff* and Kenmar to Killarney (from Cork to Bantry, 57mi. in 3hrs., for 11s., 8s.6d., 4s.9d.; from Bantry via Glengarriff to Killarney by rail 1st cl. and carriage 22s., 2nd. cl. 21s.). Or one may take a train from Cork to (24½mi. in 1½hrs.) *Macroom* and thence on a fine road via *Inchigeelagh* and the *Pass of Keimaneigh* to (36½mi.) *Glengarriff* (carriage for 4 pers. 28s. to Glengarriff and 56s. to Killarney)…

*Bantry (*Vickery's Hot.),* small town of 3000 inhab. at the upper end of *Bantry Bay*, opp. the fortified island *Whiddy,* with castle ruins. There is a fine outlook from the terraces of *Bantry House* (Earl of Bantry; one may visit the park).

The *road to Glengarriff (9½ or 10½mi.; carriage in 1½-1¾hrs.) runs round the indented upper end of *Bantry Bay,* on whose N. side the *Sugarloaf* (575m.) and the *Caha Hills* rise, culminating in Hungry Hill (686m.). At (1¼mi.) *Dunnamark Bridge,* we cross the *Mealagh* (small waterfall); we continue past (2½mi.) *Reenydonaghan Lough,* and cross the (3½mi.) *Owvane,* where, at *Ballylicky,* the road from Macroom comes in from the r. Our road turns W. over (5¼mi.) *Snave Bridge,* at the mouth of the *Coomhola,* and leaves the sea behind; to our l., a fine view of the *Sugarloaf.*

9mi. *Glengarriff.* – HOTELS: *Eccles, *Roche's, both in their own grounds and with pleasant views; in between these, Belle Vue, a good 2nd cl. establishment. The carriage stops first at (9½mi.) Roche's, and then continues to (10½mi.) Eccles. The tourist car to Killarney leaves from Roche's at 8.45 a.m.

Glengarriff ('the rough glen'), situated at the N. end of the island-studded *Glengarriff Harbour*, amid luxuriant vegetation, is one of the most attractive places in the British Isles.

There is a pretty walk from Eccles' Hot. W. to the (10min.) bridge over Glengarriff stream (lower down, the romantic remains of *Cromwell's bridge*), then r., over to a *viewpoint* (½hr.) with the best *views of the golf course and the entire area. – It is well worth ascending the *Cobduff* (369m.), 1½hrs. return from Roche's, and the *Sugarloaf* (575m.), 3½hrs. (6hrs. return) from Eccles', both offering beautiful views...

The road to Killarney crosses the *Finnihy River* by *Salaheen Bridge,* and begins to climb. At the summit of the pass, we see to our l. (NW.), the wild *Macgillycuddy Reeks* with *Carrantuohill* (1040m.), Ireland's highest mountain. We descend, soon passing the 1mi.-long *Looscaunagh Lough* (inn); ½mi. further on, there is suddenly an incomparable **view of Killarney's lakes, mountains and forests (below, l., the upper lake, connected to the Long Range by the middle or Muckross Lake. ½mi. beyond that (10mi. from Kenmare and Killarney), is *Mulgrave Police Barracks.* As we continue to descend, the road constantly offers fine views. In the valley, where an awakener of echoes receives the carriage, we skirt the foot of *Torc Mountain* (to the r., in a gorge, *Torc Waterfall*, and continue past *Muckross Lake* to the (16mi.) *Muckross* and *O'Sullivan's Hotels* (see below); thence past the entrance to Muckross Abbey (l.) and the road to *Lakeview Hotel* (r.), crossing the *Flesk* and so reaching *Killarney* station.

Killarney. – HOTELS. *Great Southern, conveniently situated at the sta., with shady grounds, rm. & service 4s., dinner 4s.6d.; *Royal Victoria, ½hr. to the W. on the N. shore of Lough Leane, with fine views; both of these are first-class. Lakeview Hotel, 1½mi. S., turning l. off the road to Kenmare; Muckross, O'Sullivan's, 1¼mi. further S. (see above). – Graham's Glebe, *Innisfallen, Slattery's, Palace, in the town (simple). – The various hotels have their own boats, boatmen, guides and ponies; tariffs are found in the hotels, where social events etc. are arranged.

CARRIAGES. (1-horse, for 1-4 pers., incl. tip) from the sta. to Ross Cas. 2s.6d.; around Ross Is., 4s.6d.; Ross Is. and West Park, 6s.6d.; ditto, Aghadoe and Deer Park, 10s.6d.; Gap of Dunloe and Ross, 11s.6d.; Aghadoe 4s.6d.; Torc Waterfall 5s.6d.; Muckross Abbey and Torc Waterfall 7s.6d…

Killarney, a quiet town of 5510 inhab., lying 1½mi. from the NE. shore of the *Lower Lake* or *Lough Leane,* is much frequented on account of its surroundings whose atmospheric beauty is not surpassed anywhere else in

Great Britain. Lakes, woods and mountains unite here in almost untouched freshness into a vista which acquires a magical charm from the rapidly changing effects of light in the hazy atmosphere. The climate is mild, the vegetation southern (myrtle, arbutus or strawberry-tree, etc.)

EXCURSIONS. If time is limited, one would do best to take the day trip to the Gap of Dunloe, returning via the lakes: carriage to Gap Cottage, 11½mi.,; ..on foot or pony (5s.) to (3½mi.) Lord Brandon's Cottage; down the lakes by boat to (3-4hrs.) *Ross Castle*… The road (many beggars) runs round the N. side of Lough Leane, past the castle of the Earl of Kenmare (l.), the Victoria Hotel and West Park and (r.) *Aghadoe House*, then, turning off l., to (5½mi.) *Ferry Bridge* over the *Laune.* From here, we continue approx. 1mi. to the W., then S. along by the small *River Loe* to (7½mi.) *Kate Kearney's Cottage* (milk and whiskey), at the beginning of the **Gap of Dunloe*, a wild, romantic gorge, through which the Loe runs, between the *Macgillycuddy Reeks* r. and the *Tomies* (735m.) and *Purple Mt.* (835m.), l.

The road repeatedly climbs and drops, passing several small lakes *(Coosaun Lough, Black Lake, Cushvally Lake, Auger Lake)* and a second, smaller, Black Lake), and then reaches (11½mi.) *Gap Cottage*, where the carriages turn. To our l. rises the steep *Purple Mountain* (834m.), the ascent of which is worthwhile for the magnificent view (with descent to the boat jetty, 2hrs.; guide recommended). – We now continue on foot or pony over the pass *(Head of the Gap)*, with a fine view l. of the upper lake, r. of the barren *Cummeenduff Glen* (the 'black valley') then sweep down in a great curve to the bridge over *Gearhameen River* and through a gate, where a toll of 1s. is exacted. We reach the so-called (3½mi.) *Lord Brandon's Cottage*, where the boat (which should be ordered previously in Killarney) lies ready in the river. The journey across the forest-girt *Upper Lake* is delightful; about 1mi. downstream is the *Arbutus Is.* The lake then narrows into the so called *Long Range*; to the l., the *Eagle's Nest,* a towering rock (335m.), to the r. Torc Mt. Near *Old Weir Bridge*, we negotiate some trifling rapids (1¼m. high), and continue to the 'Meeting of the Waters' before *Dinish Is.,* passing, r., beneath another bridge into the *Middle* or *Muckross Lake*, where the handsome outlines of *Torc Mt. (538m.) suddenly appear to our r…

Ross Castle, a rectangular ivy-covered tower on a spit of land on the lovely *Ross Bay*… 1mi. to the W., on Lough Leane, is the island Innisfallen, with the ruins of an abbey founded in the VIth c. by St Finian. Charming views. It is well worth taking the boat trip across the lake to *O'Sullivan's Cascade*, a very beautiful waterfall in a wooded gorge at the foot of the Tomies…

From Killarney to Valentia… *Mountain Stage.* Thence along the S. coast of Dingle bay, with a series of splendid views into sudden rocky gorges, to *Kells*; then down the broad valley to *Cahirciveen (*Leslie's;*

Fitzgerald's), an impoverished little town on the Valentia River, birthplace of Daniel O'Connell, to whom a noble 'Memorial Church' was erected, and *Valentia Harbour,* whence one can cross to *Valentia Is.,* starting-point of the trans-Atlantic cable to N. America. The office of the Anglo-American Telegraph Co. (which one may visit before 10 a.m.) is in *Knight's Town* (Valentia Hot.), the only settlement on the island, by Valentia Harbour. The first cable was laid in Aug. 1858, after two unsuccessful attempts, but it failed after 4 weeks. Not until 1865 was another attempt made, and success was achieved in July 1866. Since then, various cables have been laid, including one from France, and 10 cables are presently in service between Europe and America. – Valentia is worth a visit also on account of the magnificent cliffs, 180-240m. high, on the N. and W. point (*Bray Head*).

75. **From Dublin to Galway. Connemara.**

126½mi. MIDLAND GREAT WESTERN RAILWAY in 3hrs. 50min. - 5¼hrs. for 23s. 8d., 19s. 8d., 11s. 10d…

4mi. E. of Kilmessan, the *Hill of Tara,* with a number of rubble heaps, on the site of an ancient royal palace, and the *Lia Fail* or 'Stone of Destiny', an upright stone which some claim to be the real Stone of Scone…

To the S., on the Shannon, are the *Seven Churches of Clonmacnoise,* on the site of an abbey founded by St Kieran in the VIth c. The ruins (X-XIVth c.) are mostly very small; the larger cathedral possesses a well-preserved porch with ancient Irish decoration. The large round tower is called *O'Rourke's Round Tower.* In the churchyard, two old Irish crosses; the larger, *Great Cross,* or 'Cross of the Scripture', (Xth c.) is 4.5m. tall…

Galway (Railway Hot., a large establishment by the sta.; **Mack's Royal,* Eyre Sq.), a run-down town of 13,800 inhab., once prosperous through its trade with Spain, at the point where the *Corrib* leaves Lough Corrib and flows into *Galway Bay*, has nothing of special interest for the visitor, apart from the Gothic *St Nicholas Church* (XVIth c.), some old houses and the attractive *Eyre Square.*

A tram runs past the suburb of *The Claddagh* (fishing-port) to (1mi.) *Salthill (Eglinton Hot.*), a welcoming spot on *Galway Bay*, with sea-bathing. – One should pay a visit to the *Aran Is.,* to the W. of Galway Bay (steamer several times a week in 4hrs., 6s.): *Inishmore, Inishman* and *Inisheer.* On *Inishmore,* the largest (Atlantic Hot.), there are ancient castles and remarkable ruins from the beginnings of Christianity.

3-4 times weekly, a steamer plies from Galway to *Ballyvaghan* (small hot. by the pier), on the S. side of Galway Bay, whence one may reach

Lisdoonvarna either along the coast road via *Bleak Head* in 16mi., or directly by way of the 'Corkscrew Road' in 10mi.

Connemara Tour. – From Galway to *Clifden,* 49mi. by rail in 2-3hrs.; from Clifden to *Westport,* 39mi., public carriage daily in 8¼hrs. (8s.) – Circular tickets from Dublin to Galway, Clifden, Westport and back (or vice versa), 1st cl. 47s.6d., 2nd cl. 42s.

Dep. from Eyre Sq. (sit on the r.). The road crosses the *Corrib* and runs through the monotonous *Iar-Connaught,* often through forest, along by, and close to, the lower portion of *Lough Corrib*, as far as (8mi.) *Moycullen;* then via (12¼mi.) *Ross,* at the W. end of *Ross Lake,* and past the ruins of *Aughnanure Cas.* (r.) to (17mi.) *Oughterard (Murphy's, Blake House)*, a small town on the *Owenriff,* which has some falls (l.), 1mi. above its entry into *Lough Corrib* (good fishing). We continue along *Lough Baffin* and between (l.) *Lough Aunierin* and (r.) Tawnaghbeg to (27½mi.) *Maam Cross Sta.,* to the N. of, and not far from, *Lough Ardderrry*, where the road branches off (r.) to (4½mi.) *Maam* and (19½mi.) *Cong.* On our right rise the Mamturk Mts., further W. the Twelve Pins…

76. From Dublin to Belfast.

113mi. GREAT NORTHERN RAILWAY in 3-4½hrs. (Limited Mail, only 1st & 2nd cl.); fares 20s., 15s., 9s.5d. (Limited Mail 22s.6d., 17s.6d.). View to the *right,* of the sea and coastline.

Dublin (Amiens Street Sta.). The line crosses the *Royal Canal,* then *Clontarf Bay,* on a causeway 9m. high; to the r., a pleasant view of Dublin and Dublin Bay, with the Wicklow Mts. in the background. – 5mi. *Howth Junct.*

Branch-line r. to (3mi.) *Howth (Claremont,* 1st cl., by the sta.; *St Lawrence*), seaside town with fine sandy beach and a resort for the Dubliners on the peninsula of the same name, with abbey ruins and the park of *Howth Cas.* (open only Sat., 2-7; fine view). The harbour, over 20 hectares in area, is little used. Worthwhile excursion to *Bailey Lighthouse* on the SE. tip. 1mi. to the N., in the sea, is the rocky island *Ireland's Eye* (boat, 2s., only in fine weather)…

32mi. *Drogheda (White Horse,* West St.), a busy town of 11,812 inhab., in a picturesque situation at the mouth of the *Boyne,* which forms an excellent harbour. Across the deep-cut valley soars a magnificent *railway viaduct, (30m. high in the middle), beneath which the largest ships can pass. The main part of the town, with the steamer quay (steamers to Liverpool 4 times a week, in 8hrs.), lies on the N. bank. Of the old town walls, one may still see **St Lawrence's Gate,* with two tall round towers, and *West Gate. Magdalen Steeple,* a two-storeyed tower with Gothic windows, originates from a monastery founded in 1224. On the S. bank, the modern Cath. *St Peter's Church,* with a tall tower.

3mi. W. of Drogheda, an *obelisk* indicates the place where the *Battle of the Boyne* took place on 1st July 1690, in which James II's Irish troops were beaten by William III. The doughty Marshal Schomberg fell in the battle. – Those who enjoy antiquity will take the trip (carriage to Slane, 8-10s.) to the old burial mounds of *Dowth* and *Newgrange;* one continues to (12mi. from Drogheda) *Slane* (Cunningham Arms), a village attractively situated on the Boyne with the cas. and park of the Marquis of Conyngham; there is a fine view from the elevated abbey ruins… - One should also visit the ruins of *Monasterboice*, 6mi. NW. of Drogheda, with a tower 27m. high (IXth c.) and 3 beautiful Celtic crosses (the largest 8m. high) and the ruins of *Mellifont Abbey,* a Cistercian foundation (XIIth c.)…

113mi. – ***Belfast***. – HOTELS: Grand Central, Royal Avenue, rm. & service from 4s., dinner 5s.; Avenue, Royal Avenue, rm. & service 3½-5s., dinner 4s.6d.; Shaftesbury, College Sq.; Queen's, York St.; Eglinton & Winton, High St.; Commercial, Waring St.

RESTAURANTS. *Castle,* Queen's Arcade, Donegall Place; *Thompson's*, 14 Donegall Place; *Victoria*, 44 Royal Avenue; *Grand Café & Rest.,* Arthur Sq.

CARRIAGES. 2-wheeler, 6d. per mi. for 2 pers.; 3 pers. 8d.; 4 pers. 10d, etc.

STATIONS. *Belfast & County Down* (for Bangor, Donaghadee, Ballynahinch, Newcastle etc.) on the E. bank of the Lagan (over Queen's Bridge or by ferry). – *Belfast & Northern Counties* (for Larne, Scotland and England via Stranraer, Giant's Causeway etc.), York Rd. – *Great Northern of Ireland* (for Londonderry, Dublin etc.), Great Victoria St.

POST and TELEGRAPH, Royal Avenue. – THEATRE ROYAL, Castle Lane.

STEAMERS from Donegall Quay, every evening (Sundays excepted) to Glasgow (via Ardrossan or Greenock), Barrow, Fleetwood and Liverpool.

GERMAN CONSUL: *O. Jaffe.*

Belfast, Ireland's most important commercial city, with approx. 300,000 inhab., lies on the l. bank of the navigable *Lagan*, which emerges into *Belfast Lough* below the town, by way of the artificial *Victoria Channel.* Belfast is the centre of the Irish linen industry and has numerous large weaving mills; there are also some important shipyards. The town has grown up only in the last hundred years and therefore possesses little to interest the visitor.

From *Great Northern Sta.,* Victoria St. runs l. to *College Sq.* with the *Academical Institution,* a large public college. On the N. side is the *museum* (10-4; 6d.), with scientific and other collections; on the W. side is a bronze statue of the Conservative party leader *H. Cooke.* From here, we cross Wellington Place to *Donegall Sq.,* surrounded by large businesses and hotels, where a new *City Hall* is being built (at a cost of £150,000). *Donegall Place,* commencing here, is, with its continuations *Castle Place* and *Royal Avenue,* one of the most beautiful streets in the town; the latter street, in particular, possesses a row of magnificent buildings, which would adorn any major city. A tram line runs hence, NE., via York St., to the *Northern Counties* or *York Rd. Sta.*

Running E. from Castle Place, the busy *High Street* leads to Queen's Sq. with the *Albert Memorial,* a clock-tower over 30m. in height, having a statue of Prince Albert in a niche on its W. side (1868). On the N. side, its main façade fronting on to *Donegall Quay,* is the *Custom House,* a noble Renaissance building. The steamer landing-stages are on the quay; a steam ferry crosses the Lagan at this point, as does the imposing *Queen's Bridge,* to the *Belfast & County Down Sta.* on the r. bank. Further upstream are the Central Railway Bridge and the *Albert Bridge...*

It is worth ascending *Cave Hill* (330m.), 1hr. N. of Belfast (tram from Carlisle Circus to *Cave Hill Tavern,* then up to the r.). From this steeply precipitous basalt summit, there are magnificent views over Belfast and its surroundings, etc…

77. **From Belfast to Portrush (Giant's Causeway)**

To *Portrush,* 67½mi. by rail in 2¾-3hrs.; thence to the *Giant's Causeway,* 7½mi., tramway in 40min… The excursion to the **Giant's Causeway* can conveniently be done as a day-trip from Belfast…

*Portrush (*Northern Counties Hotel,* large first-class establishment; *Portrush; Osborne Temperance; Eglinton,* by the sta.), a frequented seaside resort, pleasantly set on both sides of a tongue of land, with views E. of the Giant's Causeway as far as Benbane Head, W. across the estuary of Lough Foyle to Inishowen Head and Malin Head. In the sea, 1mi. to the NE., are the *Skerries,* a series of small rocky islets.

From Portrush to the Giant's Causeway, 8mi., electric tram in 40min. The line runs by the sea, with magnificent views of the rocky coast to E. and W., then past the (3½mi.) picturesque ruins of *Dunluce Cas.,* turns l. over *Bush River,* some 5min. before (6mi.) *Bushmills* (Kane's Hot.) and climbs to its terminus at the (7mi.) *Causeway Hot.,* a large building with unimpeded views all round; nearby, **Royal Hotel,* smaller and cheaper.

The **Giant's Causeway,* 10min. N. of the hotel, one of the most remarkable and splendid basalt formations, consists of a close-packed series of about 40,000 basalt columns, stretching into the sea between Portganniay and Portnoffer Bay, 40-46m. wide and 275m. long. The columns are mostly 5-7-sided and increase in height from W. to E. (6-13m.); at the top, they are convex or concave, and they almost all consist of several pieces, which fit tightly together. The whole phenomenon gives the impression of being an artificial structure, which was ascribed to giants in antiquity.

One needs a *guide*, to visit the individual sights (the 'Long Course', then W. to the two caves and E. to Horseshoe Bay, 1-4 pers. 6s., 5-8 pers. 7s.6d.; for the 'Short Course', only to the caves and the Causeway, 1-4 pers. 4s., 5-8 6s.). – If time is limited, one should go directly to the Grand Causeway (1hr. return, with stop); the 'Long Course' (as far as Benbane Head) takes 2-3hrs, the return walk along the cliffs above, the same; Portcoon Cave, ½hr. return. Since 1896, a company has owned the Causeway, and has blocked many paths and charges for entrance.

From the hotels, the path runs down by the edge of the cliffs… From *Portnoffer*, on the E. side of the Causeway, the steep *Shepherd's Path* (no problem for those free from giddiness) climbs to the top of the cliffs and back to the hotel. The path running along the bottom of the cliffs soon peters out; visitors doing the 'Long Course' go to *Horseshoe Bay* and back by boat (the boatman names the various bays and promontories). – The basalt caves of *Portcoon* and *Runkerry* are best visited by boat from Portnabo; when the sea is calm, one can penetrate into them, 50m. and 80m. respectively…

…The **Amphitheatre*, a bay enclosed by vertical rocks, 100m. high. On the E. side is *Chimney Point*, so called from a projecting and unscaleable rock, with magnificent views to Benbane Head and the cliffs of Rathlin Island. The E. bay is called *Port-na-Spania* or *Spanish Bay* after a ship of the Spanish Armada, which is said to have been wrecked here. We continue past *Benanowan Head*, the lower *Hawk's Head* and *Lovers' Leap* to *Pleaskin Head*, the highest cliff on the Causeway (120m. above sea-level). Next comes *Benbane Head,* the northernmost point, with its chief viewpoint, **Hamilton's Seat.* There is a splendid view W. of the Pleaskin and the coast as far as Portrush and Malin Head, eastwards to Rathlin I., the Mull of Cantyre [sic] and the Scottish Islands Islay and Jura.

Londonderry, called Derry for short, in Ireland (**Imperial*, Bishop St.; *City,* Jury's Hot., Foyle St., *Ulster, Northern, Roddy's, Gowdie's Temperance*, simple), the capital of the county of the same name, with 32,893 inhab., lies picturesquely on a hill on the l. bank of the Foyle. The town, of ancient foundation (VIth c.), was rebuilt by the London merchants after its destruction by the O'Neills in 1613 (hence the name). It was remarkable for the 8-month siege in which it held out under the Rev. G. Walker in 1668-69 against the troops of James II. One should walk along the *town walls* which surround the inner town, now a promenade.

The cathedral of St Columba, built in 1633, recently underwent a complete restoration, and it makes a pleasant and harmonious impression. The nave, with a fine wooden roof, still contains 6 old choir-stalls, and is separated from the new *chancel* by a low stone screen. Stained glass, altar fittings etc. are modern. There is a broad view from the *tower* (awkward ascent).

To the W. of the Cathedral, in Bishop St., is the *Court House,* with an Ionic façade; opp. is the *Bishop's Palace.* Further NW., by the town wall, is *Walker's Monument,* a Doric column 30m. high, with the bronze statue of the courageous defender of the town, set up in 1828. From the top, there is a fine view (key from caretaker of the nearby Memorial Hall). – On the *Diamond*, a rectangular square in the town centre, is the *Government School of Art* and a bronze statue to *Sir. R. A. Ferguson* (1796-1860), who represented the town in parliament for 30 years…

In Donegal, it is well worth climbing **Slieve League* (660m.), 6-7hrs. ret. (pony 5s., guide, hardly necessary, 5s.). The path goes down the *Glen* and *Teelin Bay* for ½hr., then bears r. and up to the summit, with magnificent distant views of the mountains of Leitrim, Sligo and Mayo to the S. and Donegal to the NW., as far as Errigal, but also good close views of the jagged rock-walls and ravines of the mountain itself, which, from its full height, plunges into the Atlantic ocean. – From the summit, sharp razor edges run out in both directions, along which there are dangerous paths ('One Man's Path'). The best descent is via *Bunglass,* with splendid views of the cliffs and caves of Slieve League, and *Carrigan Head.*

Madeira

This item never appeared in the original *Baedekeriana* booklets, but might well have done, had I been in a position to continue the series in the 1990s. Because *Madeira* appeared in German in only one ed., 1934, (17 maps, 6 plans, 112pp.), and in English in only one, 1939 (23 maps and plans, xx/128pp.), both in card covers, I offer here a brief abstract from *The Mediterranean,* 1st and only ed. 1911, which devotes 10pp. to Madeira with 2 maps, one of the island, (1:400.000), the other of Funchal and its environs (1:30,000). Strangely, Madeira never featured in Baedeker's *Spain & Portugal.* The following description of Funchal and the island, as they were almost a century ago, makes intriguing reading, especially for the present-day traveller. [Madeira became an autonomous region of Portugal in 1976]. "The present English edition has been prepared by the Editor's old friend, emeritus *Professor John Kirkpatrick*, formerly of Edinburgh University".

3. Madeira.

STEAMBOAT LINES. **1.** *Union Castle Line*, steamers weekly from Southampton to Madeira in 3½days (on their way to S. and E. Africa); fares, 1st cl. 15-17 guineas, 2nd 10-12 *gs.* (return in each case about 2/3 more); also summer tours to Madeira, Las Palmas, or Teneriffe [sic] and back, 18 or 12 *gs.* Or, with a week's board in one of the islands, 20 or 14 *gn.*

2. *Royal Mail Steam Packet Co.*, fortnightly from Southampton (for Brazil) via Vigo and Lisbon to Madeira (fares 11*l.*10s. or 8*l.*); also fortnightly from London round voyage to Gibraltar, Tangier, Casablanca, Mazagan, Saffi, and Mogador, returning via Las Palmas, Teneriffe, and Madeira (fare from 22*gs.*; single to Madeira or Canary Islands from 15*gs.*).

3. *Booth Line* (for Brazil), thrice monthly from Liverpool to Madeira; 10*l.*, return 16*l.*10s.

4. *Yeoward Bros. Line*, weekly from Liverpool to the Canaries calling on alternate voyages at Madeira.

5. *Federal, Houlder & Shire Lines,* from Liverpool fortnightly, for Australia or New Zealand, calling at Madeira, Las Palmas or Teneriffe, 10*gs.*

6. *Empreza Nacional de Navegação,* from Lisbon to Madeira, 1st and 7th of each month; 5*l.*6s.3d. or 3*l.*12s.3d., return 9*l.*0s.8d. or 6*l.*3s.

7. *Empreza Insulana,* from Lisbon to Madeira, 20th of each month; 4*l.*5s. or 3*l.*3s.9d., return 7*l.*13s. or 5*l.*14s.9d.

During the winter season the Mediterranean steamers of the White Star and Cunard Lines call once monthly at Madeira, and the Transports Maritimes occasionally touch at Madeira.

The communication between Madeira and the Canary Islands is very defective.

The *Archipelago da Madeira,* or Madeira group of islands, consists of *Madeira* itself, the largest of the group, 37 by 14M., *Porto Santo* (rising 1663ft, above the sea), 6½ by 3M., which lies 26½M. to the NE. of Madeira, and the three uninhabited *Desertas.* These are the islets of *Chão* (341ft.), 12½M. to the SE. of Madeira, *Deserta Grande* (1611ft.), and *Bugio* (1349ft.).

Madeira lies in 33° lat., between the Azores and the Canary Islands, 620M. to to the SW. of Lisbon, 370M. to the NW. of Cape Juby, and 275M. to the N. of Teneriffe. The population of the islands, which are said to have been uninhabited when discovered by the Portuguese in 1419, is now, in an area of 314sq.M., about 150,000. All the islands are of volcanic origin. In Madeira, above the primeval diabase rock, numerous eruptions since the miocene epoch have formed a number of extinct craters (lagoas), and as in the Canaries have raised the soil 1150ft. above its original level. The main ridge of the island running from W. to E., and culminating in the Pico Ruivo ('red peak'; 6060ft.) frequently rises in rocky pinnacles. In examining the geological structure of the island one is struck with 'the constant mingling of solid masses of basalt and lava with strata of loose tufa and ashes, the whole being interspersed with upright dykes of lava.' The only tablelands are the *Paul da Serra*, on the W., and the smaller *Santo Antonio da Serra,* on the E. On the S. and N. slopes of the central range we observe a series of very curious and grand basins (*curraes,* sing. *curral),* which are enclosed by high rocks, and are connected with the sea by deep ravines, testifying to the enormous erosion caused by water and wind. Narrow strips of coast, strewn with round fragments of basalt, occur only at the mouths of the few streams, and on the largest of these lies *Funchal*, the capital of the island, on its SW. margin.

The mild and wonderfully equable climate of Madeira which since 1850 has attracted numberless invalids, chiefly English, to its shores, is due partly to its southern position, tempered by the surrounding ocean, but mainly to the influence of the Gulf Stream, which sends from the Azores an offshoot, known as the Canary branch, towards the W. African coast. On the sunny S. coast in particular, which is free from fog and is sheltered from the prevailing NW. wind by the above-mentioned main ridge, the mean and almost unvarying temperature of the three winter months (at Funchal 61° Fahr.; minimum 50°) is considerably higher than that of the favourite Mediterranean resorts (Nice 48° Fahr., Ajaccio 52°, Algiers 54½°, Malaga 55°), while the summer temperature is lower (at Funchal in Aug. 70½°,, maximum 92°). Dust is almost unknown. The rainfall (at Funchal 27½ inches; but more in the mountains and on the N. coast), chiefly in sudden and heavy showers, occurs mostly between October and February or March. The lowest snow-line is 1970ft. above the sea. The relative moisture of the air (67 per cent) at Funchal is moderate, notwithstanding the proximity of the sea. As in the Canaries, the mountains are generally cloud-capped about midday, except during the prevalence of the *Leste,* the wind blowing from the African desert, which in Madeira is not specially unpleasant.

Thanks to the genial climate, the abundant winter rains, and the system of irrigation by means of open channels *(levadas),* whereby water is brought down, partly through tunnels *(furos),* from its mountain sources, the fields and gardens of Madeira, 'Flor do Océano', show an almost tropical luxuriance of vegetation. Side by side with pines, junipers, and deciduous European trees, such as the plane, the chestnut, the maple, the oak, and the walnut, of which there are many splendid specimens, are seen countless evergreen trees and shrubs of tropical and subtropical origin. Among these are palms, araucarias, hickory-trees, cork-trees, camphor-trees, figs, palm-lilies (yuccas), magnolias, eucalypti, bamboos, papyrus-bushes, tree-ferns and aloes. A few isolated dragon-trees, the laurel *(vinhatico),* and the tilwood tree (Oreodaphne foetens), a kind of bay-tree scarcely occurring elsewhere, are survivals of the primeval forest destroyed by the Portuguese discoverers, and now lingering only in the remote ravines and on the slopes of the N. coast. To that forest the island owes its name (madeira, 'wood': *Isŏla di Legname* on old Italian charts). The hill-sides are now largely clothed with tree-like erica and broom (Genista madeirense, G.virgata, furze, etc.), large bilberry-bushes (Vaccinium madeirense), stemless ferns, and box, forming a kind of evergreen underwood. In the gardens of Funchal, enclosed by high walls, the traveller feasts his eyes, especially in May, on a most exuberant flora, comprising roses, rhododendrons, azaleas, camellias, callas, bignonias, daturas, fuchsias, hydrangeas, honeysuckle, and a superb red and purple bougainvillea. The garden-walls, field-roads, and hill-terraces are everywhere overgrown with vines, but, as in the Canary Islands, the wine-culture has suffered since 1852 from the grape-disease (Oïdium Tuckeri) and from the competition of port-wine. Among favourite brands are *Malvasia* or *Malmsey,* a sweet dessert-wine, *Boal,* and the astringent *Sercial.* Like the Vega of Málaga, the S. coast of Madeira yields the sugar-cane, which forms the chief crop of the island, bananas, sweet potatoes (Portug. *batata doce*), cherimolias, coffee-plants, yams (Dioscorea batatas; Portug. *inhame*), and early vegetables, which last are exported chiefly to England. Pine-apples thrive in hot-houses only. The natives live mostly on maize and the fruit of a kind of cactus (Opuntia Tuna) which grows abundantly on all the rocks.

Madeira also possesses several charming home-industries, producing embroidery, lace, silk shawls, basket-work, inlaid laurel-wood, and feather-flowers. Funchal, the only considerable harbour in the island, is an important coaling and provisioning station for steamers bound for S.Africa and for America. The heavy customs-dues, which render living dear, the over-population of the island, and the poverty of the peasantry cause a considerable emigration, chiefly to S.America.

Season and Mode of Travel. Madeira is an admirable health and rest resort at all seasons, except perhaps for sufferers from neurasthenia or gastric disorders; but in summer the Monte and Camacha are preferable to the lower sites. Tourists, on the other hand, will find July, Aug., and Sept. the best months for their purpose, as the hotels are cheaper and less crowded, the days are long, and the dry weather favours excursions into the interior. At Funchal English, French, and in the larger hotels German are much spoken, but in the interior Portuguese only. Those unacquainted with the language of the natives are then dependent on the help of their horse-attendants *(arrieiros)* or guides *(guias* or *chapas)*, many of whom speak a little English. At the principal hotels and shops English money is readily received, but small Portuguese change [*reis*, pl. of *real]* is required for fees and other minor outlays. Beggars abound, but their importunities should invariably be disregarded.

The streets of Funchal and the hill-roads are paved with round and slippery cobbles of basalt, against which india-rubber heels afford protection. The most popular vehicles are the bullock-cars *(carros de bois*; seated for 4 persons; 400-1000rs. per hour). For steep descents the *carro do monte* or *carrinho*, a kind of running sledge, is employed (400-1200rs. per drive). The longer excursions on the extremely hilly routes so characteristic of Madeira are best taken on horseback. The horses of Andalusian race are wonderfully wiry and sure-footed (per hour 500rs.; *arrieiro*, or attendant, 800-1000rs. per day). Ladies and invalids use the hammock or litter (*rede)*, a costly conveyance (2-4 bearers, at 500-600rs. each per hr.). Finger-posts are entirely lacking.

The few *Vendas,* or country-inns, and the houses of the mountain engineers (to which travellers are admitted by leave from the office of the

Obras Publicas at Funchal, Rua do Conselheiro Vieira 80) afford very primitive quarters. Travellers should therefore be provided with rugs, preserved meats, candles, insect-powder, and good drinking-water. As in the Alps, strong boots with nails and a *hasta* or *bordão*, a long stick with an iron spike, are desirable for mountaineering.

Among books on Madeira may be mentioned *A.Samler Brown's* Guide to Madeira, the Canary Islands and the Azores (10th ed., London, 1910, 2s.6d.); Leaves from a Madeira Garden, by *Chas.Thomas-Stanford* (London, 1910; 5s.); *Yate Johnson's* Handbook of Madeira (London 1885); Madeira, by *Ellen M. Taylor* (2nd ed., London, 1889); Madeira Islands, by *A.J.D.Biddle* (2nd ed., London, 1900; 2 vols.); Madeira, Old and New by *W.H.Koebel* (London, 1909; 10s.6d.); The Flowers and Gardens of Madeira, by the *Misses Du Cane* (London, 1909; 7s.6d.).

The STEAMERS arriving from the N. skirt the W. coast of **Porto Santo**, an island in the form of a tableland, surrounded by five reef-islets; its inhabitants (about 2300) live mostly in the little town of *Villa Baleira.* Beyond Porto Santo we obtain a superb view of the abrupt and furrowed N. coast of Madeira, with the curiously shaped Penha d'Aguia.

Farther on appears the long E. promontory of Madeira, a rocky peninsula worn by the surf, and connected with the islet of *Ponta de São Lourenço* by a grand rocky gateway called the *Ponta do Furado*. We steer round the *Ilheo de Fora,* an outlying islet with a lighthouse *(Farol;* 348ft.), visible from a distance of 28M., towards which the steamers from Lisbon, Gibraltar and Morocco direct their course, passing to the S. of Porto Santo.

To the S., beyond the low island of *Chão*, rise the *Deserta Grande* and *Bugio* the largest of the **Desertas**, a group of islands deserted for lack of water, and now owned by Mr C.J.Cossart, of Madeira. British sportsmen desiring to shoot wild goats, there or hunt seals (Monachus albiventer) in the ocean-caves of the Deserta Grande, must obtain permission from the owner.

The thinly peopled and somewhat bare SE. coast of **Madeira**, with the three little harbours of *Caniçal, Machico,* and *Santa Cruz,* shows clearly the geological formation of the island. Off *Porto Novo,* in particular, we are struck with the rich colouring of the *Pico dos Iroses,* where the sombre basaltic and lava rock contrasts with brick-red strata of ashes and blood-red masses of slag.

Very beautiful is the approach to the **Bay of Funchal,* which is bounded on the E. by the bold *Cabo do Garajão,* and on the W. by the *Ponta da Cruz*, a spur of the *Pico da Ponta da Cruz.* From the narrow strip of coast the lanes of the old town mount the steep hill-side between the three river-beds (which are generally dry), while several groups of houses extend up to the *Pico Fort* and the *Levada de Santa Luzia.* Farther up, stretching to the terrace of the *Monte,* are gardens and vineyards, from which peep many white *quintas* or country-houses. On the plateau behind *Forte Ilheo* are seen the charming gardens, with their tall aruacarias, belonging to the W. suburb of Funchal, the finest residential quarter. Of the barren mountains in the background, the highest peak visible from the sea is the *Pico de Santo Antonio*, to the NW. of the town.

Funchal. – ARRIVAL. The steamers cast anchor in the open roads, which are much exposed to the surf when the wind is from the S. or SW. The passenger's luggage, including hand-bags and small packages, is conveyed from the steamer, in charge of a *guarda fiscal,* direct to the Alfándega, or custom-house. Tobacco, spirits, and unused articles are specially dutiable. The charge of landing is about 500rs. for each person, but should be ascertained beforehand, with the aid of the hotel-porter, if necessary. In stormy weather passengers are landed at the *Pontinha,* a small pier beyond the Forte Ilheo. At the custom-house a declaration has to be filled up, for which the fee is 50rs.; the luggage is then usually retained till midday, and when it is finally cleared the passenger gives a receipt for it (250-300rs. more). For the transport of luggage to the hotel by bullock-car not more than 1000rs. should be paid (an agreement should be made beforehand). The Madeira clock is 59min. behind Greenwich time.

Hotels (mostly in the English style; almost all with beautiful gardens; crowded from Dec. to April). In the W. suburb *REID'S PALACE HOTEL, situated on a basalt rock and commanding fine views, with sea-baths, etc., pens. 10-25s. (or in the dépendance, VILLA VICTORIA, 8s.6d.-18s.); HOT. BELLA VISTA (Jones's), above the Rua da Imperatriz Dona Maria, pens. from 8s.; HOT. ROYAL (Adams's), Rua da Imperatriz Dona Amelia, pens. from 8s. ... Wine, always extra, is dear. The Agua Minero-Natural of Porto Santo is a good table-water (60rs. per small bottle).

Apartments for the winter in numerous quintas or villas, furnished, but without bed or table linen; from Oct. to June 40*l.* and upwards.

Restaurants. *Phenix,* Praça da Rainha; *Golden Gate,* Entrada da Cidade 7; with American bar). – ENGLISH TEA ROOMS, *Café Monaco.* – WINE. *Vaccaria do Souza*, Rua de João Tavira.

Post & Telegraph Office Estação Telegrapho-Postal; Entrada da Cidade.

Theatre. *Theatro de Dona Maria Pia*, opposite the Jardim Municipal. Evening CONCERTS twice a week in the Jardim Municipal, etc.

Shops in the Praça da Constituição, Rua do Aljube, Rua do Conselheiro Vieira, etc.; bargaining necessary; the prices are higher when the purchaser is attended by a guide. Pedlars often charge more than the shops. – EMBROIDERY, etc., at *Ad. V. Breymann's,* Rua do Conselheiro Vieira 77. – WINES, etc., sold at *Breymann's*; also by *Blandy Bros & Co.* (see below); *Cossart, Gordon & Co.,* Rua do Principe 78; *Krohn Bros. & Co.* (see below). – PHOTOGRAPHIC MATERIALS, *Bazar do Povo,* Largo de São Sebastião.

Banks. *Blandy Bros. & Co.,* Rua da Alfándega 26; *Reid, Castro, & Co.,* Largo de São Sebastião 5; *Banco de Portugal*, Largo da Sé; *Krohn Bros. & Co.,* Rua do Carmo 2; *L. da Rocha Machado*, Rua da Alfándega 27.

Physicians. *Dr. Grabham,* Valle Formoso; *Dr. Scott*, Quinta Perestrello; *Dr. Machado*, rua das Mercês 1; *Dr. Stevens*, Villa Ramose. – CHEMISTS. *Pharmacia Central*, Rua Bettencourt 2; *Botica dos Dois Amigos,* Largo do Collegio.

Carriages and **Horses** at *De Souza's*, Rua do Bispo. Bullock-cars in the Entrada da Cidade; saddle-horses (poor) in the Largo de São Pedro and the Rua de João Tavira. – LITTERS in the Largo de São Sebastião.

Motor Cabs in the Entrada da Cidade (tariff by zones; per drive 90-500rs.; to Camara de Lobos and back 800rs.).

Horse Tramway (electric line projected) from the Praça da Constituição to the railway-station of Pombal (starting ¼hr. before each train; 50rs.). – RACK & PINION RAILWAY (Caminho de Ferro do Monte) from the Estação do Pombal via Levada, Livramento, Sant'Anna and Flamengo, to the Monte; 7 trains daily in 20min., fare 300, return 400rs.

British Consul, *Capt. J. Boyle,* Reid's Palace Hotel; vice-consul, *E. Sarsfield.* – LLOYD'S AGENTS, *Blandy Bros. & Co.* (see above).

Steamboat Agents. *Blandy Bros. & Co.* (see above) for the Union Castle, Royal Mail Steam Packet Co., Booth, Hamburg-American, and Woermann Lines, the Empreza Nacional de Navegação and the Empreza Insulana de Navegação; *Leça, Gomes & Co.* for Yeowards Bros. Line; *Gonçalves & Co.,* Rua do Conselheiro Silvestre Ribeira 2, for the Hamburg & South American Line; *J. de Freitas Martins,* Rua da Alfándega 52, for the North German Lloyd. – For the coasting service (Serviço costeiro) and pleasure-trips (Viagens de Recreio), see newspapers.

Churches. *English*, Rua da Bella Vista *(Rev. C. Jones Bateman, M.A.),* services on Sun. at 8 and 11 a.m., and 5.30 p.m.; *Presbyterian*, Rua do Conselheiro; *American*, same street, lower down.

Club. *English Rooms,* in the Rua da Praia, overlooking the sea, with library and billiard-rooms. Adm. on introduction.

ONE DAY. Visit to the Monte in the forenoon; drive to Camara de Lobos in the afternoon.

Funchal ('place of fennel'; pop. 25,800), situated in 32° 38' N. lat. and 16° 55' W. long., the capital of Madeira and the seat of the Portuguese governor and a bishop, is remarkable for the luxuriant subtropical verdure of its public grounds and private gardens.

On the PRAÇA DA RAINHA, the sea-promenade, where we have a view of the Desertas, rise the *Palacio de São Lourenço*, (the governor's residence), several *Club Houses,* and a signalling tower called the *Pilar de Benger* ('Benger's Folly'). The *Varadoures Gate,* to the E. of the custom-house, is the sole survival of a town-wall built by the Spaniards early in the 17th cent.; adjacent is the *Fruit and Fish Market* (Mercado).

Opposite the pier (Caes) the Entrada da Cidade, an avenue of planes, leads to the PRAÇA DA CONSTITUIÇĂO, adorned with pleasure-grounds, in the centre of the town.

Adjacent on the W. is the ***Jardim Municipal** (public park; evening concerts twice weekly, otherwise closed in the evening), with its exuberant wealth of vegetation and flowers. On the S. side is the *Theatre.* – To the E., in the Largo da Sé, rises the insignificant CATHEDRAL *(Sé)*, with a fine ceiling of Spanish juniper (Portuguese cedro).

On the E. side of the park runs the Rua de São Francisco, leading to the long RUA DO CONSELHEIRO VIEIRA, or Rua da Carreira the busiest street, at the NW. end of which (on the left) is the entrance to the *Protestant Cemetery* (Cemiterio Britanico).

From the N. side of the Rua do Conselheiro Vieira we ascend past the church of *São Pedro* and through the steep Calçada de Santa Clara to the convent-church of *Santa Clara,* where Zarco, the discoverer of Madeira, is buried. – Farther to the N. is the Calçada do Pico, whence the Rua do Castello to the left leads to the old Spanish **Pico Fort** (Forte de São João do Pico), dating from 1632, famed for its *View.

From the end of the Rua do Conselheiro Vieira we may now cross the Largo do Collegio, with the *Jesuit Church* of that name, to the *Camara Municipal*, or town-hall, in the Rua dos Ferreiros. At the lower end of the same street, not far from the Cathedral, is the Largo de São Sebastião, where the Saturday market is held.

Crossing the neighbouring *Ribeira de Santa Luzia* we soon reach the *Carmo Church.* – Along the Ribiera de Santa Luzia ascends the horse-tramway to the station of the Monte railway, near which, to the E. (reached by the Rua do Pombal, is the *Museum,* containing valuable natural history collections and a large relief-map of the island. (Adm. on application; donation to poor-box.)

In the E. suburb of *Santa Maria Maior*, beyond the Ribeira de Santa Luzia and the *Ribeira de João Gomes* is the Campo de Dom Carlos Primeiro (drilling-ground), skirting the sea, and partly planted with trees. The Spanish *Forte de São Thiago* (now barracks), built in 1614, was dedicated to St James the Less (São Thiago Menor), the patron saint of Funchal. Near it is the church of *Nossa Senhora do Soccorro*, the scene of a great procession on 1st May.

The chief streets of the **W. Suburb,** beyond the *Ribeira de São João,* flanked with pretty villas, are the RUA DA IMPERATRIZ DONA MARIA, and the RUA DA IMPERATRIZ DONA AMELIA, which last ends at the Redondo ('round space') near the *Ribeiro Secco.* On the S. side of the road are the *Cemetery* (Cemiterio das Augustias) and the *Casino Pavão,* with a beautiful garden extending to the abrupt coast, frequented by English and American visitors. By the sea runs the Caminho da Pontinha, leading to the *Pontinha* and the harbour-battery of *Forte Ilheo* ('island fort', Engl. *Loo Rock).*

EXCURSIONS. The RACK & PINION RAILWAY, which at Levada station crosses the *Levada de Santa Luzia* and the beautiful hill-promenade of that name, connects Funchal with the ***Monte**, a village on the hill at the back of the town, with numerous villas nestling amidst beautiful groves of planes and oaks. On a spur of the hill, close to the terminus of the railway (extension projected), rises the pilgrimage-church of *Nossa Senhora do Monte*, known by English visitors as the 'Mount Church' (1962ft.). It is the scene of the Novena, a great nine-days' church-festival held in the summer. The terrace of the church (68 steps), commands a glorious *View of Funchal, the coast as far as the Cabo Girão, and the blue ocean enlivened by its passing ships. A little below the church is a sacred well.

A little to the E. of the Monte is the *Curralinho* ('little curral'), or *Curral dos Romeiros* ('pilgrims' ravine'), overgrown with erica and vaccinium. This miniature curral, a gorge of the *Ribeira de João Gomes*, gives a very imperfect idea of the grandeur of the rocky ravines of Madeira.

Those who are pressed for time may descend to the town in 10-12min. in a running sledge, by the *Caminho do Monte*; but it is preferable to walk back (in 1½hr.) by the level **Caminho das Tilias* which we reach by turning to the left above the church. After about ¼M., at the beautiful *Quinta Machado* (with a view-tower), we descend to the left by the steep *Caminho dos Saltos* (if desired, by running sledge ordered beforehand; 600rs.). The route leads to the SW., past the *Quinta Olavo,* the *Levada de Santa Luzia* and the *Quinta do Deão*, and then descends to the SE through the plane-avenue on the *Ribeira de Santa Luzia.*

A *side-path leads, above the Quinta Olavo, to the right, across the river-bed, to the church of *São Roque* (1139ft.; view; bullock-car from Funchal 800rs.), whence we may descend by the steep Caminho de São Roque to the *Pico Fort* and the *Clara Nunnery.*

The Rua da Imperatriz Dona Amelia is continued by the **Estrada Monumental,* a road which afford delightful views. It leads from the *Ponte Monumental*, a bridge across the Ribeiro Secco, past a number of sugar-cane plantations and vineyards, and, leaving the shore, proceeds to the SW. above the ocean-cave of *Forja* and the rocky islets of *Forja* and *Gorgolho.* It then crosses the S. slope of the *Pico da Ponta da Cruz* (863ft.; *View), an old crater, near the promontory of that name, and skirts the beautiful, but not very safe bathing-beach of *Praia Formosa.* Farther to the W., in full view of the bold central range backing the Gran Curral (see below), we cross the lower bridge of the *Ribeira dos Soccorridos* and an old lava-stream to (5½M.) **Camara de Lobos** (which may be reached by motor-cab), a strikingly picturesque fishing-village (pop. 6200) at the E. base of the almost perpendicular **Cabo Girão,* with a small natural harbour *(Bahia).* The best wine in the island is yielded by the slopes in the vicinity.

The EXCURSION TO THE GRAN CURRAL, on horseback or by litter, takes nearly a whole day. We start early and take provisions with us. From the W. suburb we follow the Rua das Maravilhas and the Caminho de Santo Antonio, between garden-walls and vineyards, to the NW. to the finely situated village of (2M.) *Santo Antonio* (985ft.' bullock-car from Funchal 800rs.). We descend thence to the NW. into the side-valley of the *Ribeira do Vasco Gil,* with its pine-woods and rich pastures, and soon obtain a view towards the W., extending to the Cabo Girão (see above) and the Pico da Cruz. We next ascend the steep side-valley of the *Ribeira da Lapa* to the (11M.) *Serrado Saddle* (Eira do Serrado; about 2900ft.), on the NE. margin of the *Pico Serrado* (see below). From the top of the pass we have a grand view into the great and well-watered basin of the ***Gran Curral,** or *Curral das Freiras* ('nuns' valley'; once a pasture belonging to the convent of Santa Clara), enclosed by the lofty rocks of the central mountains. Far below us, above the rock-strewn bed of the *Ribeira dos Soccorridos,* we descry the village of *Livramento* (2018ft.), with its little church and cypress-shaded churchyard.

Those who do not care to face the rugged descent to Livramento, and the steep clamber thence to Bocca dos Namorados, should now descend the ***Pico Serrado** (3347ft.; 'sawn-off peak'), whence we survey the mountain-range from the *Pico de Santo Antonio* (5725ft.) and *Pico Cidrão* (5551ft.) to the *Pico Ruivo,* the *Pico Canario* (5500ft.), and the *Pico Grande*.

Longer, but grander still, is the excursion to the W. margin of the Gran Curral. From the Estrada Monumental (see above) we turn to the NW. past the *Quinta Nazareh,* nestling amidst araucarias, to the (2M.) village of *São Martinho* (765ft.; bullock-car from Funchal 800rs.), situated among several old craters; we then cross, to the W., the ravine of the Ribeira dos Soccorridos by the upper bridge and mount in zigzags to the (7M.) village of *Estreito* (1510ft.). Our route now ascends to the N. to the (8½M.) **Bocca dos Namorados* (3445ft.), with its beautiful chestnut-wood, where we enjoy a superb view of the Gran Curral, and skirts the W. margin of the *Pico dos Bodes* (3718ft.) to the (10M.) *Cova da Cevada,* a basin offering a similar view. We next follow the top of the hill to the NW., between the Gran Curral and the E. side-valleys of the *Ribeira Brava* (see below), to (13M.) the **Bocca dos Corregos* (4466ft.), a narrow ridge at the foot of the perpendicular rocks of the *Pico Grande* or *Rocha Alta* (5420ft.). An interesting return-route is afforded by descending from the Cova da Cevada across *Jardim da Serra* (2593ft.) and past the *Pico da Cruz* (3288ft.) to *Camara de Lobos.*

The EXCURSION TO RABAÇAL can, if time presses, be accomplished in one day. It is best to go by steamboat to Calheta (8 times weekly, in 1½-2hrs.; or a small private steamer may be hired of Messrs. Blandy Bros.). The steamer calls first at *Camara de Lobos*, then skirts the sombre rocky slopes of *Cabo Girão* and steers past *Fajãa dos Padres*, a village famed for its wine, to the village of *Ribeira Brava* (inn), where we obtain, through the curral of that name, a very striking glimpse of the *Serra d'Agua* (4610ft.) and the Pico Grande (see above). We next pass the beach of *Lugar de Baixo,* formed by a landslip in 1803, the beautiful cape *Ponta do Sol* , and the village of *Magdalena*, peeping out of vines and bananas amidst the grandest scenery of the S. coast.

At the village of **Calheta** (bad landing-place; no inn) we may find litters if desired (each man 800-1000rs. per day), and we obtain provisions and torches (fachos, at 50rs.). We now walk chiefly through pine-wood via *Saldo* to the (1½hr.) narrow and wet tunnel (about 650 yards in length) of the lower *Levada Nova do Rabaçal.* At the N. end of it we obtain a very striking view of the highest part of the valley of the *Ribeira da Janella,* richly wooded with evergreen oaks and laurels. A path over the rocks (which needs a steady head) connects this levada (or conduit) with the upper *Levada Velha*, constructed in 1836-60, and with (9½M.) the engineers' houses of **Rabaçal** (3750ft.; adm. fee). A little to the NE., on the so-called *Balcão*, we enjoy an excellent survey of the **Waterfall of the Risco,* which plunges from a rock, 330ft. high, into a ravine overgrown with climbing plants and ferns, and a little lower down provides the water for the old conduit. Crossing the viaduct of the latter, we skirt the new conduit, and in a few minutes reach another luxuriantly overgrown ravine, that of the **Vinte e Cinco Fontes*, where no fewer than twenty-five waterfalls issue from a narrow basin.

From Rabaçal we may ascend towards the E. (with a guide) to the (2hrs.) plateau of *Paul da Serra* b(4656ft.; ‘mountain swamp’), where fogs often prevail, and the two *Tanquinhos Houses* (about 4900ft.; used by the engineers; poor quarters). Near them rise the *Pico dos Tanquinhos* (5260ft.) and the **Pico Ruivo do Paul* (5388ft.), both of which afford grand views of the mountains.

Scarcely less repaying is the two days’ EXCURSION TO SANTA ANNA on the N. coast, to which a third day may be added for the ascent of the Pico Ruivo or the Pico Arceiro. We start from the Campo da Barca at Funchal and follow the Estrada do Conde Carvalhal, which ascends to the NE. in windings to (3¼M.) *Palheiro do Ferreiro* (1857ft.; bullock-car from Funchal 1200rs.), the finest Quinta in the island, the property of Mr John Blandy of Funchal (adm. on application). Farther on we follow the road, uphill and downhill. To (6M.) **Camacha** (2369ft.; no inn; bullock-car 2500rs.) a well-to-do village of basket-makers in a charming wooded region, with many villas owned by English residents in Funchal. Beyond the *Pico dos Iroses* the road, now less attractive, crosses the gorges of the *Ribeira de Porto Novo* and *Ribeira de Santa Cruz*, and then, turning to the N., reaches *(13M.) Santo Antonio da Serra* (2320ft.), a poor village on a grassy tableland. We descend thence to the NW. into a sequestered valley carpeted with flowers (Amaryllis Belladonna etc.), where a rough path leads to the (15½M.) *Portella Pass* (2021ft.). which commands a superb *View of the mountains at the head of the Metade Valley (see below), of the NE. coast from the Penha d’Aguia (see below) to the Ponta de São Lourenço, and of the island of Porto Santo. We now descend, at first by a zigzag path, through vineyards and sugar-cane plantations, to (18M.) *Porto da Cruz* (no inn), a picturesque little seaport at the SE. base of the abrupt **Penha d’Aguia* (1949ft.; ‘eagle-rock’), the most curiously shaped hill in the island. We next ascend the saddle to the S. to the Penha d’Aguia, noteworthy for its marvellously rich vegetation, and descend the ravine of the *Ribeiro Frio* (see below) to *Fayal,* a village not far from the charming *Pescaria,* a little bay to the NW. of the Penha d’Aguia. The church-terrace here affords a grand survey of the valleys of the Ribeiro Frio, the Ribeiro da Metade, and the Ribeiro Secco (all mentioned above). From Fayal we then cross the *Cortadas Pass* or *Bocca do Cortado* (1985ft.), to (24M.) **Santa Anna** (1408ft.; Hot. Figueira, very fair; pop. 3200), a village well adapted for some stay, the capital of the *Comarca de Santa Anna,* the most fertile region in the island (sugar-cane, sweet potatoes, yams, etc.). From Santa Anna a rough mule-track, very indistinct at places, ascends past the curious basaltic *Homem em Pé* (‘man on foot’), and lastly over the saddle by the *Encumeada Alta* (5948ft.), to the top of the *Pico Ruivo* (6000ft.), which commands a most imposing, but seldom very clear panorama of the central chain, part of the Gran Curral and the E. half of the island.

Turning back from Santa Anna, we first wend our way towards the S. to the *Cova da Roda,* where we again overlook the NE. coast as far as the Portelle Pass and the Porto da Cruz; we then cross the *Ribeiro Secco* and the (29½M.) *Cruzinhas Ridge*, and descend into the valley of the **Ribeiro da Metade*, a gorge vying in grandeur with the Gran Curral. A zigzag path ('Quatorze Voltas'), ascends thence to the little venda (inn) of *Cedro Grodo,* and then crosses the *Serra de Caramuja* into the (33M.) valley of the *Ribeiro Frio,* with its splendid groves of tilwood trees, laurel and erica. Above the village of that name rises the *Balcão,* a rock of basalt (near the not easily accessible *Levada do Furado),* where we have a grand *View of the Metade Valley with mountain-background. Our route winds up the rocks of the Feiteiras ('ferns') and the *Pouso Saddle*, with its fine views, to the (34½M.) *Pouso* or *Poïzo Refuge* (4603ft.), situated on a dreary plateau. From the Pouzo Refuge we may without difficulty climb the *Pico Arceiro* (5893ft.; 1¼-1½hr.), a famous point of view, but almost always capped with clouds. The bridle-path ascends past the *Observatorio;* we may then descend direct to the Vista dos Navios.

The next part of our route, from the Pouso Refuge to the Monte is uninteresting. From the *Vista dos Navios* ('view of ships'), whence the bay of Funchal is visible, the track descends to the head of the valley of the *Ribeira de João Gomes*, rounds the E. slope of the *Pico do Arrebentão* (3842ft.), to which point a running sledge may be ordered from Funchal, and then descends rapidly, partly in windings, to the (39M.) *Monte.* Thence to (41½M.) *Funchal.*

[One wonders how many modern-day visitors to Madeira would undertake more than a fraction of these demanding trips, even though there is now a network of modern roads on the island!]

Baedeker on the

BAGHDAD RAILWAY

"I noticed with interest that every metal sleeper bore the name of "Krupp". This line was part of the ex-Kaiser's famous Berlin-to-Baghdad railway."

[H.V.Morton, *In the Steps of St Paul*, 1936.]

[The following extract from Baedeker's *Konstantinopel und Kleinasien*, 2nd ed., 1914, originally appeared in *Baedekeriana* no.15, Spring 1991, in my own translation. We take the train through Turkey towards Baghdad, making various interesting excursions en route.]

e. ***Baghdad Railway. From Konya to Kara Bunar*** *(11hrs.).*

Cf. the Introductory Remarks on p.270/1. The rolling-stock is still basic (no toilets). There are no buffet cars at all.

Timetable and fares. At present, only one train is running in each direction. From Konya to Eregli, 1st cl. 128¼, 2nd cl. 57 silver piastres; to Bulgurlu, 1st cl. 135, 2nd cl. 60 pi.; to Kara Bunar 1st cl. 198½, 2nd cl. 88pi.; Konya to Karaman, 1st cl. 69¾, 2nd cl, 31 pi.; Karaman to Eregli, 1st cl. 58¾, 2nd cl. 26¼pi.; Eregli to Kara Bunar, 1st cl. 70½, 2nd cl. 31¼pi.

The 36km. section beyond Kara Bunar is still under construction.

From Konya, the "Baghdad Railway" already runs 238km. onwards, SE. as far as the Taurus Mountains. It crosses the uplands of ancient *Lycaonia*, which the geographers of antiquity dubbed bare, cold, with little water, treeless and rich in salt; vast areas are prone to flooding in winter; the whole area was once covered by a salty inland sea. Only small pieces of land are cultivated; larger ones serve as pasture. For the new irrigation project, see p.294. To the N., this steppe merges into the great Salt Steppe, an undrained depression, in which lies the Tus Chol. To the E. it is joined by the *Karaman Steppe*, separated from the Lycaonian Steppe by a mountain chain of recent volcanic rock (trachyte), running from SW. to NE.; belonging to this chain are the *Kara Dag* (2170m.; partly granitic), *Karadja Dag* (1800m.) and, far off to the NE., *Hassan Dag* (2400m.). The ancient military road, along which went (for example) Kyros the Younger (Xenophon with him) and Frederick Barbarossa, runs to the S., near the edge of the Taurus range, via Karaman (Laranda) and then almost at a right-angle to Eregli (Kybistra). The railway line follows the same route, though more to the N. at first.

Soon after we have left the gardens of Konya behind, the landscape begins to take on the character of the steppe. We pass through the large village of *Hassan Köi*. – 21km. *Kashin Han* (1010m.). To the SW. is the site of *Lystra* (Acts, Ch. 14), while *Derbe* lay to the S. near *Güdelissen*. – 45km. *Chumra* (1014m.). At the sta. are the houses of the irrigation engineers. The town proper lies 7km. to the W. We cross the Charsembé Chai and head towards Kara Dag with its many jagged peaks.

63km. *Aryk Ören* (1022m.)

About 20km. E. of Aryk Ören, on the slopes and tops of the northern hills of Kara Dag, lie the ruined sites Binbirkilissé and Deïlé. One must send horses on the previous day from Konya to the station, in order to ride there (4¾hrs.); the accommodation in the odá (hostel) at Deïlé is better and cleaner than in fever-ridden Binbirkilissé; one takes one's own food; sabtié escort (gendarme). On these now almost derelict sites a large community flourished in the III-VIIIth c. A.D., which was totally destroyed by the Seljuks as late as the XIth c. Around 50 ruined churches are preserved, important to the history of architecture; the basilicas in particular display their own characteristic style: they are built of square stone blocks, not flat-roofed like other basilicas in Asia Minor but, because of the lack of wood, fully vaulted; the ground plan indicates one or three aisles, separated by columns with half-columns on the outside and inside, only one apse and, instead of an atrium, a portico between two closed chambers, cf. Ramsay & Bell, *The thousand and one churches* (London 1909). – From the sta. we reach, 2km. E., an old road from Konya to Karaman; 10km. further E., we turn off r. (S.) and, after 3km., reach the hilly plateau of *Deïlé* (Degilé, Daulé), with some yuruk (nomad) huts and the ruins of 11 churches and chapels, two monasteries and a number of graves and houses. 2km. further on, near an impoverished yuruk village, we reach the greatest ruined site, Binbirkilissé ("1001 churches"), by an Osman fortress. The whole area is also called *Maden Shehir*, town of mines, where many remains of the main church are preserved (with traces of frescoes), also many smaller basilicas and symmetrical buildings, mausoleums and secular buildings, generally older than the buildings of Deïlé. There are more ruins further to the N.

Beyond Aryk Ören, the railway runs between (l.) the Kara Dag and (r.) the *Dedem Dag* (1250m.) and *Bus Dag* (1250m.), northern prominences of the *Hadji Baba* or *Bosola Dag* (1710m.); then on to (82km.) *Mandassun* (1010m.). Thence to the S. of the *Davda Dag* (1370m.) into the eastern plain which, possessing more water, is also more fertile.

103km. **Karaman** (1025m.; Hot. Beledié with rest.). The town, with more than 5000 inhab., lies 1km. to the S. on the *Gödet Chai,* and is the seat of a kaimakam. It has seen better times: in antiquity as *Laranda,* in the middle ages under the Seljuks, and as the seat of the Karaman dynasty (1275-1466), which ruled for a long time in Konya also, being vanquished only by Mohammed II. A reminder of them is the well-preserved fort on a hill to the W. of the town, the beautiful *Hatunié Medressé* (from 1381) to the W. of the bazaar, mosques and mausoleums. In 1190, Frederick Barbarossa stopped at the town.

We continue NE. to (120km.) *Sidrova (Sidivré;* 1020m.), beneath the *Chakir Dag* (1180m.), and (149km.) *Airanji Derbend* (1119m.). The line crosses the *Divlé Chai*, reaching a summit of 1155m. between *Orbugun Dag* (1200m.) and *Ivris Dag*, then descending to the *Ak Göl,* a freshwater lake (1005m.), normally 20km. long, 8km. wide and about 4m. deep, having a subterranean outlet (duden) on the SW. side. – 173km. *Aladja* (1039m.) Fine view of the Taurus Mts. – At the plain of *Eregli* begins the territory of ancient Cappadocia.

190km. **Eregli** (1054m.; rooms available from the railway company; Turkish Hôtel de Baghdad, only for natives; the Armenian Toros Bardegyan provides coaches, horses and travel requisites). Eregli is a district town of 10,000 inhab., situated among abundant greenery on the *Kodja Chai.* One mosque is said to date from the XIIIth c. In antiquity, the place was called *Kybistra,* then *Heracleia* (whence "Eregli"); there are no remains of this. Cicero rested here, also Godfrey of Bouillon.

EXCURSIONS. 1. The village of Irvis (about 20km. SE. of Eregli) can be visited on horseback or, in the dry season, by carriage also (yaila, 2-3 mejidié) in 2-3hrs., best done when the cherry trees are in blossom at the end of April. The route crosses steppe at first, then negotiates some stony hills as far as the confluence of the dirty brown *Kodja Chai* with its tributary, the blue *Ivris Chai.* From here, one may either follow the Ivris, reaching, beyond the village of the same name, its sources; or one can branch off r. to reach the sources more directly by a more attractive but arduous way. The springs lie beneath a steep wall of rock, 5min. beyond the village; in the distance, the snow-covered mountain-range is visible.

Close by the village, a Hittite relief hewn out of the rock bears witness to the fact that the valley has always been as fertile: it shows a god with a grape and ear of corn, and a prince worshipping him (plaster cast of this at Constantinople). Half an hour's climb beyond this, up a difficult path, brings us to a second similar but more damaged image, with a ruined church nearby.

2. *Ak Öyük (Ak Hüyük:* "white hill") is a long, narrow hill 40m. high and about 12km. N. of Eregli in the plain (about 2hrs. by carriage). There are strong hot sulphur springs on the ridge, which leave behind similar petrified formations (white at first) to the springs at Hierapolis, which add to the volume of the hill itself. Nearby, a yuruk summer settlement and a mujadjur village (i.e. Turkish immigrants from the lost provinces).

3. From Eregli to Kaissarié, by carriage (see above) in 4-5, on horseback in 5-6 days; from Kaissarié to Angora, by carriage in 5-6, on horseback in 7-8 days. (Accommodation in hans or odas; one should take some provisions; sabtié escort recommended). – 1st/2nd day, Eregli to Nigdé, 75km., 12-16hrs. (For the road from Ulu Kychla to Nigdé, see p.299). We leave to our l. the wooded "White Hill" (see above) and to our r. the Baghdad Railway and Bulgurlu and continue across barren steppe, the ancient terrain of *Tyanitis*, NE. to *Bor* (1110m.; few hans – i.e. resthouses), a small town set among luxuriant greenery and enclosed by steep tufa rocks; 9400 inhab., mainly Greeks. 5km. to the S., on the road from Ulu Kychla, lies *Klissé Hissar* on the site of the ancient *Tyana,* whose foundation was traced back to Semiramis; of the old remains there still stand the arches of a Roman acqueduct and, on the "Hill of Semiramis", a marble column. – From Bor, another 2-2½hrs. to Nigdé (1190m.; hotel/hans: *Adienta-H., H. de Baghdad),* sanjak capital with over 10,000 inhab. on the threshold between Melendis Dag and Utch Kapular Dag. In antiquity, *Kadena* was probably here. A number of fine Seljuk buildings, including the mosque of Ala-eddin, the Ak Medressé and the mosque Suné Gurlu, remind one of Konya; also, entirely under its influence, is the octagonal turbë of Havanda or Fatna Hanum (dating from 1610; in the spandrels are figures of birds with female heads).

3rd/4th day (approx. 60km.): Nigdé to Develi Karahissar. 10km. beyond Nigdé we pass the old basilica (of the last century) of *Eski Andaval (Andabalis).* Half-way to Develi Karahissar, on the l. (4km.) is the dirty and inhospitable Greek village of *Misli. Develi Karahissar* lies in fertile land at the entrance to *Soganly Deré*, a valley into whose tufa walls and peaks numerous churches, arcades, cells and tombs have been cut; the cave dwellings commence 2½hrs. W. of Develi Karahissar and extend for more than an hour's journey. Here, as in Göremé, Urgub, Sinasos, Achyk Serai and others in eastern Cappadocia (to the W. and S. of Kaissarié), a Christian community of monks settled early on. The simple frescoes, with which a large number of the churches and chapels are still decorated, date from the VIII-XIIIth c., and are important to the history of Byzantine painting. (For works about the cave dwellings, see Diehl's "Manuel d'Art Byzantin" – Paris 1907, 25fr.). – From Develi Karahissar, it is possible to see Erjias Dag with its snowy summit (already visible at Nigdé), rising beyond the marshes of *Sultan Sasy*; in summer this plain is dry and salt-covered.

5th/6th day (approx. 65km.): Develi Karahissar to Kaissarié. The road crosses the Yavash Ova between Sultan Sasy and (l.) the *Sivri Dag.* About halfway, in a rocky basin at the W. foot of Erjias Dag, lies *Injé Su*, with an enormous old han. We continue along the W. margin of the *Saslyk,* a "reed marsh" which dries out almost completely in summer and is partly used for grazing. At its N. end, the road crosses the bridge Bögas Köprü over the *Kara Su,* (in antiquity *Melas),* a tributary of the Halys, and continues onwards SE. towards Kaissarié; in the dry season it is also possible to ride along the S. edge of the Saslyk.

Kaissarié (1070m.; accommodation in numerous hans, but better with recommendation in Talas or Sinjideré; several eating-places; French Jesuit mission) with 54,000 inhab. (⅓ Christian), capital of a sanjak belonging to the vilayet of Angora. It lies on a treeless plateau at the N. foot of Erjias Dag. As an important road junction (from Angora, Konya, Yosgad, Hadjin etc.) it has considerable trade, though its own industries are limited to carpets and leather. Long ago it was the capital of Cappadocia, originally called *Mazaka,* later *Eusebeia* and then dubbed *Caesarea* by Tiberius after the conquest of the country, hence the present name Kaissarié. Of the ancient town there are only a few stone ruins, 2km. SW. on the vine-covered hills by the old Turkish quarter (Eskishehir), known as Zorzat in Armenian. The present town in the plain grew up around the buildings founded by the early father Basilius of Caesarea (329-379), and was fortified by Justinian; the walls and citadel seen today were built during the Seljuk era and later restored. Opposite this imposing and extensive site, the inner town descends, with its numerous dilapidated streets, the pitifully poor huts at its edge and the tall stone buildings of the better quarters. Although none of the pre-Christian churches have survived, there are several Seljuk buildings, as in the surroundings, such as *Ulu Jami* of 1206 (a remodelled church?); the *Huen Mosque* of 1236, in fact the octagonal, pyramid-crowned turbë of Chovand between her mosque (r., with 56 pillars) and her Medressé (l.; beautiful portal); on the way to Talas, 10min.

before one reaches the town, is the round tomb *Syrtshaly Gümbet;* 200m. NE. of this, the *Köshk Önü*, a rectangular structure like a han around an octagonal tomb of 1340 with a pyramid-shaped roof. Large covered *bazaar* (Charshy); to the N. of this, on a broad square, the Konak with the post-office, the casino gardens and a large barracks. Magnificent view from the citadel (filled with Turkish houses).

1¼hrs. SE. of Kaissarié lies the little town of *Talas*, birthplace of Saint Sabas (d. 532), seat of the American mission with its schools and hospital. - ¾hr. further S., *Sinjideré,* where the Greek archbishop resides in St John's monastery, which is surrounded by well-conducted schools. – The *Erjias Dag* (3830m.) itself, on whose NE. foothills the two last-named places stand, is the ancient *Argaus,* the highest range in the Mediterranean area and the only volcano active in Asia Minor down to historically recent times; even in Strabo's time, its activity was limited to emissions of sulphuretted hydrogen, such as were still being experienced in 1880. The ascent (with alpine equipment; rock falls can be dangerous) of the highest peak of the majestic trachite cone takes about 9hrs. from the road to Everek, as it crosses a pass on the E. slope. The glaciers descend to 3100m. at one point.

The post road from Kaissarié to Angora follows the road from Eregli back as far as the bridge over the Kara Su, and runs along by the latter to its confluence with the Halys, crossing this also by a bridge, and continuing thence NW. Carriages can make *Topakly* on the first day and *Kirshehir* on the second. Riders stop at *Hadji Bektash* on the 2nd day, a flourishing town containing the chief monastery and the tomb of the founder (of the same name, d.1357) of the bektash dervishes. The order, which was once closely associated with the janissaries, has devoted itself, since the extinction of the latter, especially here to good works and agriculture. From Hadji Bektash one may go, in 1-2 days, via *Mujur* to *Kirshehir* (good hotel-han at the market), a prosperous sanjak capital of 40,000 inhab. stretching out among gardens. – From Kirshehir in 3-4 days via *Sofular* and the stone-arched bridge *Cheshmé Köprü* at Köprüköi to Angora.

Beyond Eregli, the line runs NE. at first, along the foot of the northern foothills of the *Cilician Taurus.*

The Cilician Taurus, across whose pass the road (and sometimes the railway) winds to the plain, is a recent range of fold mountains formed, in its principal summits, of massive limestone deposits. (E. of the pass: *Hadjin Dag, Ak Dag, Karanfil Dag, Ala Dag*; to the W., *Bulgar Dag* with the highest peak in the Taurus, *Aldost*, 3560m., *Karabunar Dag, Dumbelek Dag).* It stretches, 35km. in breadth, from the volcanic Erjias Dag (see above) in the NE., in a convex curve south-eastwards 230km. towards the SW., not far from Karaman. Towards the Cilician and the narrow W. coastal plain (scarp slope), this easternmost part of the S. Anatolian fringe mountains possesses, apart from the Cilician Gates pass (now crossed by the railway also), another negotiable pass road in the extreme W. (from Selefké to Karaman across the Jedi-Bel Pass).

Beyond (200km.) *Bulgurlu* (1056m.), terminus of the line from 1904 to 1911, the ascent begins. – 216km. *Chayan.* The railway veers SE. and, with many curves and steep gradients, reaches its highest point (1467m. at km. 229) between Haidar Pasha and Baghdad.

238km. **Ulu Kyshla** (1427m.; accommodation in a tolerable han; horses for 1-1¼ mejidié per day, and the local carriages, jailas, are available). The stop is called "Large Barracks", after the ruins of an enormous caravanserai, ¾hr. W., with mosque, bazaar and baths, which Selim II is said to have built; it was renovated by Ibrahim Pasha, who also built fortifications here in 1836. A new road runs N. down to Klissé Hissar (40km.) and Nigdé (a further 14km.).

The pass road through the Cilician Gates (carriage drive from Ulu Kyshla to Bosanti 6-7hrs., rather longer on horseback), joined here by the roads from Eregli and Nigdé, has followed since time immemorial the Tarbas Chai downstream from Ulu Kyshla, accompanied as far as Bosanti by the new railway line. At first we follow the l. bank to *Tosun Ali* (2¾hrs.; 1120m.), through a green gorge, with a rest house for the railway workers. Then we take the r. bank and finally descend in short curves to *Chifté Han* (1¼hrs.; see below; gendarmerie post). Back on the l. bank, the road passes the small han of *Ilidjer Hammam* (½hr.). The bath, with a 60° hot spring, the *Aquae Calidae* of antiquity, lies 5min. down the slope in a side valley to the l., invisible from the road (night accommodation in the primitive bath-house, 10 silver piastres). The valley narrows. The *Tachta Köprü* bridge (¾hr.; 870m. see below) crosses over the Kürkchi Deré which comes from far to the N. A further bridge, the white bridge (*Ak Köprü*, ¾hr.; 835m.) forms the border between the vilayets of Konya and Adana. Through a broadening valley again we reach *Bosanti* station (½hr. see below), where, for the present, the railway passengers must alight from the train, to complete the crossing of the pass by carriage.

Since the end of 1912, the railway has been operating for a further 55km. beyond Ulu Kyshla. At first it runs down alongside the *Tarbus Chai,* which rises a little above Ulu Kyshla. The pass road (see above) is often crossed. Soon, the high Taurus range comes into view. – 266km. *Chifté Han* (938m.), where the deep river gorge broadens out into a magnificent valley; the "double han" is down by the water (cf. above). – Beyond the

Ilidjer Han, the valley narrows again. At the Tachta Köprü, the Tarbas receives several streams, and is known from now on as *Bosanti Su.* Now begins the gorge in which the river breaks through the range. Beyond the Ak Köprü it continues in a valley, still broad to begin with, to (282km.) **Bosanti** (780m.; accommodation in several hans by the pass road; post office, carriages, horses, provisions available), where we alight, until the railway has been completed, to go by carriage up over the Cilician Gates pass (500m. above) by the old road which leaves the railway line here.

At Bosanti station, a new railway service road branches off the pass road and goes to Dorak, the starting-point of the next open stretch of the line. It is however hazardous, and accessible only with special permission, and can therefore not be regarded as a linking road between the two ends of the track. It is negotiable as far as a point 3km. beyond *Polemedi Kapu* or *Belemedik* (690m.; below Kara Bunar); then it climbs as a bridle-path to the prettily-situated village of *Kushjular* (1000m.), to continue again as a proper road via Hadjkiri to Dorak, where it is replaced by a fairly old carriageway to Adana. It begins, like the railway, by passing through Chakyt valley, and offers a splendid walk: ¾hr. from Bosanti we reach the superb *canyons of the “Little Gorge” and “Big Gorge”, cf. below. – In the future, it will be possible to reach the Cilician Gates pass most easily as a day’s excursion from Bosanti (by carriage, about 7hrs. return).

To avoid the further steep gradient alongside the pass road, the railway was taken on along by the river, which now bears the name *Chakyt* and until now had no room even for a path. It is the most difficult part of the entire construction of the line: with the dynamiting of the rock at many points, 70 tunnels (incl. three of 3500, 2700 and 1700m.) and viaducts, the line has to fight its way along the vertical limestone walls. The initial stretch is already open; on the E. side of the Hadjin Dag it passes through a *cleft like a canyon (see above). Beyond the temporary terminus (293km.) is **Kara Bunar** (no hotels, carriages or horses).

Then the track, still under construction, descends, almost totally through tunnels, to (313km.) *Hadjkiri.* The river rushes down in waterfalls over a deeply gouged-out bed, above which the rocky walls rise vertically for hundreds of metres. At the sharp bend before Hadjkiri is the *Yer Köprü* (“earth bridge”), where, as the result of an old landslide, the Chakyt runs underground for 175m.; beyond Hadjkiri, another 400m.-long wind-gap pierces the fringe mountains. At Hadjkiri, the railway track leaves the river and continues on W. over the foothills to (329km.) *Dorak.*

The Taurus Pass (carriage route)

Until the line is completed, the Taurus Pass itself, the Cilician Gates or Gülek Bogas must be crossed by carriage. The line has however advanced so far, that the carriage drive takes up only one extra day. One leaves the line at the penultimate stop, Bosanti, where the night is spent. An early start the next morning enables one to catch, at the stop Gülek Bogas, the afternoon trains to Adana and Mersina, which pass each other here at 5 o'clock; if one arrives later, the night is spent in Tarsus, 5km. W. of Gülek Bogas. If one intends to cross the Taurus Mts. from the S., one should spend the previous night in Tarsus, so as to be able to set off early (no accommodation or carriages at Gülek Bogas, which is the true starting-point of the pass road), reaching Bosanti in a day's travel, whence the train departs the following morning. – For the carriage one pays about £1 Turkish, often less; add 1 medjidié as tip. The road is safe, and sabtié escort unnecessary. On the way, several hans and coffee stalls are found, but the food is very basic; one should therefore equip oneself with a provision of food and wine, since one is advised to be cautious regarding the water.

Between the rail-ends at Kara Bunar and Dorak there is no carriageway, nor a public bridleway. Nor is there a proper road to the pass road from Dorak, only a very poor bridle-path (6hrs. to the Mesar Oluk han), so that it is not practical to cross the pass from here. – In winter, the passes lie under deep snow, and access is extremely difficult; one can find fresh snow as early as September.

The old pass road (bad in many places) which one must take from Bosanti to cross the Taurus Mts., ascends steeply up a deeply cut side valley on the r., past *Haivabé Han,* 1; concerning the railway service road, see p.300., to the small upland plateau of Tekir, 1hr., with the *Tekir Han* (1310m.) and the ruins of the huge entrenchments, barracks and forts which Ibrahim Pasha set up in 1836 during the occupation of Cilicia, only to dynamite them on his retreat. Fine view. – The other side of the ridge, the road enters the river valley which, as the *Tarsus Chai* flows past Tarsus to the sea. Another ¾hr. further on is the attractive *Köprü Han*. The ravine becomes narrower. In ¼hr. one reaches the pass *Gülek Bogas* (1160m.), a rocky gateway some hundreds of metres high but barely 20m. wide, through which the river roars, leaving only 4½m. breadth for the road. These famous Cilician Gates *(Pylae Ciliciae)* have often played their part in world history; Semiramis, Xerxes, Darius, Cyrus the Younger, Alexander the Great, Harun al Rashid and Godfrey of Bouillon have all passed through them; remains are still visible of Ibrahim Pasha's fortifications. The ancient road ran along the E. rock-wall, partly set into it or built out on supporting beams, whereas the modern one is blasted into the wall on the W. side. Immediately beyond the Gates, a rock resembling a castle towers up on the r., the Gülek Dag, crowned 600m. higher up with the ruins of the old Arab fortress *Assa Kaliba.*

After this, deciduous forest begins to mix with the pine forest; the vegetation takes on a southern aspect. Before *Giaúr Harman* (930m. on the r. bank) and the *Sarishak Han* (820m. on the l. bank of the river), in 2½hrs. from Gülek Bogas the *Mesar Oluk Han* is reached (670m.; not clean), where the road turns away E. from the Tarsus Chai. 20min. further on is the better *Yeni Han* (near Anastas; night stop, 10 silver piastres). The beautiful fir-trees reach down to here, but fall increasingly victim to devastation. Onwards over the bare foothills and down past numerous hans and several villages. Beyond the bridge Hökeshé Köprü (½hr. from Yeni Han) one has a splendid distant view out over the Cilician plain, the Gulf of Alexandretta and the Amanus Mts.; behind is the chain of Taurus Mts. 3hrs. from Yeni Han is *Kavak Han,* set in the shade. The pass road then crosses the increasingly cultivated plain, meeting the Mersina-Adana railway line after another 2½hrs. at *Gülek Bogas* station, 5km. from Tarsus. Here the trains from Adana and Mersina-Taurus pass one another (at present at about 9 a.m. and 5 p.m.). – Another branch of the road runs directly to Tarsus.

Continuation of the Baghdad Railway

Dorak – Adana – Mamuré, 139km., one train daily in 5hrs.

Mamuré – Radshu, 100km., under construction.

Radshu – Aleppo – Jerablüs, 204km., opened in December 1912.

Jerablüs – Tell ül Helif, 291km., and Tell ül Helif – Mossul –Baghdad, under construction.

From **Dorak** (329km.; no inns, carriages or horses) onwards, a further section of the Baghdad railway, Dorak – Adana – Mamuré, has been in operation since 1912. It passes in a southerly direction across the plain and links up at the station (346km.) *Yenidjé*, 13km. E. of Tarsus, with the Mersina-Adana line; it follows the latter E. via *Seïtunli* and *Kehia Oglu*, bears off to the l. and reaches the new station of

369km. **Adana**. – Apart from the *new sta.* of the Baghdad railway, 1½km. to the N. of the town on the r. bank of the Sihun, there is still the *old sta.*, on the W. side of the town, for the Mersina-Adana line.

ACCOMMODATION: Murad Palace Hotel, in the town near the bazaar, good beds, new, but badly run, pension 30 silver piastres; Hotel Athanassi by the Mersina sta., Greek, poor. – German *beer-hall* with garden and skittle-alley, by the new sta.; restaurant in the *Town Park.*

CONSULATES: Germany, Dr. Büge; Engl. and Fr. vice-consulate. – Branches of the *Ottoman Bank* and the *German Orient Bank.* – French Jesuit school. American Prot. Mission school.

Adăna (24m.) lies in the Cilician plain at the S. foot of the Taurus Mts., whose strategic key it is, and on the r. bank of the *Sihun,* or *Saros* of antiquity; a railway bridge and a 300m.-long many-arched bridge, dating in part back to Justinian, cross to the l. bank. The town has about 50,000 inhab., is the seat and vali of the vilayet of the same name, and chief centre of the province's crop and cotton trade; there is much cultivation of gardens and fields. The Christian Armenians, a third of the population, were decimated in the slaughter of 1909. The climate is very hot, but dry and healthy. Nothing remains of the ancient town on the same site; it was also called *Adana*, and only under the Seleucids was it called Antiocha ad Sarum. There are several attractive old *mosques* among the ten here. Some imposing modern *konak* (government buildings) by the river. Experimental garden and factory buildings of the German Levantine Cotton Co.; rolling-stock and general workshops of the Baghdad railway.

The *Cilician plain*, in the centre of which Adana lies, now called merely "low plain" or *Chukar Ova* (in antiquity *Aleïon Pedion)* is mainly composed from the sediment washed down from the limestone mountains. In winter subject to extensive flooding, it is dried up in summer, treeless away from the villages, and planted with wheat, barley, maize, rice, tobacco, cotton and sugar-cane. Now its fertility is to be enhanced by the regulation of the Jihan and Sihun and by the draining of its flood-plain; it is anticipated that 200,000 hectares will be won.

To the E. of Adana the Baghdad railway runs along the edge of the NE. (higher) part of the plain together with the road to Syria. – 382km. *Indjirlik.* A hill (140m.) rises out of the plain to the S., originally an island in the gulf which stretched as far as here. – 392km. *Kürdjiler.* – 399km. *Missis,* on the r. bank of the yellow *Jihan (Pyramas* in antiquity) which flows along between walls of loess. The village lies amid the ruined area of the ancient town of *Mopsuhestia*; Emperor Constantine's five-arched bridge is still used by traffic. – We continue on the r. bank upstream through the valley of the jackals, *Chakal Deré*, then across a massive bridge over the (420km.) *Jihan.* – 431km. *Weissié*, on the *Kara Chai*, up which the railway runs. 449km. *Toprak Kalé.* The Turkmen village of the same name lies 5km. SE. near an ancient ruined site *(Augusta?)* at the foot of a basalt cone (76m.) crowned by a half-ruined Armenian fortress. For the branch-line to Alexandretta, see below. – The Baghdad railway is in operation for the next 19km.: 459km. *Osmanié*; 468km. *Mamuré* (125m.) on the Jihan tributary *Hamus Chai.*

Toprak Kalé is the junction for the BRANCH-LINE TO ALEXANDRETTA, built in 1913, which is important particularly for goods traffic between the main area served by the Baghdad railway, and the Mediterranean. It passes by *Amanicae Pylae* at first, a 300m-long defile between basalt walls, used by Darius on the march to Issos [or "Issus"]. – Not far (12km.) from *Ersin*, the ruined site of *Gösené*, perhaps the ancient *Öniandos-Epiphaneia;* there are Roman remains (small theatre, temple, gymnasium, colonnade, acqueduct). – At 21km. *Karabasdan Chiftlik,* the railway approaches the *Gulf of Alexandretta*, continuing quite close to this along the W. foot of the Amanus Mts. To the r. we pass the tumulus *Karakaia,* which is regarded as a warrior's grave connected with the battle of Issos. – 32km. *Dört Yol*, S. of the *Deli Chai* (perhaps the ancient *Pinaros*:) here, in all probability, we may seek the *Battlefield of Issos*, where Alexander the Great won his brilliant victory over Darius III in Nov. 333 [B.C.]. The position of the Cilician town of *Issos*, from which the NE. corner of the Mediterranean used to take the name *Sinus Issicus,* has not yet been found. – 43km. *Paias (Baiae* of antiquity), now a small town of 6000 inhab., with fortress, baths and a large dilapidated han from 1544. – 52km. *Bab Yunus*, near the *Pylae Syriae*, the pass between sea and hill, through which Alexander moved towards Darius' army in the night before the battle. By the pass, the ruins of a fort and the two pillars of Jonah, whence the Turkish name derives.

60km. from Toprak Kalé, the line reaches, at Alexandretta, the best and roomiest shipyards on the Syrian coast; the railway company began the construction of a modern harbour in 1912. The small town of Alexandretta is set prettily in its ring of mountains. (Accommodation in the unpretentious Hôtel d'Orient and Hôtel de Constantinople; restaurant in the German Club; German vice-consulate; Austrian and French post-office, international telegraph). In Turkish *Iskenderun*, it has 12,000 inhab., half of them Christian, whose livelihood is the movement of goods to, and trade with, Aleppo. Fever rages for most of the year. Important harbour traffic (32 million francs-worth of exports and 35 mill. of imports in 1910); steamer of the Russian Steamship company every week; Austrian Lloyd and Khedival Mail every fortnight; Messageries Maritimes once a month, in 7-8hrs. from and to Mersina etc. The town was founded by Alexander the Great as the point of departure for the great caravan routes of Mesopotamia (but it is not clear if this was in the exact position of the present town). *Alexandria Scabiosa* was destroyed by the Persians in the IIIrd c. A.D., and has been known as "Little Alexandria" since the IVth c.

The continuation of the Baghdad railway beyond Mamuré must first conquer the *Giaúr Dag* (1840m.), the N. part of the *Amanus,* or outlier of the Taurus Mts., which extends as a mighty frontier rampart against Syria from Armenia to the Mediterranean, and consists principally of ancient volcanic rock. The track has been laid in the valley of the Hamus Chai, the *Bulanik Deré*, up to (494km.) *Bagché* (437m.). 8km. further on, the line will pierce the ridge at 870m. (W. of the bridle-way pass *Arslan Bogas*, 950m.) with a tunnel 5km. long, thence to descend by 9 smaller tunnels and 10 viaducts southwards into the plain of (529km.) *Islahié (Niboli, Nicopolis* to the ancients; 520m.). (10km. N. of Islahié, by the road to the sanjak capital *Marash*, is the ruined site of *Sendjirli*, a Hittite town excavated since 1888). We continue along the slopes of the *Kürd Dag* to (568km.) *Radshu.* – From Radshu, a further section of the Baghdad railway (as far as the Euphrates, 204km.) came into use in December 1912. It runs firstly via (649km.) *Muslimié* to (666km.) *Aleppo (Háleb),* where the (French-) Syrian rail network is reached. After the completion of the crossings of the Taurus and Amanus Mts., which is in any case not to be expected before 1915, the link, provided by the Anatolian railway, Baghdad railway, Syrian and Hedjas railways, will be complete between Constantinople and Turkey's distant Arab provinces.

From Aleppo, the Baghdad railway is now in operation, running NE. via Muslimié (see above) and (717km.) *Chobanbei* as far as the Euphrates, which is bridged at (772km.) *Jerablüs* (Jerabis, the Carchemish of the Bible). In the spring of 1913, one could travel by motor-boat from Jerablüs in 6 days to Felludja, and thence by carriage in 10hrs. to Baghdad. – The railway track continues E. via (877km.) *Harran,* where a short branch-line is to run N. to *Urfa,* (979km.) *Ras ül Ain,* (1063km.) *Tell ül Helif* (S. of Mardin) and *Nesibin* to *Mossul* on the *Tigris;* then down the r. bank of the latter via *Tekrit* to (1700km.) **Baghdad.**

From Baghdad S. to the *Persian Gulf*, there are regular sailings by the steamship companies. According to the Anglo-Turkish agreement of 1913, the Baghdad railway may build an additional section to *Basra* (585km.); the rights to build the remainder, Basra-Kuwait, about 120km., and the extending of the ports of Basra and Kuwait, are reserved by England.

Further details in Baedeker's *Palestine and Syria.*

A Handbook to the Orient

[From *Baedekeriana* no.8, Autumn 1987, being part of the text of a talk by Alex Hinrichsen at the Third Baedeker Symposium, held in Heidelberg in May 1986. Tr. MW]

In August 1872, Karl Baedeker II suggested to Dr Georg Moritz Ebers that they bring out a "Handbook to the Orient". Dr Ebers had made a lengthy journey to Egypt and Nubia in 1869-70. The volume was to contain the following routes:

I.
1. Trieste – Corfu – Alexandria – Cairo
2. Cairo – Suez, Nile delta
3. Excursion on the Nile.

II.
4. Alexandria – Jaffa - Jerusalem
5. Jaffa – Beirut - Damascus
6. Jerusalem – Damascus - Lebanon
7. Beirut – Tripoli – Cyprus - Smyrna

III.
8. Pest – Danube - Constantinople
9. Trieste – Brindisi – Corfu – Syracuse – Athens - Constantinople
10. Trieste – Corfu – Corinth - Athens
11. Messina (Marseilles) – Piraeus – Athens - Constantinople
12. Constantinople
13. Smyrna – Asia Minor

IV.
14. Athens & Greece.

The authors of the four sections were offered 30 talers per page, plus travelling expenses. The publishing house had already sent some maps and plans for Egypt to be produced, incl. 2 maps of the Nile, a map of Sinai and plans of Alexandria and Cairo.

In 1874, KB himself undertook a major tour of the East; in 1875 *Palästina und Syrien* appeared as the first part of the series.

On 30th November 1875, a 3-page agreement was signed between Dr Ebers and the firm Karl Baedeker for the issue of the volume *Unter-Ägypten* (Lower Egypt). The ms. was largely complete, but there was some disagreement about content and format. *Unter-Ägypten* was to appear under the name of the publisher, *Ober-Ägypten* (Upper Egypt) under the sole name of Dr Ebers in the firm Karl Baedeker. The publisher was decide how many to print, but Dr Ebers was assured by contract that the 1st edition would run to at least 1000 copies. The fee was set at 3000 talers (incl. the cost of Dr Ebers' travels in 1872-73). Since the Mark had been introduced as currency, it was decided that further mss. should be paid for at the rate of 100 Marks per page. Besides, Dr Ebers was entitled to 50 free copies of the 1st ed. (sale value 800 Marks).

Dr Ebers agreed to be named as principal contributor on the Preface to the guide, with reference to his ms. Karl Baedeker indicates, however, in his Preface, that he is not entirely happy with the ms.: "In preparing this volume, the editor had at his disposal a manuscript written for this purpose by Prof. Dr. G. Ebers in Leipzig; the descriptions are partly based on this." The publisher had to call upon various experts for assistance. Prof. Zittel of Munich received his proofs on 1.11.1875 for his section on "Geology & Desert"; Prof. Ascherson was asked as late as 20.10.1875 to say something concrete about "Oases in general" and, in December of that year, was requested to proof-read the entire volume – for which he was assured an initial fee of 300 Marks.

In February 1876, KB travelled to London to deliver the English translation of *Palästina und Syrien*. By the beginning of March, he was already back in Egypt, where he briefly met Prof. Ascherson (who was working on a report on Medinet el-Fayum). When he returned to Leipzig in May, KB wrote of his concern that he was losing his vitality when it came to work. He hoped that, after *Unter-Ägypten* appeared, he would experience a sense of relief.

The volume was finally announced in October 1876. Fritz Baedeker wrote in 1892: "It is unprofitable to bring out guides to the Orient, if one must entrust the writing of them to first-class authorities. I do not know if my rival Meyer is doing business with his small guides (which partly derive their information from mine). As matters are now, I regard the guides to the Orient merely as a kind of noble advertisement. What other firms spend on newspaper ads, I devote to the issue of new titles."

New titles took up much time and patience, the Egypt volumes being no exception. The guide to the Orient, mentioned above, burgeoned out into an enterprise which only took on its present form after much adaptation and re-arrangement. Time, and competition from other houses, played no small role.

1872: First ideas about a handbook for the Orient in IV sections.

1875: *Palästina und Syrien* appeared.

1877: *Unter-Ägypten* appeared, with the comment: "The second vol. - *Ober-Ägypten*, handbook for Nile travellers by Prof.Dr.G.Ebers in Leipzig and Prof.Dr.J.Dümichen in Strasbourg – is in print, and will shortly appear." (This however seems to have been wishful thinking).

1883: *Griechenland* (Greece).

1892: *Ober-Ägypten*; and, not until…

1905: *Konstantinopel und Kleinasien.*

His rival Meyer published, at the Bibliographic Institute in Leipzig, the following:

1881: *Der Orient: I. Ägypten.*

1882: II. *Syrien, Palästina, Griechenland & Türkei.*

The Russian Baedecker [sic] o*f Berlin*

A guide to Berlin and its environs was produced in 1909 in St Petersburg by the "P. Kopelmann" publishing-house. Uniform with this guide were ones to Vienna and Paris, plus Conversation Manuals (in German and French); further titles covering Italy and Switzerland were 'promised for the future'. In the Preface, the publisher said:

> "We have set before us as an example the famous Baedeker Publishing House which because of the great value of its publications has become so popular that the word 'Baedeker' has by now become synonymous with the word 'Guide-book'."

So yet another 'pseudo-Baedeker joins the collection!

Baedeker at Troy

[This extract, in my own translation, from Baedeker's *Konstantinopel und Kleinasien*, 2nd ed. 1914, appeared in *Baedekeriana* no.16, Autumn 1991]

Before leaving the comparative safety of Constantinople, the traveller bound for Turkey beyond the Bosphorus needed to acquaint himself with Baedeker's advice (and dire warnings) about travel, in the above volume:

"Public safety is mainly as good in Constantinople and its nearer surroundings as in our own large cities. The authorities have particular regard for the protection of foreigners. One will seldom have cause to complain about a lack of civility from officials; if the execution of one's wishes tends to try one's patience, one must take into account the Oriental ways with their more leisurely concept of time. If one requires police escort for occasional excursions over greater distances, one should apply to the consulate, where one's needs will be willingly fulfilled (the mounted gendarme, *Sabtié*, receives about 1 medjidié per day; he also helps to give the European some standing). – The Turk is quite tolerant of foreigners who respect his views, who behave in a seemly fashion in the mosques etc., do not stare at veiled women (nor photograph them; this may only occur in the case of men and children with permission), and above all keep the peace. It goes without saying that one does not venture into the port areas after dark; one must also be especially on one's guard against guides who offer their services for the visit of the 'sights' there, gambling dens and places of entertainment. Nocturnal adventures are to be shunned in the Orient, where all kinds of diseases are much more prevalent than in the West. One should watch out for pickpockets, especially in Galata and Pera. It is wiser to go for walks in company, more to avoid the feeling of loneliness than because of possible danger. The stern refusal of access to military areas, the handing over of *Bakshish* (tips) to officials and other deplorable practices have eased in Constantinople since the onset of the new era. Begging is nowhere near as importunate as elsewhere in the Orient. Those desiring any kind of information are advised to approach Turks in European dress, who usually understand a few words of French. The old traditional Turk seldom has any understanding for things that interest the tourist. Annoyance is caused by people taking many notes, drawing or photographing, and these must not be done near military installations, or inside mosques or museums…

Well-versed travellers can dispense with the services of a dragoman (guide and interpreter) in Constantinople and its nearer environs. Also, the excursions on the Bosphorus, to the Princes' Islands, Haidar Pasha etc., are simple enough for the traveller to undertake on his own. The kind of trip which goes beyond the usual objectives of natives and foreigners makes the company of a dragoman essential. This profession is normally carried out by native Jews. However well informed they may be on many topics, one cannot expect them to have a real understanding of history, or the significance of works of art. Dragomans who casually offer their services in the street often only do so with the intention of taking the foreigner into some shop or other, where they enjoy a percentage of the sale."

14. Troy

Introductory note. The excursion to Troy is not one which the layman will normally undertake: the journey is arduous in itself, the accommodation primitive, and the excavations (in keeping with these particular conditions) do not lend themselves to a clear over-view, and they impress the observer only partially; some intensive study is required, both before and during the visit. What does make a direct impression is however the landscape, the setting for Homer's battles. The traveller who has no knowledge of Greek or Turkish must employ a *guide,* either a dragoman from Constantinople or, preferably, a recommended guide from Dardanelles (the name given to the town of Kalé Sultanié), e.g. from an archeological institute, though he may speak only Greek and Italian. Travellers with a knowledge of Greek may use the services of Georgios Jannakis Tsakkiri at Renköi, who will also bring rugs; on request, the German vice-consul in Dardanelles will arrange for him to be available; also, if necessary, a sabtié escort (gendarmes). One must provide one's own food.

The point of departure for the excursion is the town of *Dardanelles*, where almost all the steamers from the Aegean Sea, and many from

Constantinople, put in, offering almost daily the opportunity to return in either direction; one should inquire in the agencies beforehand.

Distribution of time. From Dardanelles, one can make the trip by carriage, with a 2-3hr. stop at the ruins, in a day at most. It is better to devote two days, spending the night in one of the villages near Troy (Kalifatli, where decent accommodation may be found with a Greek peasant, or Chiblak). Or one may ride off in the afternoon, spend the night in the large Greek village of *Renköi,* visit *Troy* the next morning, returning that afternoon. The rewarding excursions into the surrounding countryside, e.g. to *Bunarbashy* or the *tumuli,* require more time. The traveller who intends to visit the wooded *Ida Mts.* to the S., must obtain special permission from the authorities.

The journey from Constantinople through the Sea of Marmara to Dardanelles takes 14 to 30hrs., depending on the steamer.

The town **Dardanelles.** – Disembarcation 5 piastres; passport and customs examination. – HOT., Greek: H. Hellespont at Gerasimos, tolerable (the landlord also provides everything necessary for the excursion to Troy), H. des Etrangers, Pand. Christidēs, bed 2fr. in both (make agreement).

POST OFFICES: *Turkish, French, Austrian* and *Russian* post office.

VICE-CONSULS: for *Germany* (Mich. Christidēs), *Austro-Hungary* (C. Xanthopulos, repr. Austrian Lloyd). *Italy* (de Caravel, repr. of the Società Italiana di Servizi Marittimi), *England, France, Greece, Netherlands* and *USA.*

Branches of the Ottoman Bank, correspondent of the German Orient Bank.

Dardanelles, Turkish *Kalé Sultanié* after the fortress around which the town grew, or *Chanak Kalessí* ("pottery castle") after the once thriving ceramic industry, is the capital of the Dardanelles sanjak, including the Troas area, with over 16,000 inhab., 20,000 if the garrison is included. Most of the stone houses were destroyed on the 9th Aug. 1912 by earthquakes. – An excursion to *Abydos* (2hrs. on foot) scarcely repays the effort and is not to be recommended because of the nearby Turkish fortifications; better, therefore, to make for *Hissarlik (Troy).*

One can generally ride to *Hissarlik* on good horses (6fr., possibly only 1 medjidié) in 6hrs. – Two other possibilities are less likely to be chosen: a) by carriage in 5hrs. (poss. there and back in a day); b) in a sailing-boat, with a favourable wind, to *Kum Kalé* with the current, thence on horseback for 1½hrs. (the individual will find horses there, and everywhere in the villages) to Hissarlik. Returning (by boat) from Kum Kalé to Dardanelles, one is entirely dependent upon a good wind. – A railway is planned from Dardanelles via Esiné to Soma, with a branch via Bairamitch to Biga.

The road to Hissarlik. One follows the Turkish military road, which runs along the S. shore of the Hellespont to Renköi. Just outside the town, we cross the *Kodja Chai*, the ancient *Rhodios*, whose fertile valley opens up on the l. We continue round the bay of Sari Siglar to the peninsula *Kefes Burnu* (Dardinis Akroterion, Trapeza), reaching, after this, the site of ancient *Dardanos* on the small bay of Kefes. In 2hrs. we reach *Karantina.* The view across the straits to the Thracian Chersmes opposite [i.e. the Gallipoli peninsula, tr.], and the islands of the Aegean, becomes ever more extensive and beautiful. Gradually we climb the foothills, where the large Greek village of *Renköi* (or *Erenköi)* lies amid fields and deciduous woods (15km. in 3hrs.; poss. accommodation for the night). From here we have our first view of the excavated site of Hissarlik, the plain of Troy and the coast as far as Sigeion. 1km. to the N., the site of the ancient *Ophrynion.* After a short rest at Renköi, we descend SW., at first on the road (built in 1906) to Esiné; to our r., on a hill, the remains of a *palaeokastro.* Then the way divides, the r. arm leading westwards past the Tumulus of Ajax, to Kum Kalé; l., the new road, which travellers generally take; southwards through the valley of a tributary and then the Simoeis, to the range of hills on whose summit, 3-4km. W. of the road, lies Hissarlik-Troy. Riders take the middle, older path N., just by the edge of the uplands, where now only pools and marshes betray the silted upper courses of the *Kalifatli Asmak*, the ancient river-bed, which once received here the Simoeis, and had its estuary close by the W. side of the foothill range of *Rhoiteion*, where today the *Tepé Asmak*, full of sea-water, stretches inland. Later, after its union with the Simoeis, it made a new bed further to the W. and, at the time of Pliny and Strabo, came out into the Stoma Limne, as it does today. In the middle ages, however, the Scamander completely altered its course below its confluence with the Thymbrios, and flowed further to the west, to enter the sea E. of Cape Sigeion. This western arm carries the old name of *Menderé*; the Simoeis did not reach it any more, but flowed as an independent river through the lower reaches of the Kalifatli Asmak into the Stoma Limne. Since 1895, the main course of the Scamander has chosen an estuary further E. again; it makes a confluence with the Kalifatli Asmak, the lower course of the Simoeis, and flows with this through the Stoma Limne into the sea, while the former mouth near Kum Kalé is silting up. So now, where the valleys of the Scamander and Simoeis meet, stands the height of Hissarlik today, the site of Troy, (though once to the S. of their confluence and closer to the Scamander), about 5km. S. of the Straits of the Dardanelles. The castle mound [*this is perhaps a misleading tr. of "Burghügel", since the "castle" has disappeared. A fairer tr. must be the* *(alas more cumbersome) "hill on which the palace and town once stood" tr.*] offers a magnificent *View across the whole terrain, Homer's battlefield: to the SW., the mount of Tenedos (190m.), to the W. the Hagios Dimitrios Tepé (223m.); then, to the N., the village Jenishehr, the Turkish batteries, the grave-mounds of Achilles and Patroclus and the sandy tongue of Kum Kalé; in the evening, the Sidd el-Bahr lighthouse shines across from the other shore of the Dardanelles. Beyond, to the NW., the island Imbros and the mighty mountain of Samothrace, Poseidon's standpoint. To the W., below the castle, the plain of the Scamander. The present chief estuary can be discerned from the sailing-boats which lie in front of it, loading wood that has been floated down. It was here, roughly from the tumulus of Achilles to that of Ajax, that the Greeks had their port, not far from the Homeric estuary of the Scamander. (A. Brueckner has recently placed it on the bay of Besika). The Scamander divided the battleground into a western (Greek) and an eastern (Trojan) part. The ford near Ilos' tomb in the centre of the plain (Iliad XI. 166, 371), which the Greeks always had to pass through, when they advanced on Troy, is alleged to be located near the Turkish cemetery of Kum Köi. – From the ancient Scamander estuary, a wooded line of hills runs E.; approximately half-way between Troy and these hills, one can see a darker strip running over the plain to the Scamander: the marshy course of the Simoeis. At Renköi, the uplands are joined by a range of hills which run in a broad arc round Troy to the E.; to the SE., behind it, Ida towers up, Zeus' lofty seat; on the offshoot of one of the lines of hills descending from there, lies the plateau of Troy and, on the NW. side of this, separated by a small valley, and marginally higher, the castle.

EXCAVATIONS. To have established by excavation for all time that the height of Hissarlik was the site of Priam's palace (castle), is the unforgettable achievement of Heinrich Schliemann. (Of his numerous publications, we mention only the following here: "Troja", Leipzig 1883 and the report, issued posthumously in 1891, of the excavations of 1890. *Dörpfeld* published further reports in 1893 and 1894, and a concluding work about the excavations to date: Troja und Ilion", 2 vols., Athens 1902, 40*M.*); the equally great merit of W. Dörpfeld derives from his scientific formulation of the excavations and their completion for the time being. In antiquity, the town of *Ilion* on the height of Hissarlik was almost universally regarded to be the successor to Priam's city, as is seen from the historical sketch. Only Demetrios of Skepsis, in the IInd c. B.C., and a few scholars, placed the site at *Iliéŏn Kome*, approx. 6km. SE. of Hissarlik. In more recent times, only a few researchers had decided in favour of Hissarlik, the most important of them, including Moltke, choosing instead, for strategic reasons, ("Letters about the state of things and events in

Turkey", Berlin 1841), the height of *Bunarbashy*. Schliemann, after a brief trial dig at Bunarbashy in 1888, had indicated only a shallow depth of deposited material, so turned to Hissarlik and, through a series of excavations in 1870-90, brilliantly proved the correctness of his choice, solidly defending himself against E. Bötticher, who had maintained in 1883 that he, Schliemann, had turned up nothing more than a "crematorium". It must be admitted that up to 1882 too little had been properly noted down and preserved, and the broad north-south trench had destroyed some remains for all time. But, with Dörpfeld's assistance, the treasure-seekers became scientific researchers. A quirk of fate did not permit Schliemann to live to see the finest result (see below). He regarded the second layer to be the remains of Priam's palace; but the excavatons of 1890 hinted, and those of 1893 and 1894 confirmed, that it was the *sixth* layer (the Mycenean) which merited that title. Kaiser Wilhelm II provided the funds for this last campaign.

The most important FINDS, e.g. the so-called Treasure of Priam, were presented by Schliemann to the *Museum für Völkerkunde in Berlin* [Museum of Ethnology]. Other material, particularly the finds from the last campaign, are in the *museum at Constantinople.*

HISTORY. The excavations at the castle brought to light nine different layers of habitation, stacked upon one another. These nine layers do not run horizontally, but follow the profile of the hill. From the results of the excavations and the historical notes handed down, one can piece together the following history of the site. The oldest small settlement (first layer), whose unimpressive and only partly uncovered remains can be divided into two periods, dates back to the Stone Age and up to the IVth c. B.C.; it had been situated on the rock, 26m. above sea-level. The resulting rubble raised the hill by about 5m.; after this had been levelled, a castle approx. 300m. in circumference, with a strong fortifying wall, was built on the horizontal plateau, along with dwellings made only of dried (not fired) clay bricks ('air bricks'); on the S. side, the castle was twice extended (this being impossible to the N.) by taking the defensive wall further out, so that this layer II falls into three periods, comprising the period (approx.) 2500-2000 B.C. This prehistoric "brick or clay castle" (second layer), the chief example of an E. Mediterranean culture advancing out of the Stone Age into the Bronze Age, was destroyed by a conflagration (and so also is known as the "burnt city"). Upon its rubble stood, between about 2000 and 1500 B.C., three small prehistoric villages (3rd to 5th layers). The hill rose at the centre to about 36m. already, falling away gradually at the sides. Between about 1500 and 1000 B.C., it carried a terraced Mycenean stone castle, with a perimeter of about 540m., the Troy of Homer (sixth layer).

The dating was established by fragments of Mycenean vessels. Schliemann had not discovered these (see above), because a) in the Roman era (layer IX) the hill had been levelled again, and the uppermost terrace thereby destroyed, and b) according to an ancient report, Archaeanax built the walls of Sigeion and Achilleion in the VIth c. B.C. with stones from Troy, demolishing the latter's walls on the NW. side, so that barely a trace of them remained. It is a matter of doubt whether the castle already possessed a lower town.

On the site of the destroyed castle, and using the walls that had remained standing, a pre- or ancient-Greek village (seventh layer) stood between about 1000 and 700 B.C., which also covered two periods; in the second of these, the inhabitants were perhaps already Aeolian Greeks, who then for a while had to flee from barbarians penetrating from the N., Trers or Trars. A fortified village of Aeolian Greeks (eighth layer) stood, from about 700 B.C. onwards, on the hill, which had gradually risen by 15m. (41m. above sea-level). It contained a temple of Athene, which was visited by Xerxes (Herodotus VII, 43) and Alexander the Great, who also made a sacrifice at Achilles' tumulus. His plan, to make the site more beautiful and magnificent with buildings, was not carried out until King Lysimachos (in part) and then the Romans (fully) were involved in it. The new sanctuary to Athene built by Lysimachos was the sacred centre of the union of the cities of Ilium. Probably, at that time, the hill was already only the acropolis of a small town, which grew up on the plateau beneath. After suffering much at the hands of the Galatians, and enjoying the favours of Hellenic kings, then smarting from the siege and destruction wrought by Fimbria, Sulla's rival commander (85 B.C.), Sulla commenced the long line of Roman benefactors, who honoured Ilium as the cradle of their race. Caesar made sacrifices here, but his far-reaching plans were realised even here only under Augustus. Thus one can reckon, with some confidence, the final period to be from about the birth of Christ to 500 A.D.; during this time, the site was the acropolis of the Roman city of Ilion (ninth layer), with the large temple of Athene. All the regularly vertical and smoothly hewn stone blocks, remains of buildings found, belong to this layer. To create space for the temple area, the hill was levelled again, destroying the greater part of the remains of levels VIII and VII, and a good deal of level VI; only at the edge could traces of these three layers be found, protected by the rubble thrown down from the sides. Rome's "mother city" became the goal of travellers; Hadrian and Caracalla stayed there (in 214 A.D.), Marcus Aurelius probably had the sanctuary renovated; Constantine the Great (323-337), taking up one of Caesar's plans, wanted at first to build his imperial city here; Julian visited the well-preserved temple in 355. During the Byzantine era, both city and castle fell into disrepair; the stones were dragged off for dwellings and tombs; but Ilium was a bishop's seat for almost a thousand years. The Turks (since 1306) did not settle here. The fields extended up the hill until Schliemann arrived.

A tour of the excavations.

One's view of the excavations is, as already said, impeded by the destruction caused by the first diggings, and the fact that the layers are so numerous and do not all run horizontally. Gradually, however, one acquires an eye for the distinguishing features of the individual layers in building methods and materials. The most clearly recognisable are the layers **II** (the horizontal prehistoric clay castle), **VI** (the Homeric terraced stone castle) and **IX** (the horizontal Roman acropolis). They should be awarded closer inspection, while the remaining layers are to be dealt with only cursorily. To serve one's orientation, when inside, there are Schliemann's N-S trench and the double oak-tree.

From the excavators' huts we go N., coming first to three chambers with a fallen granite column, the uncovered part of the Roman *theatre C.* Immediately to the r. of this, the *south gate tower* of the *Mycenean castle* (layer VI), intersected on the front side by a marble-clad Roman wall. Let into its front are two upright stones, doubtless for ritual use. This was the main entrance to the castle in Mycenean and later times (according to Dörpfeld, this is Homer's Dardanic Gate, while the Scaeic would be found to the NW.). The paved road to the r. of the tower is 3.3m. wide; the *east wall* abuts on to it. It once consisted of a sloping substructure about 6m. high and 5m. thick, and visible to the outside, whose stone blocks were hewn almost regularly, forming fairly horizontal bands. Above this, from 1m. above the castle floor, rose a vertical superstructure composed of flat, rectangular stones, again almost regularly cut; this superstructure was only 2m. thick, to leave a walk-way on the inside, on the broader substructure.

In the original wall-building in layer VI, a superstructure of air-dried clay bricks of the same thickness was erected on the substructure; in a later period in layer VI, this upper wall was replaced by another built of the flat oblong stones which, in shape, resemble the clay bricks (and so are called 'stone bricks'); this preserved upper work did not therefore need to be so solidly constructed as the one made of the weaker clay bricks.

9m. from the main gate, to the E., we encounter for the first time the characteristic feature, which recurs at intervals of 9-10m., of this ring-wall; a neatly-worked corner, 0.10–0.15m. deep; these corners form an effective interruption to the wall, transforming the ring into a polygon. The first corner already lies within the Roman "*theatre B*", beneath which the wall runs.

The lowest level of seating is marble; the position of the stage house is occupied by a marble bema (platform); the whole is enclosed within the rectangle of the walls and was, by analogy with the corresponding buildings at Priene, Miletus etc., the *Buleuterion* (assembly house of the council) of the Hellenic city.

After this, we follow the wall further. Beyond the long Roman transverse wall of regular stone blocks comes the formerly two-storeyed *south-west tower.* All of the towers were built on afterwards in front of the Mycenean wall, more or less at the time when the thinner stone brick superstructure replaced the thicker air brick structure on the wall.

To the l. (W.) of the tower, and separated from the wall by a street's breadth, lie *houses of the Mycenean level*: site VI G, which is cut by a thick Roman ashlar wall (the southern stylobate wall of the temple area), then abutting on to this to the N., and set back rather further from the ring-wall. VI F with VI E and VI C adjacent to it to the N. again. [These numbers refer to Dörpfeld's plan, which it has not been possible to reproduce in this book. According to him, the site of Troy measured approx. 200 X 160 m. tr.] The houses of layer VI lay around the hill in several concentric terraces; one must imagine that the king's palace would occupy the highest point; but nothing has been found of the upper terraces, since the ground was levelled in later times. The chief roads ran round; from the gates, radial ramps led up, and alley-ways separated the dwellings. The buildings consisted of a vestibule between end-walls, and the inner chamber. The house walls were originally perhaps also thick clay brick walls, which were then later replaced by thinner stone ones. They supported flat earth roofs; the surviving walls, mainly only a few metres high, often display the surface decoration referred to in the case of the east wall, through vertical projections added on. VI F is a room of 12 by 8.4m., with two doors but without a vestibule. VI E is particularly well constructed; the east wall goes deeply into the ground, in carefully fitted ashlar blocks. – To the r. (E.) of VI F and E., chambers can be seen, with *pithoi* (jars for provisions) let into the floor; they belong to *level VII* and are laid out where there had been a street in layer VI. Near VI F there was also a deep rock wall here. – Adjacent to the W. side of VI E is the rear wall of VI C, a building of the second terrace, whose front part may be seen beyond the trench. In the front portion, preserved in its original place, is the stone foundation of a wooden column; from this one may assume that three wooden supports stood along the axis of the room, which measured 15.3m. by 8.4m. The ground-plan of the temple of Neanrheia (to the S. of Troy) is similar; one might therefore take VI C to have been a temple also.

To the N., from the front of VI E, we reach (r.), by one of the radial ramps, the *east gate* VI S and, passing through a breach in the Roman ashlar wall (which carried the columns of the east hall of the temple area), we come to a section of wall which projects from the N.; this, together with the wall coming from the S., formed a curved walk about 10m. long, in front of the 1.8m. wide gate. Following the outside of this external wall, we reach the substantial *north-east tower* of the Mycenean wall which, with a breadth of 18m., projects 8m. On top of the 6m. high sloping substructure (composed of fine ashlar blocks) there once rose vertical clay brick walls, so that the tower would have offered a panoramic view into the distance. Within it, where a 1.25m. gate allowed entry, is a rectangular rock well or cistern, which was in use over a long period, and which descnded deeply to a watercourse. – Behind the N. side of the tower, a *flight of steps* led down, in the period of *level VIII,* to a well outside the tower. The large retaining wall to the SE. dates back to Roman times.

If one climbs up behind the tower, one continues straight on from the main stairs, then l., at the end of a corridor paved with slabs, to a *well* which, like the one in the north-east tower, leads down to a watercourse in the rock, and still yields water today. Above it doubtless stood the round marble well-house from Roman times, of which a ring lies next to the corridor, on the r., as one ascends. – Above this comes the plateau of the *Temple of Athene.* The temple of the Ilian Athene was famous from antiquity. Alexander promised a magnificent rebuild, and Lysimachos carried it out; but little of it still stands today. The columns which one can see, metopes (Helios on the quadriga) and other marble architectural pieces doubtless come from the temple which was erected by Augustus, and restored several times. Its outline (35.2m. by 16.4m.) can be made out by the deep ditches, in which the foundations were laid upon compacted sand. It possibly did not possess an ambulatory but only six Doric columns at the front and rear and, from the E., a broad open staircase. In front of it, beyond the corridor, the large *altar foundation* remains. In Roman times there extended around the temple a level *area*, approx. 80 sq.m., produced by removing earth at the centre and depositing it at the sides; colonnades enclosed it on three sides, and a simple wall to the N. The centre of the southern colonnade was occupied by a *gatehouse* with four columns on its front, similar to the main gate of the acropolis.

We return to the *theatre C* and turn W., alongside or on the western section of the Mycenean ring-wall. About 70 paces from the theatre we reach a large building of the Mycenean layer, set on a terrace 4m. high, which is called the *kitchen building* on account of the large pithoi for provisions, and other finds in the third room; behind this, a flight of steps led to the second terrace (VI N). Its long frontage, facing the ring-wall, which is very carefully constructed at this point, repeats, particularly clearly, the latter's method of building with the added projections. 25 paces further on, the broad ring-wall comes to an end. After a filled-in section of 7 paces, which corresponds to an earlier *west gate*, there follows a narrower wall section, very well constructed, of the 'stone bricks' mentioned above. The *house VI A,* large and well built, comes almost up to this wall, consisting of atrium and main room; in the middle of the latter, a layer of ashes was found, which suggests that the hearth was here. The house is squeezed into the space between wall and terrace, and the wall was doubtless adapted at the same time, so that both can be ascribed to the latter period of layer VI. Opposite the northern corner of VI A are the remains of the even larger but similar structure VI B. – Here, the *Mycenean wall* ends. It surrounded the whole castle with a perimeter of approx. 540m., of which 2/3 remain; the N. section and a part of the W. wall were removed.

To the E. of houses VI A and B one can see, below, a broad paved *ramp* leading up to the inner castle mound to the gate *F M* from a lower ring (uncovered again by the excavations; one reaches it from the S. side). The ramp, 5.55m. wide, with parapets 1m. thick (destroyed), had a 1:4 gradient and was therefore not intended for chariots. It led, as a side access on the W. side, to the *prehistoric castle* (layer II), the clay brick castle which succumbed in the fire, and which Schliemann took to be Priam's fortress. It measured about 300m., and has been almost totally uncovered. In the untouched earth mounds, it appears as a layer, 1-2m. deep, of yellow, red or black burnt debris. – Its *ring-wall* stretches on both sides of the ramp. It consisted of a substructure 1-8m. tall of pieces of virtually unworked limestone with earth mortar; it slopes, so that one can easily climb up it. On top of this was a vertical wall, more than 3m. tall, of air-dried bricks, and on top of this again there was perhaps a wooden walkway in the form of an arcade. – At the top of the ramp, the *gatehouse* F M, 5.25m. wide, with a double gate catch. Turning to the r. inside, we can see three different ranges of the ring-wall. It was thrust outwards twice at this point. The ramp, up which we came, and the outer wall, must therefore belong to the last period of layer II, and presupposes that the two inner ranges of wall were already covered over by them. The low *gate passage* FN (continuing r. – that is, E.) was, on the other hand, the main entry point in the earlier period. With a width of approx. 3m., it has a gentle gradient, calculated for chariots, and a clay surface, and was covered with tree-trunks; above this rose a substantial tower building of the early wall. – Immediately beyond this (E., down by the mound of earth with the double oak), is the *gatehouse F O,* the main gate of the earlier period of layer II which, on a larger scale, corresponds to the gate F M, described above. (At the S. end of the large gatehouse F O, the clay bricks of the walls can clearly be made out). The clay brick ring-wall, which bordered this gatehouse on both sides, was 4m. thick here (the Themistoklean wall at Athens being only about 2½m.), and has tower-like projections, of which two, immediately to the r. (E.) are visible. Their continuation was found under the large temple of Athene. – Proceeding NW., 15 paces from the large gatehouse F O, across a yard once covered with gravel, we come upon a small *Propylaeon*; it formed the entrance to a group of buildings in the middle of the castle of layer II, which one might designate the *Court of the Ruler.* The Propylaeon has a single door-opening, 1.82m. wide, and consists of a larger atrium and a smaller rear hall. Its massive stone porch, 3m. long and 1.1m. broad, still occupies its original position. To protect the walls of clay bricks, wooden posts were set against the free-standing ends, which stand on stone pedestals, bearing in mind the dampness of the earth; this was the common practice in layer II. These then gave way to the end-walls in the later stone structure. The second layer probably did not possess any free-standing columns. The dwellings of the commander of the castle, his wife, children and relatives opened on to the courtyard adjacent on the inside, which again was covered with gravel. The *main structure* II A, immediately opposite the Propylaeon, the *Megaron,* as in Tiryns and Mycenae, is composed of an atrium and room (about 20m. deep and 10.2m. wide, half destroyed by the great N-S. trench), at whose centre rose a hearth 4m. in diameter. The walls, whose construction can be seen particularly clearly at this point, are 1.44m. thick; upon a stone base (to protect against damp) 1.3m. high, there is one layer of bricks set lengthwise and the next breadthwise (each about 0.67m. long, 0.45m. broad, 0.12m. high), which consist of clay mixed with straw and merely air-dried. To give greater solidity, beams were inserted lengthways into the first layer, transverse pieces of wood in the second to fourth, and lengthwise again in the fifth; these can be made out in the depressions in the clay bricks, or where they have been more strongly fired (into bricks proper). The height of this room is not known. The only opening in the flat earth roof was doubtless above the hearth. On the r. is a smaller building, consisting of atrium, middle room, rear room and a small rear hall. To r. and l., other similar buildings opened on to the courtyard. If we return to the gate by the first-named ramp (F M), we find, beyond, a similar group of smaller dwellings; one may assume that there was a third group in the northern (destroyed) part of the castle. Blocked up in a hollow space in the clay-brick superstructure of the ring-wall, about 6m. NW. of the ramp, Schliemann discovered the so-called *Treasure of Priam,* which is now preserved in the Museum für Völkerkunde at Berlin. Similar discoveries of jewellery and vessels, weapons and tools of gold, silver, electron and bronze were also made at other points in layer II, dating back to the fully developed Bronze Age. The clay vessels betray a knowledge of the potter's wheel and kiln only from the second period of this layer. Beakers bearing two fairly large handles were popular; stone idols were numerous, and clay spindle weights were found in quantity.

In Schliemann's great N-S. trench which, at this point, thrusts between the first and second groups of dwellings of the second castle, some dwelling walls survive (of small stones with earth mortar) from the two original ancient settlements of layer I. Because of the narrowness of the trench, an outline is not recognisable. Numerous stone and clay utensils for everyday use were found here, produced without a potter's wheel, but betraying considerable use, and the remains of meals.

Only the specialist researcher will be interested in layers III, IV, V, VII and VIII, scarcely mentioned here. To the l. of the inner front structure of the gate over the ramp are walls of dwellings, partly of undressed stone, which Schliemann took to be Priam's palace, but which belong to the *layer III dwellings.* The peasants of this village overhauled the castle wall again. Their small rooms usually lie round a courtyard, and their walls were largely composed of alternating layers of varying thickness, of undressed stones and clay bricks. Large egg-shaped earthenware vessels (pithoi) served them (as earlier, and later on) for the storage of provisions. – Others occupied their abandoned dwelling-places (layer IV) without building a castle wall (remains of poorly-built dwellings to the SW.). – The *fifth settlement,* on the other hand, had a thin wall again (1-1.3m.; also the piece of the wall with a small flight of steps), which was gradually replaced by the better one in layer VI.

Seventh layer. Walls have remained standing, chiefly between the castle wall of layer VI and the first terrace walls, and can be divided into two quite distinct periods: a) simple country people, who were still using "Mycenean" earthenware, renovated the walls and gates of VI and built their dwellings (similar in ground-plan to those of VI) against the inside of the castle wall; these are preserved to l. and r. of the gate VI S, with numerous earthenware vessels for provisions and, at the west gate VI U, also, the remains of a second inner circle of dwellings. – b) At the same places stand walls of a different kind, which are recognisable above the foundations by the irregular stones (orthostats) set up on end. They formed largish dwellings, whose rooms were grouped around a courtyard. Early geometric and embossed vases were found in them.

Eighth layer. Aeolian Greeks then fashioned themselves a fortified settlement, making the remnants of the old wall of layer VI serviceable again by inserting small stones. Because of the levelling in Roman times, there is less to be seen of this eighth layer than anything else. The dwellings were very simple; their walls consist of irregular or good polygonal undressed stonework with earth mortar.

Lower town. The plateau to S. and E. below the hill has been but little investigated. It seems to have been only very sparsely populated in early times. It is likely that a small town did not come into being here until the Hellenic era, which grew to a town under Roman rule, and whose ring-wall, of length about 3500m., and thickness 2.5m., can still be discerned. The theatre in the NE. is part of it. Trial diggings to the S. of theatres B and C brought to light the walls and granite columns of a stoa (portico). It is to be assumed that the agora (public square) was on this terrain, where the huts now stand.

[*So where is King Priam's treasure now?* We begin the trail with the following piece, taken from Baedeker's *Berlin* (Engl. 3rd ed., 1908)]

"***Ethnographical Museum**, designed by *Ende* and opened in 1886… On the ground-floor are the Prehistoric Collections (director, Prof. K. Schuchardt) and Schliemann's Trojan Collections; the two upper floors are devoted to the Ethnographical Collections, which rival in extent and scientific value those in the British Museum. The official guide (1906; 50pf.) is not clearly arranged. As the collections are constantly being added to and the arrangement of the exhibits altered, visitors are referred to the directing arrows and instructions on the door-posts of the rooms and to the labels attached to the various objects…

The Rooms to the right of the court contain the **Schliemann Collections,* presented by the distinguished discoverer (d.1890) to the German Empire. Most of the objects were excavated in 1871-82 on the site of ancient Troy, including the famous series of gold articles, formerly called the 'Treasure of Priam' (in the 2nd Room). In 1909 this collection is to be transferred to the Antiquarium in the Old Museum."

Later on, Schliemann's right to remove these artefacts to Germany was disputed by the Ottoman government of the time. What happened to them? During World War 2, Berlin was devastated by bombing attacks, and, although many museum treasures were brought to safety, much was irretrievably damaged or destroyed. From Baedeker's *Berlin,* 7th Engl. ed. 1965:

"The destruction of or damage to many of the well-beloved buildings of Berlin, still partly in ruins in the E. part of the city, the distribution of the treasures of the museums and art galleries between West and East Berlin, the loss of many famous sculptures, prevent the newcomer from forming an adequate idea of Berlin's former artistic wealth and of what it could once again become in happier circumstances."

In other words, there was a very messy divorce, with both parties picking over the goods and chattels (many of which had fortunately been stored safely away during the war). Elsewhere, in the same volume, he gives an answer, of sorts, concerning their whereabouts:

"The new **Museum of Pre- and Proto-History** *Museum für Vor- und Früh-geschichte*), housed in the Langhaus block of the Charlottenburg palace, originated (like most of the other Berlin museums) in the Hohenzollern collections of art and archaeology and is based on antiquities brought to Berlin since the time of the Great Elector. When in 1945 the museum was destroyed by bombs and fire, one of the largest collections of the kind in the world vanished in smoke and ashes. The great gold treasures, Schliemann's finds from Troy (1890), the Eberswalde treasure, and very much else have disappeared."

That was exactly 20 years after the bombs fell. Were Schliemann's incomparable gold, silver, copper, bronze and terra cotta treasures – vases, gold bottles, necklaces, bracelets, goblets and much else – all pulverised in the rubble? I turned to Wikipedia for help. Until the bombing raids, the Schliemann Collections were housed in the Pergamon Museum, situated in what became East Berlin. It seems that the treasures were not lost after all, but removed by the Red Army to the Soviet Union, turning up in 1993 in the Pushkin Museum in Moscow! Lengthy, and not very productive, negotiations have been going on, for their return to Germany.

All I can add is that, if you go on line, select Wikipedia and then *Priam's Treasure,* you will find the topic dealt with in more depth than I can allow myself here. Call up *Troy*, and you can see a useful map of the site, and a cross-section of it, which Baedeker included in his own description.

Finally, if you are planning to visit Troy from Istanbul, you can do as follows (my sincere thanks to Tom Brosnahan at www. turkeytravelplanner.com for this information): take the bus from Istanbul to Çanakkale [our old friend Kum Kalé] in 5hrs. Thence by taxi for the 19-mile trip to the site of Troy. The entire excursion may take 14-16hrs, with 2hrs. at Troy. Better to stay a night in Çanakkale and do it in style. It's not cheap!!

Gradus ad Parnassum

(or the Ascent of Mount Parnassus)

[This extract, which never appeared in *Baedekeriana*, comes from Baedeker's *Greece*, 4th revised ed., 1909, which devotes almost 90 pp. to Athens, a section which was printed as a book on its own from the 2nd ed. of 1896 – and has become very collectable. It was "intended for sale solely within the kingdom of Greece". One of my customers used to ring me up constantly, to ask if I had *Athens* in stock – he claimed he dreamed about it! I was, alas, never able to satisfy his demands. As *Greece* may not be in *your* collection, dear reader, I intend to take you climbing instead!]

Parnassos.

The ascent of the famous *Parnassos*, which well repays the exertion, may be accomplished from Delphi in 7½hrs... From Aráchova it takes 5¾hrs.; this route is specially recommended for the descent. As the view is best early in the morning, it is advisable to devote two days to the ascent, the night being spent at the ruined huts about 2hrs. below the top.

Warm coverings for the night must be taken, as well as an abundant supply of provisions and even water for the latter part of the ascent, as there are no springs on the upper part of the mountain; the guides have also to be provided for. In other respects the ascent, in fine weather, is comparatively easy, and it is possible to ride almost to the summit *(horse*, ordered through the landlord at Kastri, about 7 dr. for the day; blankets and provisions for the same amount; pack-horse extra). The expedition is best made in July; before June there is too much snow on the ground and after July the days favourable for the view become fewer. It is important to ascertain beforehand that the guide is really acquainted with the way and is prepared to cross snow if necessary.

FROM DELPHI a steep winding path *(Kakē Skala),* beginning near the stadion, ascends in 1hr. to a ridge (2970ft.) where the walking is easier. Farther on we traverse a flat eminence and descend slightly to the *Livádi,* an upland plain shaded by beautiful pinewoods, belonging to Aráchova. Above this plateau lies the stalactite cave of *Sarantáli* or *Sarávli* (4660ft.; 3hrs. from Delphi; ½hr. from the halting-place at the foot of the mountain), the *Korykian Grotto* of the ancients, described by Pausanias, in and around which wild Bacchic festivals were celebrated. Candles are not required in daylight. To the right of the usual entrance is a rough cube of rock with inscriptions in honour of Pan and the Nymphs. From the cave we proceed, passing a spring of good water, to (1hr.) the Kalývia Arachovítika (see below).

A pleasant route, diverging to the left from the path to the Korykian Grotto above Kasatri, leads via (3hrs. more) the prettily situated *Epano-Agóryani.* Thence we descend rapidly, crossing the foaming *Agoranitza,* to (1½hr.) *Kato-Agóryani,* immediately to the S. of which lies the ruined town of *Lilaea.* The walls and towers of the citadel are in good preservation, but the remains of the rest of the town are unimportant. Several large springs here form the source of the *Kephisos.* – From Kato-Agóryani to *Graviá,* 2¼hrs.; to *Kato-Souvála,* 1hr.

FROM ARACHOVA (horse about 10 dr.) we ascend in 1hr. to the plateau of *Livádi.* We then pass the village of *Kalývia Arachovítica*, which lies in the NE. part of the plain and is inhabited in summer by the Arachovians. We next ascend two steep pine-clad slopes, keeping steadily towards the NW.; when the wood ceases (2hrs.) the W. summit of Parnassos appears close to us on the right. In 20min. more the path turns sharp to the E., and in another ½hr. we reach two ruined chalets where the night may be spent. The upper part of the mountain is covered with blocks of stone, across which we make our way (no path) to the (1hr.) depression beneath the (1hr.) *Lykéri* or highest summit (marked with a cross).

The highest summit of ***Parnassos** (8070ft.; according to others 8270ft.) rises at the S. end of a ridge stretching from N. to S., while the four other peaks, detached from the main peak but connected with each other, are arranged in a wide semicircle from E. to W. As the magnificent view is generally clearest just before sunrise the traveller should start in time to be on the summit at daybreak.

**View. To the E. across the narrow strait which separates *Euboea* from the mainland and over the serrated peaks of that island, may be distinctly seen (in clear weather) the outlines of the *N. Sporades*, rising from the wide expanse of sea, which stretches beyond them until it is met on the horizon by the mountain-lines of the more distant islands of the Archipelago. – To the NE. the steep promontory of *Athos*, the ‘sacred mountain’ of the Greeks, is visible. – To the N. rises the usually snowclad *Olympos,* beside which even the Thessalian *Ossa* and *Pelion* are dwarfed; the *Gulf of Volo* is full in view, while in the immediate foreground are the *Bay of Lamia* and the mountains to the N. of the plain of the Spercheios. As the sun rises the more distant prospect becomes veiled in mist, but the lakes and rivers in the plains of Phokis and Bœotia, which before were barely visible, sparkle and glitter in the sunlight. – To the SE. appears the broad-backed *Helikon* and beyond it the heights on the *Attic Peninsula*, the line of which appears to be continued by the row of islands at its S. extremity. – Nowhere is the importance of the *Isthmus of Corinth* so distinctly visible as here, where an extensive survey is obtained of the two parts of the country which it joins. – The view of the *Peloponnesus* is bounded by the mountains on the N. margin of *Arcadia: Kyllene,Chelmos, Erymanthos,* and, at the bend of the Corinthian Gulf, *Panachaikon;* while beyond, to the SW., stretches the open sea. – Quite different from this wide panorama is the view to the W., embracing the lofty range of *Korax,* separated from Parnassos only by the *Valley of Amphissa;* its summits, *Kióna* and *Vardoúsi*, are the highest in modern Greece and tower several hundred feet above Parnassos itself. To the NW. the most prominent points are *Tymphrestos* and *Œta.*

Items awarded 2 stars in Baedeker’s *Athens:*

Monument of Lysikrates
Acropolis
Temple of Athena Nike
Propylæa; Parthenon
Erechtheion
Portico of the Caryatides
Frieze from the Parthenon, in *Acropolis Museum
Theseion, ‘the best preserved edifice not only of ancient Athens but… the whole of the ancient Greek world
National Archælogical Museum

Correspondence between Karl Baedeker IV and Michael Wild

[From *Baedekeriana* no.17, Spring 1992]

In the 1970s, I discovered that the Baedeker firm had an address in Freiburg, on the edge of the Black Forest, and that Karl Baedeker was living and working there. I asked my friend Michael Tocha, who was living in the area, to investigate. Here is a portion of his letter to me, written on 21st May, 1974, in his excellent English:

> "I had not known that the Baedeker publishing house is domiciled in Freiburg. The other day I went there and had the chance to talk with Karl Baedeker IV himself for nearly an hour. He showed me the first Baedeker ever published (1839, I think) and also a few reprints of special interest: e.g. *Berlin* (1880) which a large bank had undertaken to reprint on the occasion of their 25th anniversary at a cost of over 25,000 DM. Even more interesting was *Jerusalem and Surroundings* which is an excerpt from *Palestine and Syria* (1876). That old volume is of special significance for the Israelis because it is more or less the only documentary proof of the fact that there were considerable Jewish communities in Palestine already in the 19th century. For that reason they would have liked to reprint the whole volume, had not the title been *Palestine and Syria* which, of course, is politically unbearable in Israel today. So the excerpt is a compromise.
>
> Mr Baedeker is still trying to rebuild the archive of his house which has been destroyed in an air raid. He does not only need all the volumes ever published, but of each volume each single edition. When I told him that time and again you have a look into second-hand bookshops in England he said he would appreciate your help in completing his archive. He gave me a list of the

editions he is still looking for, and asked me to pass it on to you. If you discover one of those old editions, let Mr Badeker know, or send him the book right away; in return he will give you volumes you need for your own collection. In any case he would be glad if you contacted him yourself. He really is a polite gentleman, proud of the reputation of his firm, which is family property in the 5th generation.

For me it was very interesting to get in touch with the owner of an old, almost venerable publishing house (I would never have gone there if you had not asked for information), and I hope that for you too, the outcome of this errand is of some use."

Little did Michael Tocha or I know what he had begun on that fortunate day! My ensuing correspondence (in German) with Karl Baedeker is printed below, in my own translation.

"27th May, 1974.

Dear Herr Baedeker,

In the last few days I received a letter from my friend Herr Tocha, in which he reports the conversation which he had with you. I understand that he mentioned me and my collection of Baedeker guides, and also that I am always searching for missing titles in second-hand bookshops. He sent me your catalogue, and also the lists of the editions missing in your archive.

I have been looking for Baedeker guides for the last 10 years and I enclose a list of the titles which are now in my collection. When I began, they could be had for 25 pence! Nowadays the price has risen about 6 times (more, in the case of the rarer titles), and the old guides are more and more treasured and harder to find. When I buy a title twice, I try to have the greatest possible gap between the two editions, since a comparison of the editions becomes more interesting. I also like comparing editions in different languages (e.g. German and English), since the text can differ greatly.

I have read your list of the English editions which you need for your archive, and compared it with my collection. I was very pleased to find Paris (1876), and enclose this book for you.

In the next few months I shall try to find other titles which are not in your archive. If you send me the lists of the French and German titles which you need, I might be able to find some of these also.

I will close with a remark about the reprint of Russia, which recently appeared. A few years ago I found this title (in French) in a shop in southern England. I held the book in my hand, but alas could not afford to buy it (for it cost £10, even in those days). When David & Charles produced their reprint, I bought that instead. A pity, though, that the maps lost a lot of detail in the copying. Otherwise the book is excellent."

Herr Baedeker's answer shows that he must have acquired, in his genes, the first KB's close attention to minutiae!

"6th June, 1974.

Dear Mr Wild,

Thank you for your letter, your list of your collection and, above all, for Paris (English), 5th edition 1876, which is indeed missing in my archive. These early editions are not easy to find. I hope that you will not take it amiss if I point out that the 'General Map of Northern France' is missing from the front, also, at the back, the 'Plan of Paris in three sections'. Plans are often removed from Baedekers as soon as they are used, and these get lost. When purchasing, one must pay close attention to this point. Until I find a complete 5th edition, yours will go into my archive.

In your list are another 2 volumes which I do not have:

Londres, 10th ed. 1899;
Austria-Hungary, 8th ed. 1896

Please write and tell me what you are looking for, then I will make you an offer. For the Paris volume I should like to give you a book in exchange, which you want yourself.

An omission from my list of wants is: The Mediterranean 1st (and last) edition 1911. I am anxious to acquire this.

I am gladly following your request for my French and German wants lists, and enclose these.

It will interest you, that the following has just appeared as reprint: Baedeker's Egypt, 8th ed. 1929. It is similar to Russia 1914, but bound in yellow linen. Publisher David & Charles, retail price £6.

I am pleased to have got to know you as a passionate collector of Baedekers.

Best wishes,
Yours,
Karl Baedeker."

"10th June 1974.

Dear Herr Baedeker,

Many thanks for your nice letter, which I received yesterday. I am pleased that the Paris volume can fill a gap in your archive, even if only temporarily. I regret that a few maps were missing. In the case of the older editions, which have journeyed far with their owners, the collector must often make a difficult choice: either take a volume that leaves something to be desired, or reject it out of hand.

It is very kind of you to offer me a volume in exchange. As you see from my own list, the rarer titles are missing: Konstantinopel, Greece, Russia, Indien and Canada.

I am of course very anxious to acquire these titles. (The edition is unimportant).

As far as Londres 10th ed. 1899 and Austria-Hungary 8th ed. 1896 are concerned, I can send you Londres immediately, if you can replace it for me (in English, French or German – any edition). I must however point out to you that, although the volume is in excellent condition, the plans of London and the supplement are missing. I don't really want to part with Austria-Hungary at this point: I found it only after a good deal of searching, and the volume is not in good condition, since the individual sections have been separated and lie loosely in the cover.

Thank you also for the other wants list. As promised, I will try to acquire something for you, and will sniff around everywhere for The Mediterranean. (I don't recall ever having seen this title). Do you by any chance have a list showing how many copies of each title and edition were printed? I would find that most interesting and helpful.

Thank you for your news about the reprint of Egypt. I see that the retail price over here is much cheaper, on the current exchange rate, than in Germany!

With best wishes,
Yours,
Michael Wild."

Things now really began to take off… The letters – and books - fly thick and fast!

"18th June 1974.

Dear Mr Wild,

Thank you very much for your letter. I am sending you, per Printed Paper Rate:

Konstantinopel und Kleinasien, 2nd ed. 1914.

Some pages and plans have been stuck back in. This is a swap for the Paris volume.

For Londres 1899 I am sending you:

London und Umgebungen, 14th ed. 1901,

in good condition but without the Supplement of maps.

Please send me Londres by Printed Paper Rate.

Since the firm was destroyed in 1943, there has been no list of the print-runs for the various editions.

With good wishes,
Yours,
KB."

"25th June 1974.

Dear Herr Baedeker,

Thank you very much indeed for your parcel with the two books Konstantinopel and London. The former brought me especial pleasure.

I enclose Londres, as agreed, and also two other volumes, which are on your English wants list:

Paris and environs, 13th ed. 1898
Southern Italy, 9th ed. 1887.

In both cases, all maps and plans are intact."

At this point, I had the temerity to make a suggestion about how the firm might mark its imminent 150th anniversary of the foundation in 1827:

"When I was recently reading about the history of your firm, it occurred to me that you will be celebrating, in 1977, the 150th anniversary of its foundation. That gave me some ideas, which I should like to pass on to you. If this strikes you as importunate, or if you have plans of your own, please ignore what follows!

i) a short history of the firm in 3 languages (German,. French & English) with pictures of the members of the family then working in it, where these are available;

ii) a selection of coloured maps in facsimile (e.g. Rhine, 10th ed. 1886, p.123 – Rüdesheim/Bingen, Egypt, 7th ed. 1914, p.190-1 – The Fayum, Paris, 13th ed. 1898 – Asnières) and also some panoramas (Mont Blanc, Snowdon, Jerusalem etc.);

iii) Part of the oldest Baedeker guide, in facsimile;

iv) Extracts (in 4 languages, German, French, English, Italian,) from the Conversation Manual, and also from the older guides. Much of this is found amusing today.

v) A short essay in 3 languages about the changes in travelling since 1827 (the emergence of the motor car, the spread of travel through all social classes, etc.)"

Karl Baedeker responded to this with a hand-written postcard, which I am proud to have in *my* archive:

"Dear Mr Wild,

Thank you for the 3 volumes and for your letter. Paris 1898 and Southern Italy 1887 take their places in the archive. I'm sending Londres back, as my son bought a Londres 1899 back from Strasbourg a few days ago, complete with Supplement.

Regarding a Jubiläumsschrift [jubilee commemorative book], we have done some work on your ideas, and make two suggestions of our own: 1. Extracts from the first Karl Baedeker's travel logs. 2. Letters from KB to John Murray, his competitor. Thank you for your stimulating suggestions.

With cordial greetings,

Karl Baedeker. 9th June 1974."

The Jubilee was in fact commemorated differently, with a reprint, (the *Handbook for Travellers through Germany and the Austrian Empire,* 3rd. German ed. 1846) but that is another story, and does not detract from Karl Baedeker's warm response to me. Summer holidays then ensued…

"21st September 1974.

Dear Herr Baedeker,

Please forgive me for this late answer to your card. I have been very busy during the holiday period. I was glad to hear that the three books reached you, and was very touched that you approved of my suggestions for a Jubiläumsschrift. I was very interested to hear that Karl Baedeker's travel logs are still in existence.

I am also sorry that I was not able to visit Freiburg… In the past few months I have had virtually no opportunity to be in bookshops, and so I unfortunately have nothing for you at present. But I shall pursue my inquiries and I hope to be successful again before Christmas, so that we can continue to help one another to make inroads into the wants lists."

As stated elsewhere in this book, Baedeker (the first) almost met Murray, but not quite. It seems to have been fated that the same should happen to Wild. We never met, and our correspondence then lapsed for almost a decade. Then I wrote again:

"Dear Herr Baedeker,

You have not heard from me for a long time, which is not to say that I am not here any more! I have noticed, during the last 10 years, how rare the Baedeker guides have been getting. I was lucky with The Mediterranean a few years ago: I found one for £3 in a book fair and knew at once that the dealer had no idea how valuable this treasure really was. I hope that you managed to find yourself a copy in the interim.

In the last few weeks I have begun to build up a largish stock of Baedeker guides, with the intention of becoming a dealer myself. I shall probably not make much out of it, but it will be interesting. I might even be lucky enough, in the course of the years, to become one of the main specialists in England. The problem is always that one wants to keep the best books for oneself! If you still have wants, please let me know. I have 71 Baedekers in the house at the moment, and the number is always growing.

I am still looking for Indien, partly because it is still a gap in my collection, partly because public interest in England has been sparked off by a television series. As the book was only issued in German, I simply cannot find it over here. Could you suggest a dealer, who might have it on the shelf?

I should be most grateful for any help. If someone were thinking of a reprint, I should be pleased to suggest myself as translator!

I hope that you are well, and that our correspondence will soon flourish again."

The world is not so kind. The reply to the above letter was poignant. Signed by a G. Heim, and with the "Karl Baedeker Reisehandbücher" letterhead, it read:

"9th May, 1984

Dear Mr Wild,

Many thanks for your letter of 30th April. Unfortunately we have to inform you that Herr Karl Baedeker died in June 1979. His son Florian, who took over the firm, was involved in a fatal accident in October 1980. After that, Frau Eva Baedeker took on the running of the firm. She died in March this year. Despite these blows of fate, the editorial work on the short red City Guides continues as before.

Frau Corinne Schmidt-Thomé, Herr Karl Baedeker's daughter, is now looking after the old guides. Please write to her about wants, duplicates, etc. [A Freiburg address was then given].

The wants list has shrunk, but a number of volumes are still missing. We were able to acquire a copy of The Mediterranean.

[Two German bookdealers, both in Berlin, are mentioned].

Herr Alex Hinrichsen is another collector, who could perhaps help you further. He has brought out a catalogue, "Baedeker's Reisehandbücher 1828-1945" and also issues a journal "Mitteilungen für Baedeker-Sammler" [information for Baedeker collectors]. Through these, Herr Hinrichsen has very many contacts with other Baedeker collectors.

We wish you all the best in your plan to become a bookdealer, and remain, with cordial greetings, …."

This was a sad blow, in the sense that I had lost a charming and helpful contact in Karl Baedeker IV. The above letter did however prove very useful, in that it put me in touch with Alex Hinrichsen. More of that later…

I exchanged a few letters, and books, with Frau Schmidt-Thomé, who wrote in a polite and helpful way. The mint copy of *The United*

States, 4th revised ed. 1909, which she sent me, still occupies a proud place on my shelves. In a letter of 26th November 1984, she referred to the transfer of the firm to Langenscheidt, which drew a line under that part of the history of the house of Baedeker.

Mention was made above of the often amusing quality of the material in Baedeker's *Traveller's Manual of Conversation*, stereotype edition. After the earliest (three) editions, 1836 onwards (Coblence), it settled down into the "Stereotype" format which did not change from one printing to another. My own copy was sold by W.E.Franklin, bookseller, Newcastle on Tyne, and the date in the front end-paper is April 1878, when *The East. Lower Egypt, the Fayûm and the Peninsula of Sinai*, with 16 Maps, 7 Views, and 76 Woodcuts was announced as "In preparation for the summer".

The *Manual of Conversation*, quite apart from being unintentionally hilarious in places, casts interesting lights upon the aspirations and needs of the middle-class traveller to foreign parts. There was no need to speak slowly and loudly in English, when you had, at your fingertips, a store of remarkable expressions in German, French and Italian as well. The drawback was that the person whom you were addressing might also need to have the book in his/her hand, in order to keep up the conversation – which was bound to follow a pre-arranged script. Woe betide anyone who departed from it! I have selected some plums, of which the first one strongly indicates the perils of catching a packet (in more senses than one!):

On embarking, and of what happens at sea.

Gentlemen, they are going to sail and are only waiting for you.

Come; we are ready: take these two portmanteaus.

Get into the boat, Gentlemen; take care not to hurt yourselves.

I think the sea is very rough. The vessel is a great way out; and, if a gale of wind come on, the boat might upset before we could reach her.

There is nothing to fear.

Well, here we are at the ship; but not without a great deal of trouble; you were obliged to row hard.

The wind increases. See that great wave which is coming to break against our vessel. I fear we shall have a storm: the sky is very dark towards the west… The waves are very high; the rolling of the vessel makes me sick; I have got a headache. The smell of tar affects me.

Smell some *eau de Cologne,* it will do you good.

I am very much inclined to be sick *(J'ai une grande envie de vomir)*.

Drink some Hollands; it will strengthen your stomach, and you will feel relieved.

I am very weak *(Ich bin sehr schwach)*; I must lie down in my hammock.

Yes, lie down *(Sì, si corichi)*, that will do you good.

I am better again, the rest has refreshed me… What bird is that?

It is a sea-gull.

I think we ought soon to see the coast now; we have been ten hours on the way already.

The coast has long been in sight.

Where then?

Yonder, that misty bluish line.

Oh yes! I can distinguish the land quite plainly now with my telescope…. Well, here we are safe and sound; but not without having run some risk: what do you say to it, Captain?

On the contrary, gentlemen, we have had a very good voyage… You must have all your trunks, portmanteaus, parcels, and effects carried to the custom-house, to see if there is anything contraband in them, before they are taken to the inn.

[After all that excitement, our Englishmen sit down to supper, and are pleasantly surprised to find some congenial company at table:]

Supper.

Gentlemen, supper is ready.

Let us make haste, as it is late. We must get up very early to-morrow morning.

I have no appetite; I could willingly go to bed without any supper.

Your appetite will improve as you eat. Come, come, there is some agreeable society, you will be amused.

Good evening, Gentlemen. Oh! Lord A., are you here! What has brought you into this country?

I have just come from Italy with my wife and the Marquis.

Lady A., I have the honour to present my respects to you. How did you enjoy yourself in Italy? Did you like the country?

Yes, extremely. We were there for three months without being dull for a single moment. I could have stayed there a year.

Let us sit down; the supper is getting cold. We can talk at supper.

Sit here beside my wife. And you, Sir, here between the lady and me.

I shall be very well placed here opposite the Countess.

Will you allow me to help you to some vermicelli?

No, thank you. I ate it so good in Italy, that I do not choose to run the risk of eating it bad in France. Give me something to drink.

What wine do you choose?

Give us a bottle of Burgundy. My neighbour and I will easily finish it; it will not be too much. Give me a plate. Madam, will you have some of this ragout?

[The meal continued with endives, haricots, a mutton-cutlet, pigeon, quail, partridge, hare, roast beef, a pike "which was swimming in the river five hours ago" and spinach, all washed down with two bottles of Bordeaux and a bottle of sparkling Champagne, not to speak of a "flask covered with straw", containing the liqueur maraschino. After the dishes were cleared away, the grapes were rejected as being unripe, "quite green", but Mrs N. was urged to taste the apricot-jam, and someone else tucked into a "sweet and juicy peach". The Countess's opinions were, alas, not recorded…]

The master, before getting up.

[We know all too well that he had a drop too much last night, has woken with a thick head, and is searching for his glasses, so as to find the right page in his *Manual* for the role-play with his long-suffering valet:]

Peter, what o'clock is it?

It is past eight, Sir.

What! Eight? Why do you come to my room so late?

You told me last night not to come before nine.

Yes, it is true; now I recollect. It was very late when I went to bed.

Will you shave to-day, Sir?

No, I shaved yesterday, and shall not shave again till to-morrow. What kind of weather is it?

Bad weather, Sir; it rains.

Then give me my boots, as the streets must be dirty. You must give me cotton-stockings to wear with my boots, and kerseymere trowsers *(Ger. Kasimirhosen, Fr. pantalon de casimir, It. pantaloni di casimiro)*.

With a washerwoman.

Please to return this linen on Thursday evening without fail at 7 o'clock punctually, as I start immediately after.

You must also get my stockings mended…

Well, you have come at last! You were to have brought me my linen three days ago. You are never punctual, and have always very bad excuses to give. Let me see if my linen is white.

I beg you not to boil my linen too much, and especially not to leave it too long wet, before it is ironed, as that ruins it.

The tailor.

Who is knocking? See who it is.

It is your tailor, sir.

Good morning to you; you have kept me waiting long enough.

I beg a thousand pardons; but your clothes were not finished.

Well: I will first try on my nankeen pantaloons, and afterwards my trowsers and coat. But where are my waistcoats?

You shall have them to-morrow without fail.

These pantaloons are too tight and too short.

They are not worn now so wide and so long, as they were a fortnight ago.

Is the fashion changed already?

It changes every week, sir… The trowsers fit you very well.

On the contrary, they fit very badly. They are not high enough round the waist: they are tight between the legs, and too wide at the knees.

I can remedy that, Sir; I will take them away with me, and bring you back everything to-morrow with your waistcoats.

To make inquiries before undertaking a journey.

How many leagues is it from here to X?

A hundred leagues.

How many English miles is that?

Nearly three hundred.

Is the road good?

Sometimes good, sometimes bad.

Can one go on the riding-path without driving on the pavement?

In this season the riding-path is generally good every-where.

Are the inns good?

Tolerable. There are good and bad.

Are the beds clean?

In some places they are, in others not.
May one get clean sheets easily?
Sometimes it is difficult to get them.
Is the road safe? Do you ever hear of robbers?
It is very safe, but still it is not prudent to travel after sunset.
Are the postilions insolent?
No, never when they are well paid.
Is the road over the mountains very steep?
In some places it is.
Is it necessary to get out of the carriage?
Yes, it is prudent to get out.
I have my own carriage; can I hire horses cheap?
You may easily get them in this town.

Just on setting out.

[It is to be assumed that not only each passenger in the carriage will have this famous little red book in his hand, but the long-suffering postilion also!]

Are the horses come? Have them put to directly, for we wish to set off immediately.

They are to already, sir.

Is the trunk well fastened? Have you not put the chain around it?

Yes, sir; that was the first thing we did.

I should not like the trunk to be stolen on the road.

Come, let us go down, gentlemen; it is time to set off. Take these two hats, and put them in the net. Put this cane and umbrella into the case; and these shoes and boots into the boot.

But, my dear sir, what must we do with these books?

We will carry them down ourselves, and put them in the pockets… Postilion, mind you go slowly when the road is bad, and when you make a turn; we do not wish either to be jolted or overturned.

I shall obey your orders, sir.

Go on the side of the road as much as you can, to avoid jolting, and then drive quick.

Yes, sir.

Where there are ruts or stones, drive on the pavement.

I shall try to please you.

How do you call the village situated on that hill?

It is a market town; we shall go through it.

Is this road safe? Are there any robbers on this road?

It is very safe here; but when we have passed the bridge, we enter a thick wood which is not very safe at night.

To whom does that large country-house belong? The palace seems very fine.

It belongs to prince N.

Postilion, stop; we wish to get down: a spoke of one of the wheels is broken; some of the harness is undone; a spring is also broken; one of the horses' shoes is come off. It begins to get dark. Do not leave us in the middle of the road during the night: whip your horses, get on, and take care not to overturn us.

You need not be afraid.

But the road is very steep and hilly; it is full of stones; there are precipices. Keep away from that ditch: it is full of mud. You must put on the drag.

There's no danger, sir, and I shall go gently.

We should do well to get out, I think.

I advise you not, for it has been raining, and the road is slippery; in advancing one step, you lose two.

I shall ask these peasants who are coming towards us, if the road by which they have come is bad.

It is unnecessary; here we are, thank God, at the inn safe and sound.

Where travellers pass the night.

Waiter, give us four rooms with four good beds directly.

I can only give you two double-bedded rooms. We have many strangers tonight, and all the rooms are occupied. Do you wish to sup alone, or at the table d'hôte?

We will sup at the table d'hôte, and shall thus hear some news. How much do we pay?

Four francs a head.

That's very dear.

On the contrary, it is very cheap; for the table is very good.

Bring some warm water for washing and two bottles of good wine into our room, with a decanter of water; we are very thirsty… Anthony, listen: when they put the sheets on our beds, be there, to see that they are clean.

Do not be afraid, Gentlemen: in our house the same sheets are never given to two persons.

"Let us go and see the king" [from "Imperative Phrases" in Baedeker's *Traveller's Manual of Conversation*, p. 160]

The "Indien" Translation

[This article did not appear in the original *Baedekeriana* series. It bridges the gap between my correspondence with Karl Baedeker, and the coming into being of my complete translation of Baedeker's *Indien*, thanks to the assistance and support of Alex Hinrichsen.]

The final letter to me from the house of Baedeker not only gave me the sad news of the deaths in the family, but also pointed me in a very useful direction. Alex and Ursula Hinrichsen, then of Holzminden near Hamelin, were not only Baedeker collectors and dealers, but also publishers. My own postal 'Baedeker business' was taking off very nicely, with contacts not just in this country but all over the world. (I sometimes wondered how I managed to fit in my teaching career as well!) I began by purchasing the *Baedeker*-Katalog (listing all the Baedeker guides 1832-1987, with illustrations, publ. by URSULA HINRICHSEN VERLAG, in 1988). This work (later superseded by their "Baedeker's Reisehandbücher 1828-1990), does for Baedeker what Köchel did for Mozart: every work has its number, e.g. the 1st ed. of *Central Italy and* Rome is E143, while *Konstantinopel u. Kleinasien*, 1st ed. 1905, is D497.

Soon, I was having dealings with the Hinrichsens on the purchase/sale front, but then, one day, I happened to mention to Alex that I was interested in translating *Indien*, of which he had at least two copies in stock. He described my suggestion as *verführerisch* [seductive!]: he would supply me with a copy at half price (DM 350, approx. £97), and I would translate it so that it could then be issued as a reprint, as had been done by others with *Russia, Egypt* and so on. He would see to the securing of the necessary rights from the firm Baedeker.

My copy duly arrived and was in fact a 1928 binding. (Baedeker held a stock of the guides *unbound*, and sent them to the binders according to demand. The front endpapers were updated to the date of binding, rather than that of first publication.)

I set to work. *Indien* being one of his fatter guides, I devoted many months to the task, finding, as I did so, that I was becoming remarkably closely acquainted with a country which I had never visited, but which was full of wonderful scenery, colourful people and superb buildings.

A copy of my typescript duly went off to Holzminden. To my consternation, Alex then informed me sadly that, since the take-over of the Baedeker firm by Langenscheidt, a new policy had been formulated there: in order to market Baedekers as new, up-to-date and in strong competition with all the other guides proliferating the shelves of bookshops, the image of Baedeker must henceforth be *modern* – which meant that they had no time at all for reprints of the "older titles". So I had a dead duck on my hands. Alex was suitably shattered also. We both understood the reasoning behind the decision. Karl Baedeker I, and his descendants, had always striven to produce books that really were up-to-date (look how KB took John Murray to task on that score!)

In two of my *Baedekeriana* booklets, Langenscheidt kindly allowed me to print long extracts from *Indien*, and that is precisely how I shall finish this present book. Had my series of booklets continued to the present day, I should doubtless have taken you, with Baedeker, to many other parts of the world, to which he wrote guides: USA, Canada, Norway, Spain and, in the Autoguides, Bulgaria and Yugoslavia, to mention but a few. I hope, though, that this present offering will have whetted your appetite for more information about **Baedeker** (Wikipedia gives good coverage, and E-Bay comes up with Baedekers for sale). I wish you good hunting!

India

[From *Baedekeriana* no. 11, Spring 1989]

In his *Baedeker's Reisehandbücher 1828-1990* (Ursula Hinrichsen Verlag, Bevern, 1991), Alex Hinrichsen gives *Indien* the following entry:

"D499 **Indien**
22 Karten [maps]/33 Pläne/8 Grundrisse [outlines]... 12 Abb. [illustrations] auf S. 17-19 [on pp. 17-19]; LXXIV/358 S. [pages]; Leipzig 1914. Tasche mit Indienkarte im Rückendeckel. [Map of India in rear pocket.]"

In this bulky volume, Baedeker is ambitious in his coverage of not only the Indian sub-continent but also further afield. Briefly, he starts by attributing the footwork to Dr Georg Wegener, who travelled a great deal over the area, especially in 1911, "in the retinue of His Royal Highness, the Crown Prince" and duly furnished Baedeker with a manuscript.

The guide proper begins with Ceylon, as then it was, then moves to the mainland, taking in Madras, Calcutta, Ootacamund, Bangalore, Mysore, Bombay and the Ghats, Bijapur, Hyerabad, Jaipur, Delhi, Agra, Lahore, Karachi, Lucknow and Darjeeling (plus a host of smaller places en route).

He then moves on to Burma, covering Rangoon, Mandalay etc. Thence to the Malayan Peninsula, with Penang and Singapore, and onward to what was then still Siam, homing in on Bangkok Still not tired of the Far East, he continues on to Java, with its volcanoes, and helpfully provides an appendix of the Malayan language for the traveller, (who was supposed to do his homework on this during the long voyage via the Suez Canal.)

In typical Baedeker fashion, we begin our series of extracts with some Practical Notes for the intrepid German tourist, who is about to find himself in a very foreign world inhabited by all classes of natives and, of course, members of the British *raj*, (whose benign influence on the previously less tame sub-continent he secretly envies):

"Among the non-European countries, India is one where travel is comparatively straightforward. Excellent steamer connections are available for the return journey by sea (3 weeks each way). The whole country is covered by an extensive network of railways, and even if, because of the vast distances to be covered, journeys of 30hrs. or more are unavoidable, they are generally easier to bear than in Europe. All the places worth a visit are either on a railway line or can quickly be reached from one. The officials, especially the station masters, are instructed to give every assistance and advice to the travelling public, and they carry out this task in truly exemplary fashion. Accommodation is provided even in the more remote districts. While, up to 10 years ago, it was still regarded as out of the question to travel through India without a native servant, travelling conditions are now so far developed that one can manage on one's own, if one has a sufficient knowledge of English and is already used to foreign travel. Thanks to the rapid progress of popular education, one finds the occasional English-speaking native almost everywhere, especially in southern India, and anyone who has, during the long sea voyage, taken a little trouble to assimilate a few words of Hindustani, will hardly ever run into difficulties. The people are neither hostile to strangers nor importunate, and far less likely to beg, than is the case, for instance, in Egypt. Public safety is guaranteed. Every native knows that any attack upon a European is punished severely, and that the culprit very rarely remains undetected. The carrying of weapons is therefore unnecessary. One gets by everywhere (in normal times) with a calm and assured demeanour. It is only when very incautious travellers leave their things lying about for all to see, that minor pilfering occurs…

When Baedeker gets down to the *nitti gritti,* however, the picture becomes a shade less rosy. He even contradicts himself at times:

One's **equipment** must be more carefully considered than for the usual journeys in the Near East. One must take into account the alternation of heat and cold here, the special travelling conditions in India, the long rail journeys, the often inadequate accommodation and also the social customs of the English, which are more or less standard to everyone. The following hints to gentlemen will give ladies at least a clue as to how they should best equip themselves according to custom and needs.

In general, the following are sufficient for gentlemen: two light-weight European summer suits and a thick autumn or winter suit (to be packed in one's hand luggage on railway journeys, to facilitate rapid changing); a light-weight dinner jacket for dinner on board ship and in the better hotels; a particularly light-weight suit for the journey through the Red Sea and the stay in Colombo; a summer overcoat; a warm overcoat and a good travelling rug for northern India and sea voyages, also a light-weight dust-coat for railway travel. If one needs to extend one's wardrobe while in India, this should be done exclusively at good European firms in the major cities. The local tailors, particularly the so-called "Cheap Jacks" set up in hotels or nearby, demand the same or higher prices as the former for much inferior workmanship. If need be, one can get them to make up suits of raw silk in Colombo or Bombay (average price 35R.; give the tailor a well-fitting suit as a pattern, and the service will be better than if the customer's measurements were taken, however thoroughly). For those who wish to attend social gatherings, tails are obligatory. A frock-coat is required only at receptions by the Viceroy, governors, etc. One can go visiting in any suit apart from white, which on the Indian mainland is usually worn only by officials of lower rank, or as military uniform. Nor is it a suitable colour to wear for travelling, because of the dirty state of the railways.

One should keep to the same linen and underclothing as one wears at home during a hot summer; if necessary, one can purchase very light-weight items in Colombo or Bombay. In the daytime, comfortable shirts (also coloured and other types) are worn, usually with soft double collars and self-knotted ties; with the dinner jacket in the evening only a fine white shirt and simple stiff collar with a black necktie are worn. One's supply of underclothing must last for at least 3 weeks without the need to have washing done, not to mention that in the hands of the native washermen (Dhobies), many items of clothing become unserviceable after being washed only twice. For night attire the so-called *pyjamas* are usual and, on trains, almost indispensable. Here, as in the smaller hotels and Dak bungalows one should take at least half a dozen towels and a few sheets, since one very often comes across dirty bed linen. Under no circumstances should a woollen belt be forgotten, which is needed in bed also.

Good footwear is essential. One should equip oneself with two pairs of sound brown lace-up boots, a pair of canvas shoes for the sea voyages and for Ceylon, and patent leather shoes to wear with one's suit at social gatherings.

The indispensable tropical hat *(sola topi)* should be purchased either in a good German store for tropical equipment, e.g. Dingeldey & Werres (Berlin W9, Potsdamer Strasse 127/128), or in transit through Port Said, this avoiding the inconvenience of having to convey it thus far. Good English cork helmets may be purchased for 16-18 shillings, with pith hats for 12-14 shillings. The German prices are similar, if somewhat lower. One should always select a better quality helmet, since the cheaper ones rapidly fade. In the morning and evening one wears a light felt or straw hat, or a cap.

In addition, the usual small items, such as slippers, cap, binoculars, pocket thermometer, aluminium drinking beaker, knife with a corkscrew, electric torch, a pair of spectacles with tinted lenses for bright sunlight, a pocket compass and similar articles.

One should get one's family doctor to make up a small medicine chest, containing the following: quinine in pill form, potassium permanganate or similar substance as an additive to water used for rinsing the mouth; aloetic pills for chronic constipation; a laxative for diahrrhoea, some opium; bandages for external injuries, mercury chloride pastilles and iodoform as disinfectant; lanolin; an eyebath etc.; a small clinical thermometer whose use should be explained by the doctor.

Above all, one should not forget to take ample reading-matter, especially if one is is not used or disposed to read English books.

Finally, one will have to equip oneself with bedding in a furnishing shop in Colombo (or Bombay), both for night travel by train (where it is unnecessary only in carriages on certain main lines) and for occasional use in poor accommodation. One needs at least a thickly padded quilt *(razai)* as underlay, a lighter blanket or plaid as top cover, and a pillow, all of which can be properly stowed away in the laundry bag or bedding roll. Whoever wishes for greater comfort, travelling of course with a servant, can take a complete bed with him, following the example of Europeans living in India. This consists of a good mattress of the same length and width as the couch in the train, a decent blanket and several pillows with the requisite linen. Many take their own wash-basin with them, since the basins on the trains are often really dirty, and unusable for reasons of hygiene (in any case one should wash one's face only with hand or sponge). These extra items of course greatly increase the quantity of luggage.

Photographic articles, fresh films and plates may be purchased in any of the larger tourist centres, but only in English sizes, for which one should be prepared. For developing one pays 1½-2R. per dozen. One should be cautious when handing over exposed films for development by natives, and it is best to make a trial first.

Good travelling companions increase one's pleasure and, as an alternative to reading, help one to bear the monotony of rail travel and the bleak evenings spent in hotels. In contrast to the convenience offered by the tours which a wide variety of travel bureaux arrange nowadays, is the disadvantage of being tied to one's travelling companions, even if one finds them uncongenial, and to a fixed programme. In any case such tours, provided that one has sufficient command of the English language and previous experience of travelling, are no cheaper than going about in one's own chosen party of two or three people, where in any case the cost of coach journeys and a servant are shared out.

It is pleasant, but by no means essential, to have an English-speaking native servant (*boy;* Hindustani *Chokra* or *Naukra)* who packs, unpacks and guards the cases, sees to their handing in and recovery on trains, makes up the bed on night journeys and provides room service in hotels. In dealings with porters, drivers, launderers and other people he acts as interpreter and also helps to effect savings. On the other hand, one has to resign oneself to the fact that he receives fairly high commission from the shopkeepers, which one has to pay on top of one's purchases. The Madrassi make the best servants. Of course they must be able to speak the major Indian languages. There are even a few who can speak some German, but one should not rely upon being able to obtain one of these. One should not engage a servant purely by virtue of the certificates he proffers (Hindust. Chîtîs), which are often forged, but use the mediation of the manager of a European hotel or Cook's office (gratis). After engaging a servant one should take possession of his references and keep them under lock and key, to protect oneself from his possible breaking of his contract by absconding. The usual rates are 35-45R. per month. The servant provides his own food, except that he is to be paid a small amount towards this when on a steamer. All his other expenses for the journey fall to the traveller, these normally including the return journey to the place where the servant was hired; third class railway fares are however low. It is customary to make him a gift of about 10R. in advance for a new suit and, when visiting places at higher altitudes, to buy him a blanket. At the end of the tour a tip is generally given in recognition of the fact that one was satisfied. All in all the servant will thus receive some 250-300*M* for the 10-week round trip, an amount which is excellent value for 2 people.

Coinage. The Indian coin is the rupee, formerly of pure silver. To counter the severe currency fluctuations between English and Indian money, the value of 15R. was fixed at 1 pound sterling (£) in 1899. This rate applies however only to gold; English banknotes are subject to the rate of sight-bills. If one reckons that £1 averages 20*M* 40Pfennig, then the value of the rupee in German money is 1*M* 36Pf., so 100R. = 136*M.*; in reality, the owner of a credit note to the value of 100R. will seldom have to pay less than 137*M.*, sometimes over 140*M.*, where this is issued in German currency.

The rupee is divided into 16 *annas*, the anna into 4 *pice*, and this again into 3 *pies*... The only gold coin in circulation is the English sovereign (£1)... Banknotes appear in denominations of 5, 10, 20, 50, 100, 500 and 1000 rupees, which are issued in Madras, Bombay and Calcutta, and are subject to small deductions outside the presidency for which they are primarily valid...

(Railway) tickets. One is recommended to secure these from the agencies of *Thos.Cook & Son*. One can thereby avoid having to jostle about at the often dirty ticket counters, and one also enjoys the advantage of the reduction for distances over 300 miles... Before commencing a lengthy journey, one should request the station master the previous day for a sleeping berth, which can only be guaranteed in this way. One pays a small fee and finds one's berth indicated on the train by a reservation ticket.

The carriages are very broad and have double roofs against the sun, which overhang at the sides. They are equipped with electric ventilation and lighting. The windows often have 3-4 different means of closure (light glass, dull glass, wire mesh and wooden blinds) which one can alternate at will. The first class compartments have leather upholstered seats along the side where the windows are, rather too wide for comfortable sitting; above them, a sleeping cushion strapped up lengthways in the daytime, and a broad aisle down the middle. They accommodate 8 people but, except in emergency, are given to only 4. Next to the compartment is a spacious toilet with washing facilities and, on some fast and luxury trains, even a bath. The second class is not greatly different from the first; the compartments are larger and more crowded. In the daytime they can be used by Europeans who are content with the more simple accommodation, although one finds oneself sitting next to half-castes and better-class (though not always very clean) natives. To use a second class compartment by night is out of the question for the European. – There are no sleeping cars as such. The first class passenger who gives notice in good time receives a long sleeping-cushion for himself alone, on which his bedding may be spread out.

Dining cars form part of the train on a few major lines only. Meals are mostly taken in Refreshment Rooms at main stations, where the appropriate stops are made: early morning tea *(chota hazri)*, as a rule between 6 and 7, *breakfast* about 9, *tiffin* between 12 and 1 o'clock, both for 1R. 8a., *dinner* at 7-8 o'clock for 2R. The guard generally inquires beforehand and issues meal tickets. There is no charge for advance orders made by telegraph. The meals leave a good deal to be desired, by European standards, although they have improved in the last few years.

It is up to the passenger to see that he gets off at the right point when his destination is reached. Larger towns have several stations, and one must consult the information in one's itinerary. If only two stations are named, *city* and *cantonment*, the latter (European quarter) is almost always the correct one for the hotels...

Electric trams are found in most of the larger towns. They are rarely used by the resident Europeans and then usually only where there are special first class compartments. The stranger may however quite well make occasional use of them; regular use is to be avoided, for reasons of hygiene...

If one does not fear the uncomfortable seat and the violent bumping, then carriages may also be used in towns... Mounts and litters for ladies are usual virtually only in the hill resorts. The Indian litter is intended exclusively for lying down, though there are chairs also...

In a few Indian royal cities, for example Jaipur, Gwalior and Udaipur, one may have the opportunity to ride on an *elephant,* at a high price or in exchange for a very generous tip. Mounting and dismounting is admittedly complicated, and not everyone finds the swaying seat pleasant, up on these great animals.

Accommodation and Fare. The hotels do not match the standards of furnishing and cuisine which one is accustomed to find in Europe. The prices are therefore more modest in scale. Apart from a few large cities, only full Pension is offered, calculated in days from the hour of one's arrival. Part of a day is reckoned as a whole one, but any meals missed are deducted if claimed for. Service is exclusively by natives. Sometimes these people are forbidden to enter the room without permission from the traveller or his servant. Clothes and shoes are cleaned only superficially, but one should not expect much greater efforts from one's own servant... It is usual to pay the coolies directly, for fetching and carrying one's luggage... First class, by Indian standards, are the better hotels in Agra, Delhi, Calcutta (here hardly worthy of the former capital), Lucknow and a few other towns, as well as the hill stations. Comfortable public reception rooms are rare, electric lighting is a recent innovaton. The guest rooms are often very spartan in their furnishing, being linked to a so-called toilet-cum-bathroom, a dark closet with rough cement walls. In place of the bath there is mostly a low tin tub, 100 X 60cm. in size, and a huge earthenware jug filled with water, from which one pours water over oneself with the aid of a small tin basin. Hot water is provided only very sparingly. A simple commode completes the fittings. One should always remove the door-key.

The price for Pension accommodation is 8-13R. The first meal *(chota hazri),* consisting of tea, buttered toast and bananas, is brought to one's room between 6 and 7 by the room-boy, who asks when one wishes to take one's bath. Breakfast proper, consisting of eggs, meat etc., occurs between 8 and 10, lunch (tiffin) between 1 and 2 o'clock, and the dinner usually at 7.30 p.m. A good selection of wines is normally available, but the prices are understandably high. Even the better-known brands of mineral water are dear, as is German beer, which is sold bottled. One will soon adopt the habit of drinking whisky and soda…

There are also a number of second class hotels, under European management, run on similar lines to the above grade, but their furnishing and cuisine is of an even lower standard. Pension 6-8R.

The third class of hotel is made up of establishments which are run by natives, but which look to a European clientele. A small number of them are good, but one often finds soiled and torn bed linen, and no proper covers. The bedstead, being only of solid wood, lacks either straps or elastic supports. In these circumstances it is imperative to take one's own bedding with one. It hardly needs to be said that the remaining furniture is limited to barest essentials. Doors do not always lock properly. All these things are annoyances which must be cheerfully borne.

Guides and daily programme. The traveller who keeps to the main tourist circuits will, in using this handbook, seldom need any other guide, such as is naturally required in the remoter regions. There are very few really good guides for the whole of India who possess a certain amount of education and reliable knowledge of the subject. The explanations and romantic stories given by inferior guides are worthless…

One should go out of doors only before 11 a.m. or after 3.30 p.m., remaining indoors during the interim. From 5 p.m. one need no longer wear one's tropical hat. The sun sets at approximately 6 p.m. The visitor who wishes to become acquainted with the interesting life of the people can safely wander about on foot, with the aid of our town plans, even through the native quarters, except during times of political upheaval, and religious festivals (.e.g. the Mohammedan Moharram and Ramadan days, and some Hindu festivals which are akin to carnivals). One must however respect the feelings of the natives, act strictly according to instructions when visiting temples and mosques, and behave always in a considerate fashion. As is well-known, shoes must be removed as one enters a mosque, though one can usually keep the slippers, which one wears in their stead, tied over one's shoes, and then it is simply a case of guarding against the slippers' becoming detached too soon. In Hindu and Jaina temples, the holy place is not to be entered. The Parsees' prayer houses are utterly prohibited to the European. In Mohammedan districts, one must also refrain from photographing women or entering cemeteries.

Apart from in a few major places, the evenings are boring. Dinner ends at 8 or 8.30 p.m. There is no kind of evening entertainment. The hotels mostly lie some distance from the native town, preventing a stroll to the latter. One will only watch a performance of dancing girls *(nautch)* once. The illumination in the smaller hotels and bungalows is often so pitiful, that even reading and writing are rendered almost impossible. At 10 p.m. at the latest, silence reigns everywhere. So, early to bed and early to rise!

Medical precautions. The large majority of travellers will get to know India only in the winter months. One can live very much as one does at home, by dressing according to the suggestion on p.XIV, paying particular heed to good protective headgear (that is, by avoiding going out bare-headed even for a short while between 8 a.m. and 5 p.m.), and by avoiding long walks, or any walking whatsoever around midday. The wise traveller will hardly need to be reminded about moderation in eating and drinking. One should never, under any circumstances, touch ordinary water, not even in mountainous areas. One should slake one's thirst with the well-known mineral waters, which admittedly are expensive, or with the thoroughly unexceptionable Indian soda water, whose stale taste may be improved by a tiny sprinkling of table salt or a small quantity of whisky. Whisky and soda, enjoyed in moderation, may be regarded as the cheapest and most wholesome drink, and is everywhere available. Strong spirits are particularly harmful in the tropics.

One should ensure regularity of the bowel and sufficient sleep. Stomach disorders must not be neglected. A powerful laxative usually cures diahrrhoea; if this fails, one should consult the doctor and not hamper his treatment by self-administered opium. If diahrrhoea and fever occur together, one should contact the doctor immediately.

In areas where fever is prevalent, beds are protected by nets against mosquitoes (malaria!); they are provided even in the bungalows. They are not however always in good repair, and cautious travellers will take their own with them.

During outbreaks of cholera, one should enjoy drinks of fresh uncorked water only, and take soda water with one, for cleaning the teeth. The plague is less infectious to Europeans. Since it is however very widespread, one should as far as possible avoid direct contact with natives. Smallpox is more serious, for it occurs in a particularly dangerous form. The best protection is to renew one's vaccination before beginning one's journey. Many Europeans have already fallen victim to disease because they neglected to take these precautions…

If one uses the services of native washermen one runs the risk of contracting the contagious if harmless inflammation of the skin known as ringworm (Hindust. Dhobie itch), for which medicine can be obtained from chemists.

If, after reading all that, the German traveller was still dead set on going to the sub-continent, Baedeker started him off in Sri Lanka - still Ceylon in those days. We join him on the rewarding climb up Adam's Peak, bearing in mind his decision to give heights in metres, but distances in miles!):

Adam's Peak

This excursion takes 2-2½ days, either from Kandy or Nuwara Eliya. Best seasons: October, and December to March. From the railway station *Hatton*, a mail coach leaves after the arrival of the important trains, approx. 2 p.m., for *Laxpana* (in 2hrs., return seat 14R.). Return the next day at 3 p.m., staying in Hatton. Pleasanter, and no more expensive for 3 people, is to have one's own car (27R. return) with which one can connect with the afternoon train for Nuwara Eliya the following day. For both methods of travel, one should reserve by telegraph at least one day in advance, with the hotel manager or with Pates Livery Stables at Hatton. The actual ascent (4hrs. up, 3½ down) is no more exacting for mountain-walkers free from vertigo, than ordinary Alpine walking. One must have stout walking shoes or boots; one will also appreciate leggings, a change of underclothing and a warm coat or rug for the summit; for night ascents, a cap is useful, for day ascents, a pith helmet. Everything else will be provided by the landlord at Laxpana, to whom one should also telegraph one's arrival time: guide (3R.), coolies with lanterns as bearers (1R.50 each), lights (50cts.), a bamboo cane as walking-stick (may be loaned, 25cts.), and provisions (tea, toast, eggs, 1R.25cts.).

Adam's Peak (2241m.), a steep gneiss pyramid, wooded to the summit, rising alone out of one of the mountain chains in the SW. of the Ceylon uplands, is admittedly not the highest, but, because of its striking shape, visible over great distances, has been the most famous mountain on the island from time immemorial. A mark in the rock at its summit (similar to the Rosstrappe in the Harz mountains) has endowed it with a religious significance and made it a place of pilgrimage for the faithful of three religions: the Buddhists see in it the footprint of Buddha who, after propagating his teaching, left the island again from this spot; the Hindus connect it with Shiva or Vishnu; the Mohammedans attribute the mark to

Adam, whom the archangel set down here after his expulsion from Paradise. The mountain is mentioned as a holy place in the Mahawansa chronicle around 150 B.C. by its Sinhalese name *Sammala.* The legend about Adam is pre-Mohammedan, mentioned already in a Coptic ms. of the IVth c. A.D. Ceylon sources of the XIIIth c. report a new access route to the summit. The Venetian *Marco Polo*, who called at Ceylon in 1293, reports that the mountain was only climbable with the help of fixed chains. The Arab *Ibn Batuta,* who was on the summit in 1340, saw both the chains and the rock steps, which still exist.

From Hatton to Laxapana, 14M., excellent road. First through the valley of a tributary of the Kelani Ganga down to *Dickoya*, a bustling place among excellently managed tea estates. Adam's Peak is glimpsed only once more. Then in a romantic ravine over the water-course and descending in cleverly engineered curves to the E. edge of the main valley to (6M.) the *bridge over the Kelani Ganga.* Beyond the bridge, in *Norwood*, change of horses and carriages for the mail coach. Now uphill again and, with ever more superb views of the Peak to the r., on through prosperous tea plantations to (12M.) *Maskeliya,* another lively place. 2M. further on, the little town of

Laxapana (about 1250m.), where *Peak View Hotel* offers very decent accommodation for 10 pers. and food (Rm. 1½, with 2 Bd. 3½, B. 2¼, L.2, D.3R.). One should have an early dinner and retire immediately. One is woken at midnight, and the march begins at 1 a.m. One should ascertain that everything carried by the bearers is protected from the wet.

The ascent (4hrs.) begins on a good bridle-path, which winds upwards through the plantations towards Maskeliya and, beyond an iron bridge, continues on the r. bank. After 1¾hrs. one reaches the narrow and bad pilgrim path, which often only the guide can make out. A few giant blocks of gneiss, towering like roofs, serve exhausted pilgrims as shelter in bad weather. After a further ½hr., at the foot of the mountain-face upon which sits the summit pyramid, one crosses the ravine of the stream *Sita Gangula,* full of tree ferns. Now begins the most difficult part of the ascent, over loose pebbles and tree roots in the virgin forest. One should take great care where one places one's feet, and allow the guide to assist. The place where, after 1hr., one reaches the top of the rock-face, is called *Indikatupana* and is marked by rest-houses (ambalams) for pilgrims. The summit pyramid is surrounded by a thick profusion of myrtle, laurel, magnolias, rhododendrons etc., which protect one from giddiness on ascent and descent. In many places, irregular steps are cut in the rock and, in the steepest places, iron rails or chains are fixed. After ¾hr. appears a small pool r. ("Adam's Tears"), from which the coolies fetch fresh water for making tea. Immediately below the summit, 10min. higher, a few hovels offer protection from rain and cold, and the opportunity to change one's underclothing. A small flight of steps leads to the very top.

The summit is a small area of about 25 paces in an irregular square, and surrounded by a low whitewashed wall. In the N. corner, four small bells hang on frames; in the S., the pilgrims' path from Ratnapura ends here (see below). In the centre, a 4m. high (approx.) mass of rock juts out, the *Sripada* of the Buddhists. The impression in the rock is 1.62m. long and 0.74-0.79m. wide; an added stone edging and weak painting-in of the shape support the fancy: it is a left foot, the toes facing the onlooker, and extending a little beyond the protective railing; a slight rise, where the ball of the foot should make a depression, proves that the artifice of Man has assisted but little. Priests and guardians are up here mostly only from January to April. The ancient shrine is open to everyone. The faithful offer blossoms, fruit, incense etc. – The **View, if the sunrise is unobscured, is of indescribable magnificence. As soon as the sun comes up, one can often see, to the W., the famous shadow of the summit, which stands out in the form of a gigantic triangle on the fine morning vapour. One seems to hover like a bird over the white ocean of mist which covers the depths. All around, a fantastic labyrinth of jagged mountain chains and fertile valleys. Pidarattallagalla rises out of the mighty mountain group to E. and NE. To the ESE., the group, to which belong Horton Plains. To the W., one can make out the long coastal strip, to the WNW. Colombo, to the ENE., far below, Laxapana; to the SE., the coastal lagoons of Hambatota.

The descent in daylight discovers new delights, but is rather exhausting. In any case, one should not begin too late, so as to avoid the midday heat.

The descent to Ratnapura is advisable only for strong walkers who are quite free from giddiness (8-10hrs.). On the way one passes 5 government rest-houses, of which *Palabathara,* not quite half-way, is the most important. Here, and 2hrs. further on at *Gillemala,* are Buddhist temples and tame elephants.

[About 30 mi. from Adam's Peak, near Kandy, the tourist who has successfully climbed the Peak can relax among the beauties of Ceylon's answer to Kew. The text is slightly abridged.]

The ****Botanical Gardens of Peradeniya** (*pera:* the guava; *deniya:* area), the most beautiful among the numerous gardens of this type in S. and E. Asia, competing with Buitenzorg in Java in scientific importance, covers an area of 150 acres (60ha.), washed on three sides by the Mahawelliganga. Situated at an altitude of 479m. above sea-level on the moist W. slopes of the mountain range, it produces a superb abundance of tropical flora, being particularly rich in lianas, palms, bamboo, pandanus, orchids, ferns and giant broadleaf trees. The garden was first established in 1821 for the observation of the native vegetation, but later also was used for experiments in acclimatising useful plants from other tropical countries. The professional staff comprises seven persons who are engaged in the production of a comprehensive "Flora of Ceylon" (the section on phanerogams was completed by Sir Joseph Hooker in 1900; that on ferns, mosses and fungi is in preparation). The Director is F. Macmillan. A special laboratory equipped on modern lines is available for scholars. There are some 3000 visitors per annum. Entrance free. One inscribes one's name in the visitors' book in the *Lodge,* to the r. after the entrance.

Outside the entrance l., a group of Assam rubber trees *(Ficus elastica)*, with strange roots; on the triangular lawn a mahogany tree from the Honduras *(Swietenia mahagoni).*

Passing the lodge, one reaches a group of palm-trees, comprising 50-60 different species, incl. areka, date, corozo, sago and oil palms. Walking around this ova-shaped group, one notices… an *Amherstia nobilis*, then a Durian *(Durio zibethinus),* the producer of the evil-smelling but tasty civet. Crossing Main Central Drive, one follows Liana Drive, lined with profuse garlands of lianas, mainly of the climbing palm variety *Calamus,* which provides the material for cane chairs. Leave the carriage by the round pool, which is enlivened by a fountain, and continue on foot S. to the spice section, which includes nutmeg *(Myristica fragrans).* Returning, note, l., the insect-eating plants *(Nepenthes)* and, on the trees, the large-leaved Mexican creeper *Monstera deliciosa.* Of particular interest is the *orchid house,* N. of the round pond.

By the Mahawelliganga there is a pretty view E. to Hantane Peak. The drive follows the river bank N. To the l., the *Nurseries,* for the cultivation of useful and ornamental plants, then *Palmyra Avenue*, whose palms are about 30 years old… On the l., the *Experimental Plots,* where cocoa, coffee, cardamom, banana, mulberry, vanilla, cocaine plants and sugar cane are grown. Further down the avenue, giant *bamboos.* In the treetops by the river one sees flocks of large bats, so-called flying foxes *(Pteropus medius)*, which sleep in the daytime, hanging from the branches. The drive passes round the *Arboretum,* a large plantation of trees occupying the whole N. part of the peninsula. (Just before the NW. curve of the Mahawelliganga, a ferry crosses to the *Experimental Station* on the opposite bank, where experiments are made with useful plants for the Ceylonese plantations.) The drive, S. along by the river, offers excellent views, such as "Bridge View", towards the railway bridge.

We turn l. along West Road to the centre of the gardens, the *Great Circle,* a large expanse of lawn surrounded by magnificent tropical trees, the centre of which is bisected by Main Central Drive and its N. continuation, *Royal Palm Avenue*, planted in 1898. Of the trees, one's eye is particularly taken by the S. African *Spathodea campanulata* with its scarlet blossom. Some trees were planted by royal visitors, e.g. a Flamboyant *(Poinciana regia)* in 1899 by Princess Henry of Prussia, a Bo-tree in 1875 by the (later) King Edward VII of England, and an *Amherstia nobilis* (1898, by Prince Henry of Prussia.)…

West River Drive continues S. to the lake, which contains beautiful water-plants (incl. *Victoria regia* from Brazil) and is surrounded by clusters of bamboo. To the l., the giant bamboo *(Dendrocalamus giganteus)* from Burma, which here attains the rare height of approx. 37m. and girth of 30cm. From Lake Road, *Talypot Avenue* heads S., a splendid drive planted in 1885, ending in a loop, in the middle of which is a classified collection of palms. R., a collection of bamboos and pandanus. One follows the path Hill Walk N. to *Herbaceous Ground*, a collection of herbs and low brushwood, then back to the lake and the entrance once more.

[Intrigued to see if these English names had been changed, after Ceylon shed its British status and became Sri Lanka, I consulted John Murray's *Handbook for travellers in India, Pakistan, Nepal, Bangladesh & Sri Lanka,* 22nd ed. 1982, and was pleased to see that the original names have been retained, and that there had been more post-Baedeker royal planters here, including "George V, Prince of Wales (later Duke of Windsor), and Queen Elizabeth in 1954."]

19. Agra.

[The very name naturally evokes the Taj Mahal – which is dealt with at the end of this extract – but the inner town itself has some superb buildings. First, though, Baedeker gives us his customary thorough general information:]

STATIONS: *Cantonment Junction*, for the railway Bombay-Gwalior-Muttra-Delhi; *Fort Station,* between Fort and Jama Masjid, for the lines to Bombay via Jaipur and from Tundla. The station *Idagah* lies on the connecting line between Cantonment Junction and Fort Station. – *City Station*, also for Tundla.

Hotels (1½-3km. from the stations [for mainland India, Baedeker has reverted to metric distances!]): *Cecil Hotel, Mall Rd., new and comfortably furnished, open only from the end of Oct. to the end of Mar., Swiss proprietor, German spoken, 50 Rm., P. 8-12R.; Laurie's Great Northern Hot., also aspiring to the first class, quite good. P. from 7R.; Metropole Hot., Drummond Rd.; Savoy Hot.; Dak bungalow, W. of the main Post Office, well spoken of.

Carriages: within the town limits, 2-horse landau 2R. per hr., one-horse phaeton 1R. for the 1st hr., and 12a. for each succeeding one; ½ day, 3½R., 3R., whole day 5R., 4R.; Taj Mahal and back, 3R., 2R... The hotels charge higher prices, but do not allow carriages hired elsewhere to drive up to them. – MOTOR CARS from *H. Pestonji & Co.,* opp. Laurie's Hotel, especially recommended for Fatepur Sikri, approx. 40R. there and back.

GUIDE: 3R. per day. There are also special guides for most of the places of interest.

Post: main office, Mall Rd., near the hotels. – TELEGRAPH: a few mins. to the SE. – BANKS: *Bank of Bengal, Alliance Bank of Simla.* – CLUB: *Agra Club,* S. of the post office. – DOCTORS: the civilian surgeon at the English station.

Shops. Jewellery, embroidery using gold, silver and precious gems: *Alla Bux, Chutton Lal Jahori Bazar*, both in the city; *Ganeshi Lal & Son*, Drummond Rd., near the Metropole Hotel (esp. good for thin silk fabrics shot through with gold, and Indian miniatures). – Soapstone and marble items, mosaics: *Nathooram*, Drummond Rd. – Photographic articles at *Raina & Co.,* in Perthapura. – Provisions at the *Agra Co-operated Stores.*

– Carpets at the factory of *Otto Weylandt & Co.*; German prop., who is also happy to give information. One can watch the carpets being made. The knotwork is done mainly by boys…

Agra (204m.), the older seat of the Grand Moguls, now the blossoming capital of a division of the British "United Provinces", with a pop. of 185,000, of whom 62% are Hindus and 20% Mohammedans, lies in a plain planted with crops and cotton, though dusty during the dry season, on the right bank of the 40-70m.-wide *Jumna (*or *Jamna)*, which at this point curves sharply towards the E. Junction for several railway lines, it is an important cotton depot, also a centre for some cotton mills and ancient crafts. The powerful *Fort* overlooks the river… The native quarter *(city)*, lying N. and W. of the Fort, contains winding but well-kept streets busy with traffic. The *Cantonment,* with many gardens, extends to the S., containing most of the European dwellings, barracks and administrative buildings. – Agra possesses some buildings which rank not only among the noblest creations of Mohammedan architecture, but of architecture in general.

The name (from "agur", i.e. salt-pan) indicates salt trading in the past. The town originally lay on the l. bank of the river. The first Grand Mogul, *Baber,* who conquered it in 1526, also took up residence there. The founder of the present town was his grandson *Jelala-ud-din Mohammed,* known as *Akbar,* i.e. *The Great* (1556-1605), whose powerful personality confronts us especially in his other residence at Fatepur Sikri, nearby. He mounted the throne at the age of 13, and, by the time he was 25, had subjected the numerous separate states of N. India and incorporated the entire area into his empire. By good administration and the development of trade and agriculture, he raised the standard of living. By tolerating those of other religious persuasions, he tried to weld the various elements of the people together and, himself, took as his legitimate wives a Hindu prince's daughter and apparently also an Armenian or Portuguese Christian girl. He organised debates between the representatives of different faiths, and finally founded a latitudinarian cult. Numerous artists came to his court, also painters, whom he permitted (against Islamic law) to depict human figures. His original and powerful buildings, done in the red sandstone of the area, unite the forms of Hindu and Jain style with those of Mohammedan art. His son *Jehangir*, born at Sikri in 1569 who, as prince, bore the name *Selim*, moved the residence to Lahore in 1618. Just as the Italian Renaissance was spreading through Europe at that time, Persian art made a breakthrough at the court of the Grand Mogul where, in any case, Persian was favoured as a language. Marble, dragged here from great distances, became the preferred building material. Massiveness of form gave way to simple elegance, especially under *Shah Jehan* (1627-

58), the first ten years of whose reign can be described as Agra's period of greatest glory. The walls of buildings were incrusted with pietra dura, likewise in the Persian style, and perhaps executed in part by Italian artists. Also, in his later residence at Delhi, Jehan still showed favour to Agra, where he spent the last years of his life as a prisoner of state (1658-66). Then, Agra declined into a provincial town, being several times sacked in the wars of the XVIIIth c., and passing in 1803 from the command of the Mahrattas into the possession of the English, who successfully defended the Fort against the mutineers in 1857. – The maintenance of the monuments and the laying out of the gardens around them is to Lord Curzon's credit…

The ****Moti Masjid** or *Pearl Mosque*, built at the Fort's highest point by Shah Jehan in 1648-55, may be regarded as one of the noblest places of worship in the Mohammedan world. The outside walls, which enclose a rectangle of 72 X 57m., are simple and made of red sandstone. The principal gate is on the E. side; a double staircase of 49 steps leads up. As we enter through the low, vaulted gateway, the whole splendour of the building is unfolded. Everything is of white marble, without any decorative carving, but perfect in the harmony of its forms. The courtyard (47 X 48m.) is bordered by arcades, partly open and partly closed, and paved with marble slabs; in the middle, the basin for ablutions. The Mosque itself, on the W. side, opens in seven arches. The Persian inscription, in black marble on the frieze, praises the building's beauty which, it says, is like that of a valuable pearl. The interior is only 17m. deep, consisting of three transverse aisles, with three domes above the centre one. At the back wall, the prayer niche (mihrab) with the pulpit (mimbar). Behind the delicately pierced marble grilles, on the N. and S. sides, the women of the court attended the service. The mosaic floor bears a pattern that resembles prayer mats.

The Palace of Shah Jehan, oppposite the Mosque, to the S., is similar in plan to that ruler's later palace at Delhi. The buildings are grouped around three large courtyards.

The outer court, which we enter first, measures 150 X 112m. and is bounded by arcades on three sides. On the E. side, the *Divan-I-Am opens off, a pillared hall 58.5m. broad and 13.5m. deep, built of sandstone with a white covering of stucco. Here, the ruler's public audiences were held. The throne stood against the E. wall in the raised niche (decorated in marble and pietra dura), whose access was from the Machhi Bhawan behind (see below; a narrow little flight of steps leads up). The pierced marble windows to r. and l. permitted the women to see what was going on in the hall. – The two-storeyed pavilion in Hindu style on the W. side of the arcaded court, called *Selimgarh*, is presumably the remnant of one of Jehangir's larger buildings. – To the N., near the Divan-i-Am, one enters the *Inner Mina Bazaar*, a small courtyard with a delightful marble loggia for the women, when they personally wished to purchase finery and jewellery from the brocade and jewel dealers. Also worthy of our attention, near the *temple* added by the Hindu conquerors of the XVIIIth c., are the fine bronze gates which Akbar removed from Chitorgarh as booty. They form the entrance to the Machhi Bhawan, but are generally shut. We therefore return to the Divan-I-Am and ascend the staircase mentioned above.

The Machhi Bhawan (pron. Match-hi) is the second courtyard of the palace, much smaller than the first, and mainly in ruins. The name ("fish place") seems to indicate that it once contained fish tanks, possibly also fountains and flower beds. It is enclosed by two-storeyed arcades. The small staircase finishes at the upper arcade, in whose NW. corner Aurangzeb added a mosque for domestic use, the *Najina Masjid* ("jewel Mosque"). We also visit a room which the guides claim to be Shah Jehan's prison, and the upper loggia by the Inner Mina Bazaar, and then reach a *Terrace,* offering a magnificent view towards the Taj Mahal. A polished black stone block with a carved edge, known as Jehangir's throne, is supposed to have served at the nomination of Prince Selim as heir to the throne (1603). Opposite, a white marble seat for the Grand Vizier. To the E., below the terrace, a cage in which animal fights were held. – Adjacent, to the S., is the *Divan-I-Khas, the private audience hall built in 1637, 20 X 10.4m. in size, and thus smaller than the hall at Delhi but, in its fashion, also a work of beauty and perfection. The material is white marble, and style and decoration are nobly simple. The marble slabs (dados) on the lower part of walls and pillars are decorated with flower reliefs. – To the E., on a projecting bastion, stands an octagonal pavilion in marble, **Sam man Burj*, i.e. Jasmin Tower. This charming structure was probably built by Jehangir for his favourite wife Nur Mahal. Later, her niece Mumtaz-i-Mahal lived there, who was Shah Jehan's favourite wife. The lowness of the marble parapet round the balcony can be explained by the oriental custom of sitting on the floor…

The third great court of the Palace, lying SW. of the Divan-I-Khas, a square of side 85m., with a fountain in the middle, is called *Anguri Bagh*, i.e. court of grapes, because vines might perhaps have been planted here. Its E. side is bounded by the **Khas Mahal,* a marble structure of 1636, in whose splendid rooms lived the women of the harem; the two flanking pavilions, with gilded roofs and white marble courts on front, contained the bedchambers. The building's basement, to which a staircase leads down from the S. platform, served as a refuge during the intense heat of mid-summer. The *Shish Mahal*, in the NE. corner of the Anguri court, with the baths for the harem (opened on demand), possesses mirror decoration similar to that in the palace at Amber. Three attractive rooms in the SE. corner of the court are said to be *Shah Jehan's private apartments,* the E. one being an octagonal pavilion like the Jasmine Tower. According to the story handed down, Jehan died here within sight of Mumtaz-i-Mahal's tomb, in the arms of his faithful daughter Jehanara. – Along the S. wall of Anguri court, behind railings, are kept the carved doors seized during the Afghan war of 1842. At that time, they were mistakenly regarded as old Indian temple doors removed by the Afghans in 1025, when in fact they are later Mohammedan work…

*Tomb of Itimad-ud-Daula, erected in 1622-28 by the empress Nur Mahal to her father Mirza Ghiyas Beg, who was Jehangir's Grand Vizier and Treasurer. We pass through the garden in front and, by a pretty gate, enter the main garden which, with its lawns and decorative water channels, surrounds the monument. At the four corners of the garden wall are towers with pavilions made of red sandstone, and mosque-like structures on the long sides. The Tomb, entirely of marble, stands on a plinth and resembles, in shape, a single-storeyed garden pavilion of sides 21m., with round corner towers topped by pavilions, and a beautiful central pavilion, whose roof still displays the Hindu style, while Mohammedan styles predominate everywhere else. For the first time we find here the Persian type of decoration with inlays of coloured stone. The pierced marble windows are also notable. The central pavilion above contains the cenotaphs of Itimad and his wife, while the graves themselves are in the gloomy basement. – The W. garden gate, facing the river, is a pretty viewpoint…

From the Fort and the Cantonment there are good roads leading, in 2½km. to the E., by the Jumna, to the most splendid building in the entire canon of Mohammedan art, upon which warm praise has been lavished down the centuries: the

Taj Mahal, tomb of Shah Jehan's favourite wife Arjumand Banu (called *Mumtaz-i-Mahal,* i.e. the chosen one of the palace), who died in childbirth in 1629. She was a grand-daughter of Itimad-ud-Daula and niece of Nur Mahal, and in 1612 became the wife of the future emperor, upon whom she exerted a considerable influence by virtue of her beauty and her nobility of sentiment. The building was begun in 1630 and completed in 1648. Its plan and elevation are reminiscent of the older tomb of Humayan and probably hark back to Persian master-builders; there is no authentic indication that western craftsmen had any hand in it. The grounds form a rectangle of approx. 567 X 305m. in area, and consist of a forecourt 137m. deep, a garden 288m. square and the low terrace to the N., upon which stands the mausoleum itself. The buildings are in an excellent state of preservation; the damage, which they suffered in the wars of the XVIIIth c. and in 1857, has been repaired, and the entire complex restored to its original form.

The first court *(Taj Ganj),* which we now enter from the W., between rows of colonnades, is surrounded by magnificent buildings in red sandstone, containing the assembly rooms and guest quarters for pilgrims. In the middle of the N. side is the splendid *Main Gate,* (giving access to the garden), a square sandstone structure, 43m. high, clad in white and coloured marble, with lofty gate recesses and smaller side niches. The central portion has, at the front and on the garden side, an upper part with eleven pretty little domes in the style of the Fort gates at Delhi. The four corner towers are crowned by pavilions., The l. wing contains a collection of old plans of Agra, photographs of the Taj since 1860, and experiments with pietra dura material. Superb view from the roof. – A few steps lead down into the garden. There is a breathtaking view, along the main avenue, of the marble domed mausoleum rising in the distance, and reflecting in the clear water of the ornamental channels. The present growth of trees in the garden is, despite recent cutting-back, undoubtedly fuller than it was many years ago, a factor which impairs the general effect. At the intersection of the two main avenues is a marble platform with fountains and seats. At each end of the transverse avenue, an ornamental pavilion.

The N. end of the garden is shut off by the 1.20m. high paved terrace, which supports the main building. In the centre, the mausoleum; r., a *meeting hall*, l. a **mosque,* both of great beauty, in red sandstone with marble inlay (from the interior of the mosque we have a magnificent view of the Mausoleum, which is seen here standing alone and divorced, as it were, from its surroundings).

The ****Mausoleum,** of white marble with blueish veins, and bearing noble pietra dura decoration and delicate bas-reliefs on its base, rises from a marble sub-structure, 50.50m. high and 94.40m. square, between four marble minarets, 41.75m. high. Its plan is a square of side 56.70m., cut off at the corners. On all four sides, huge outer arches open at the centre, rising to a shallow point, with windows of similar shape next to them on two floors. The cornice is 32.92m. above the ground. The large central dome, which is flanked by four smaller ones, is 26m. in diameter and rises to a height of 65m., or 75m. with its gilded spike. The general effect surpasses the imagination. The Mausoleum's simplicity of design, together with the splendour of its artistic execution, combine into a marvel of art which competes, in its sublime beauty, with the temples of the Greeks, and the most famous cathedrals of medieval and Renaissance times. The same harmony prevails within the building, where the octagonal central hall, vaulted with a 24m.-high intermediate dome, contains the cenotaphs of Mumtaz Mahal and Shah Jehan. The solemn atmosphere is heightened by the subdued light which seeps in. Both cenotaphs, that of Mumtaz in the centre, a shining polished block of marble inlaid with floral mosaics and sayings from the Koran, and the rather larger cenotaph of Jehan to one side, are surrounded by alabaster screens pierced in a wonderfully delicate lace-like pattern. The silver doors, the priceless jewels and the carpets which covered the stones, were stolen in the XVIIIth c. The guide draws attention to the remarkable acoustic inside the building. The sarcophagi, containing the couple's mortal remains, are shown in the basement.

[After the delights of Baedeker's often quite flowery description of Agra, we move on to the capital city, already several times mentioned.]

21. Delhi.

STATION; (given as *Delhi Junction* in the timetables, with a good restaurant and some accommodation serving all lines. Carriages and hotel representatives meet the trains. – The new *Kingsway Station*, out to the N., and the suburban stations, play no part in the more important rail traffic.

HOTELS: *Maiden's Metropolitan Hotel, good cuisine also, P. 8-10R.; *Cecil Hot. (prop. Hotz, Swiss, German spoken), open only from the end of Oct. to the end of Mar., 50Rm., P. 8-12R.; Woodland Hot., Civil & Military Hot., both near Kashmir Gate, P. 6-7R.

CABS: 1st cl. 1R. per hr., each succ. hr. 12a., all day 5R.; 2nd cl. 8a., 6a. – Better but dearer are the carriages of the large hotels, e.g. at Maiden's: landau or phaeton, within the city confines 2R. per hr., 1R. for each succ. hr.; all day, phaeton 6, landau 7R.; excursion to Kutb Minar, phaeton 12R., landau 14.

GUIDES, at the hotels, dispensable, since special guides present themselves at the chief places of interest, most of whom speak some English. – POLICE: Hamilton Rd.

TRAVEL AGENCY: *Thos. Cook & Son*, by Kashmir gate. Party excursions by car in the surrounding country: 20-30R. per person.

POST & TELEGRAPH OFFICES to the E. of the sta. The new *General Post Office* near Kingsway Sta.

DOCTOR: the British Government Civil Surgeon. – CHEMIST: by Kashmir Gate, in the town.

SHOPS: famous are: jewellery and silver objects, carvings in ivory, embroidery with silver and gold thread (already influenced by European patterns), woven muslin, painting of miniatures and the production of brass and copper articles. Most of these shops are to be found in or near Chandni Chauk. Jewellery from *Chota Lal & Semt Lal, Hurjeemal;* ivory carvings from *Fakir Chand & Rughnat Das,* Bara Dariba St.; embroidered silk (good quality) from *Kishen Chand* and *Manik Chand.* – There is a wide selection of various items, also carpets etc. at *Imre Schwaiger* (formerly Tellery), not far from Kashmir Gate. – PHOTOGRAPHY: *Sultan Ahmed Khan,* in the Fort, Lahore Gate; *Fakir Chand.*

Delhi, more properly *Dehli* (252m.), has been for almost 3000 years, as go-between for trade for the Punjab and the states bordering the Ganges, the focal point of culture and seat of government; in the XVII/XVIIIth c., the famous seat of the Grand Moguls, then chosen in 1877 for the proclamation of the Indo-British Empire and, on the 12th of December 1911, elevated to capital status in place of Calcutta. It has a pop. of 232,800 (40% Mohammedan, 55% Hindu), vigorous trade, ancient arts and crafts, and modern cotton, sugar and milling industries. It lies on lat. 28° 40' N., and long. 77° 12' E., on the r. bank of the *River Jumna* which at this point is 180-300m. broad, and dotted with several islands. The city has changed its name and location 7 times during its history, partly because of devastating wars, and partly at the whim of its rulers. New Delhi (the *modern city* or *Shahjehanabad)* dates from the XVIIth c. It has a circumference of 9km. and consists of the *Fort,* the former residence of the Grand Moguls, and the densely populated *native town,* with ten well-maintained roads and a jumble of narrow winding streets and blind alleys. The sta. lies in the N. part, and more or less to the SE. of this is the splendid main mosque. The city walls, built in 1648 and strengthened and given a moat in 1807 by British engineers, possess 7 gates, of which the most important are *Kashmir Gate* to the N., *Farash Khana Gate* to the W., *Ajmer Gate* to the SW. and *Delhi Gate* to the S. The river crossing, where the former bridge of boats was replaced in 1864 by a railway bridge 1km. long, was protected by the fort *Selimgarh* (1546), now in ruins. Outside the N. city gate stretches the *Civil Station,* the older part to the E. of the Ridge, the newer to the W., with the *Viceroy's Residence.* The construction of a new European town is being planned to the SW. of Shahjehanabad. *Ancient Delhi,* outside the city walls to the S., is an enormous tract of ruins, 14-15km. long and 9-10km. wide. Its mosques and superb tombs, with their numberless domes, arches and pillars, poking up between the trees or half-hidden in the brush, the mighty ruins of dilapidated city walls and the soaring victory tower of the

Mohammedan conquerors – all these present a marvellous picture of former power and magnificence…

Delhi played a large part in the military uprising or *Mutiny* of 1857. The revolt began at Meerut; from there, the mutinous regiments turned upon Delhi. On the 11th of May, the native troops here renounced their loyalty, murdered English officers and officials, seized all war materials and proclaimed the 90-year-old Bahadur as independent emperor. About 30,000 mutinous troops collected together in Delhi, the suppression of whom by the numerically much inferior English within the fortified city belongs among the most glorious acts of war in recent times. On the 7th of June, General *Barnard* moved up from the Punjab with 3000 men and 22 field-guns, beat the enemy to the N. of the town and took up position on the Ridge overlooking the plain. Here, the courageous band of soldiers stood its ground, strengthened by reinforcements, finally under General *Wilson,* against almost daily fanatical attacks by the troops occupying the town until, at the beginning of August, further reinforcements under General *Nicholson* arrived, raising their number to about 10,000, of whom more than half were native troops who had remained loyal. After some heavier artillery had been moved up, the bombardment began on the 7th of September of Mori Gate, Kashmir Gate and the Water Bastion. At the storming of the city on the 14th of September, General Nicholson brought the left wing of the English columns, only about 1000 men strong, up to Kashmir Gate and, despite the heaviest of fire from the defenders, forced a way through the breach, storming thence to the W., where he was mortally wounded at Kabul Gate. On the W. city wall and in the streets of the town the struggle continued until, on September 20th, Lahore Gate and then the Fort fell into the hands of the English. The remnants of the defenders retreated to the S., with the grand Mogul Bahadur, who was captured the next day in Humayan's Tomb. He died in Burma in 1862.

Not far from the hotels, the so-called *Ludlow Castle* in the Civil Station catches the eye, with its blue walls and white battlements, headquarters of the Delhi Club. In the road leading to Kashmir Gate are: to the E., *Kudsia Garden*, a park of the XVIIIth c., with fine trees and picturesque building remains (the batteries which made the breach in the gate were sited here); to the W., *Nicholson Garden*, with a statue to the heroic general; his grave is in the cemetery opposite, to the N.

Kashmir Gate has two passages and still bears signs of the breaching action. A tablet gives the names of the brave soldiers who dragged up the sacks of powder and met their deaths in the explosion. – We follow the road SE. To our l., *St James's Church,* completed in 1836, in the form of a Greek cross surmounted by a tall central dome; the former adornment above the dome (ball and cross, showing signs of the bombardment of

1857) stands on the ground next to the building. Further on, the *Telegraph and Post Offices*, and a few European shops.

Beyond the railway crossing, we reach the Fort, then, to the r., turn into the broad Queen's Road which, following the railway line, traverses the N. part of the city from side to side. On the far side of the road stretches the superb Queen's Garden, the "Hyde Park" of Delhi. To the S. of its central part lies the modern *Town Hall* with the *Delhi Institute,* assembly rooms, library and a small museum which includes, among other things, photographic views of the city taken in the days after the siege of 1857. In front, a *bronze statue of Queen Victoria.*

The 21m.-broad Chandni Chauk or "Silver Street", always busy, which crosses the city from W. to E. (S. of the Town Hall), is Delhi's main traffic artery, with the most elegant shops for native arts and crafts. In the centre, near the Town Hall, a modern bell tower and, opp. to the S., the great *Caravanserai* established by Shah Jehan's daughter Jehanara. At the W. end of the road we see the *Fathpuri Mosque* in red sandstone. The E. end of the road emerges into the extensive open area which divides city from Fort, opp. the latter's main entrance.

The ***Fort**, the imperial palace built in 1628-58 by Shah Jehan on the model at Agra, constitutes a town in itself with its 16m.-high crenellated walls of red sandstone, its numerous low towers and two projecting bastion gates. It measures almost 1km. in length and 490m. in width. At its transformation into a citadel, a large proportion of the old buildings inside the Fort had to make way for stores and barracks for the European garrison, but the preserved parts of the actual palace still testify to the fairy-tale splendour of the Grand Moguls' court, of which the French travellers Tavernier and Bernier reported, in approx. 1660 and 1699 respectively. At Lord Curzon's suggestion, the entire E. side has recently been cleared and enclosed by railings. The gardens, also, have been restored to their original plan.

From *Lahore Gate,* to the W., a majestic, vaulted arcade (104m. in length), leads to the forecourt, which itself was originally surrounded by arcades. Through the next, richly decorated gate, which served as a music room *(Haubat Khana)* for the reception of guests, we reach the main courtyard and the **Divan-i-Am,* a pillared hall, open on three sides and 30.5m. long and 18.3m. deep, for the daily public audiences, to which all subjects, regardless of rank, could bring their petitions before their sovereign. The columns, formerly covered in white stucco, support tall toothed arches; in the outer row they are coupled in pairs, and linked in fours in the corners to pillars. In the rear wall is the splendid niche, accessible only from the rear, where the famous jewel-encrusted throne stood, of which Tavernier gives a detailed description. Its decoration, with rich pietra dura mosaics on black marble, in the style of the work at Agra, is ascribed to the Frenchman Austin de Bordeaux who, during Shah Jehan's time, had been thrown ashore in India. The flowers, fruits and animals thus portrayed and, as chef d'oeuvre, Orpheus with his lyre, were made quite realistic, exploiting excellently the colours of the stones. They were recently restored by an Italian artist, when the picture of Orpheus, taken to London in 1857, returned to its old place. Beneath the throne niche was the Grand Vizier's seat.

Behind the Divan-i-Am, on the bank of the river (now greatly receded), lay the imperial dwellings and staterooms. The visit commences with the ***Divan-i-Khas* or private audience hall, open on all sides, of white marble, 27m. X 20 in size, and restored in 1891. The pillars, large in girth, are adorned with splendid pietra dura mosaics and rich gold decoration, the ceiling is radiant with blue and gold. The whole effect is quite superb. One can understand the builder's pride, who announced in Persian script over the N. and S. entrances: "If there be a paradise on Earth, then it is here, then it is here, then it is here". A water-channel, partly covered, runs through the hall and through most of the palace. – To the N. of the Divan-i-Khas lies the *Hamman*, or imperial baths. The walls and floors of the 3 main rooms are of white marble decorated with pietra dura. The light descends from coloured windows above. Fountains and seats complete the impression of luxurious comfort. The bottoms of the water-basins are decorated in wave-like patterns. The small **Moti Masjid* or Pearl Mosque, adjoining on the W. side, was built in 1659 by Aurangzeb, of white and pearl-grey marble, with a courtyard 12.2m. X 10.7, a double-aisled hall and three gilded domes; the bronze door was given by Bahadur Shah. The area is enclosed by red sandstone walls. – The N. limit of the palace buildings is marked by the monumental gardens *Hayat Bakhsh,* recently restored. They measure approx. 183m. square with, at the centre, a four-cornered basin, to which broad sandstone paths lead from S., E. and N., each containing a water-course. The basin is surrounded by decorative stone slabs and contains a small island palace *(Zafar Mahal).* At the end of the N. and S. paths are open marble halls: to the S., the *Bhadon Pavilion,* to the N., the *Sawan Pavilion,* with a marble basin and a veil-like waterfall in front of niches which are designed to hold lamps. At the NE. corner of the garden rises the tower *Shah Burj,* whence emanate the palace's water-courses; the (restored) chute is grooved, to make the water sparkle.

To the S. of the Divan-i-Khas lies the ***Khas Mahal*, or dwelling quarters of the emperor. In front, two small rooms and an open hall with fountains. The three main rooms are sumptuous, especially the middle one, whose walls are clad in rich pietra dura work; in the N. wall is a famous pointed grille window; inscriptions praise God, who granted power to the rulers from Timur's race. From the E. room, a polygonal pavilion, the *Samman Burj,* juts out on a bastion, where we have a view of the river frontage of the Fort. To the S., adjacent to the centre room, is an open hall, with fine windows and a richly decorated ceiling, whose faded colours make it look like an old carpet. – Further S., the women's palace or *Rang Mahal,* which takes its name ("painted palace") from its former decoration. It has a fountain in the middle. Also, the Small or *Mumtaz Mahal,* which now contains a small but valuable collection illustrating the history of Delhi, with items mainly from the time of the Grand Moguls…

**Jama Masjid*, built in 1644-58 by Shah Jehan, the largest and, by virtue of its effective external design, the most outstanding mosque, still, in the Mohammedan world. It stands on a base 10m. high and approx. 100m. square, and is surrounded on 3 sides by open arcades of red sandstone, with pavilions at the corners. Magnificent flights of steps lead to the huge entrance gates, of which the E. one would formerly open its doors only to the Grand Mogul. The paved courtyard, with the fountain of purification at its centre, is bordered by arcades on the N. and S. sides. On the W. side, the Mosque itself, built of red sandstone with white marble inlay, framed on both sides by minarets 33m. high, and surmounted by 3 large onion-shaped domes, whose snowy white marble is subtly broken up by black lines, and whose points are gilded. One must don over-shoes in order to enter. The interior is 60m. wide, 27.5m. deep; the decoration, incl. that of the prayer niche (mihrab) is simple and dignified.

In the NE. corner pavilion of the courtyard, a few relics will be shown if a tip is offered: fine mss. from Mecca and Kerbela, a hair of the prophet's beard, his slipper, etc.

There is a splendid *View from the S. minaret (stairs in the S. gate of the courtyard), esp. in the evening light, because of the view of the Fort; to the r. of this, the Golden Mosque, behind it among gardens the so-called Mosque of Jehan and the River Jumna. To the S. one can make out, within the Pahari quarter (set on a hill), the gloomy Black Mosque; beyond the city walls to the SE., Firozabad and, further, Purana Kila; beyond the latter again, rather to the l., the white dome of Humayan's Tomb; to the S., in the middle distance, the Tomb of Safdar Jang; on the skyline, the Kutb Minar and, to its l., Tughlakabad. To the W. one has a view of the main part of the city, with the street Chauri Bazaar in the foreground. To the NW., close by, the vaulted roof of the Jain Temple, surmounted by three golden spires; further off, the red Town Hall, with the Bell Tower in front. Beyond the city walls, the Ridge with its memorial. In clear weather it is said that one can make out the Himalayas, 200-250km. distant.

In the narrow streets NW. of the Jama Masjid, a remarkable *Jain temple* is worthy of mention, dating from the XVI-XVIIth c., which, in contrast to the older Jain buildings, borrows its plan and style from Mogul architecture. Narrow steps and a prettily carved wooden gate lead into a courtyard surrounded by stucco arcades with double marble pillars. Behind this, a hall with a garishly painted dome and a beautifully carved portal. The interior, with 3 aisles, is rich and tastefully done; on an altar dais, a Tirthankar statue beneath an ivory baldaquin…

Excursions in the environs.

To the W. and NW. of the Civil Station, a long-drawn-out rocky spine rises about 20m. above the plain: the Ridge, well-known from the fighting of 1857. The road goes past the barracks of the native cavalry regiment. Near the S. end of the Ridge, the *Mutiny Memorial* has stood since 1870, a pointed Gothic column of sandstone. To the N. of this, one of the two *Ashoka pilllars*, more than 2200 years old, which Firoz Shah brought to Delhi; it stood here in one of his palaces and was blown into 5 pieces in a gunpowder explosion in the XVIIth c. Re-erected in 1867 by the English Government, it is now 12m. tall. Further on, *Hindu Rao's House,* built in 1830 for a Mahratta of high birth, the so-called *Observatory* and the *Chauburji Mosque*, (dating from Firoz Shah's time), of whose domes only one survives. These three buildings were the strongpoints of the English position in 1857.

Further to the N. along the Ridge rises *Flagstaff Tower,* also much alluded to in connection with the siege.

The view of Delhi nestling in its bed of greenery is a beautiful one. Especially prominent are the Jama Masjid and the Lahore Gate of the fort and, in the foreground, the yellowish pointed dome of St James's Church. Far to the S., one can make out the Kutb Minar (see below). To the E., below, is the older part of the Civil Station, in its midst the so-called *Ludlow Castle*; to the W., the newer part, with the *Viceroy's Residency* and *Circuit House,* in fine positions on a hill. Nearby, the quarters of the Governor of the Punjab. – 3-4km. to the N. of Flagstaff Tower, on the r. bank of the River Jumna, the splendid durbars were held in 1877, 1903 and 1911, the first for the proclamation of Queen Victoria as Empress, the second for King Edward VII and the third one for King George V, (both of the latter as Emperor of India). On all three occasions, the Indian princes appeared, with large retinues…

[Near Lalkot…] The *Mosque Kuwwat-ul-Islam, i.e. "Power of Islam", begun in 1193 by Kutb-ud-din, continued by his successor Altamsh and completed around 1300 by Ala-ud-din, 46m. wide and 53m. long, occupies the site of a Hindu temple, whose pillars were used. The main entrance, to which some stone steps lead up, is on the E. side. The inner court is bordered at the front by a fourfold pillared hall with a dome at the centre and two at the corners, and by three-fold pillared halls to the

r. and l., of red sandstone, but only partly preserved; the pillars, which support the flat roofs, are similar, in the richness of their carved figures, to those in the temple at Mount Abu. The chef d'oeuvre is the façade of the mosque itself, on the W. side of the courtyard, with a noble centre arch 16m. high and 6.70m. broad, flanked by two lower side arches and splendidly executed bas-relief work, which is equalled in the whole of Mohammedan art only in the rather more recent mosque at Ajmer. Here also, the arches are built up from horizontally placed corbel stones, since the indigenous workers, who had to carry out the architectural concepts of the Mohammedan conquerors, were not conversant with the construction of vaulting with wedge-shaped stones. The interior of the mosque is in ruins. In the courtyard, before the centre arch, stands the remarkable *Iron Pillar,* set up here probably in the IVth c. A.D. It consists of a single piece of pure wrought iron (and therefore not susceptible to rust), over 7m. long, of which 0.60m. is set in the ground; its diameter is 0.40m. at its base, and 0.30m. at the capital (about 1m. high). The clean-cut Sanskrit inscription describes it as the victory monument of a Chandra prince, but is undated. A later inscription contains the name of Anag Pal and the date 1052.

The ****Kutb Minar**, set up by Kutb-ud-din, both as minaret and victory column, and completed by Altamsh, is one of the world's proudest monuments, and in a marvellous state of preservation. It is 72.54m. in height (Victory Column in Berlin together with the figure of Victory, 61.5m.), 14.64m. in diameter at the bottom, and 2.74m. at the top. Of the five storeys (which taper as they rise), the first three are of red sandstone, the lowest having round and sharp-edged vertical ribs, the second sharp-edged, and the third round ones. The two upper stages, struck by lightning in 1368 and entirely renewed, perhaps by Firoz Shah, are of white marble with layers of sandstone between, and smooth of surface. Each stage is terminated by a splendid balcony, running right round. On the three lower stages, the broad bands of inscription with verses from the Koran in elegant Arabic script make a very decorative effect. The pavilion which once crowned the column was dashed to the ground by an earthquake in 1803 and has been set up again at the bottom.

Inside the tower, a spiral staircase with 156, 78, 62, 41 and 42 steps leads upwards (379 in all). The *View, even from the balcony of the lowest storey, embraces the entire ruin-strewn site of Ancient Delhi and the present city, in which the white domes of the Jama Masjid are particularly prominent. In the middle distance, Safdar Jang's Tomb; NE., the white dome of Humayan's Tomb; to the r. of this, and rather closer, the Begampur Mosque and tower of *Bedi Mandal*, then the light-coloured domes of the Tomb of the holy man *Roshan Chiragi Delhi,* built in 1373. To the r. of the latter, and surrounded by trees, the village of Khirki with its mosque; in the distance, in the same direction, the Hindu *Kalika Temple* and, to its r. again, Tughlakabad, the dome of Tughlak Shah's Tomb and the fortress Adilabad. Close at hand, S. and W., the village Mahrauli, with domed tombs. – The view from the topmost platform is said, in clear conditions, to extend NE. to the Ganges (100km.) and the Himalayas (250km.).

[The above-mentioned Viceroy and Governor of Punjab, along with their retinues, did not need to spend the hot summers down in Delhi. Up in the hills, **Simla** was the ideal *Anglicised* place to be, at that time. Here is Baedeker's description, which did not in fact appear in *Baedekeriana.* Note that distances are usually in miles, but this is not always consistent!]

The continuation of the East Indian Railway proceeds N., with through carriages from Calcutta and Bombay, to (39M.) *Kalka* (sta. rest., Lawrie's Hot.), at the foot of the Siwalik Hills, a spur of the Himalayas, where the narrow-gauge mountain railway begins (Simla State Railway): 70M. in 6½-7hrs., for 18R., 10R.; maximum gradient 3%, more than 100 tunnels; 36km. *Barogh* (stop for breakfast).

Simla. – HOT. (consistently good); Grand Hot., only in the summer; Cecil Hot., P. 7-10R.; Carlton Hot., 42 Rm., P. 7-10R.; Corstorphen's Hot., P. 7R.; Hot. Metropole etc. – *United Service Club.* – *Rickshaw:* in winter, carriage hire ½R. per day, additionally 2a. for each coolie up to 2hrs., 4a. up to 8hrs.

Simla, a British enclave in the Simla Hill States (under the rule of native princes), situated in the foothills of the Himalayas at an average altitude of 2150m., with an excellent climate (March 13°C, June 23°; Dec.-Feb. 7-10°, occasional frost and snow), is the summer residence of the Viceroy of India, as well as the Governor of the Province of Punjab and the Commander-in-Chief of the Indian Army, also of the German and Austro-Hungarian general consuls for India. During this time, a brilliant social life develops; the number of residents rises from approx. 14,000 to 30-40,000, incl. 3500 Europeans. The imposing government buildings, private bungalows, club-houses, sanatoria, hospitals and sports fields lie in magnificent surroundings. Among the rich vegetation, one notices in particular the graceful deodar cedars and, during their flowering time in

February, the rhododendrons (Kipling's book "Under the Deodars" is set in Simla). In winter, the place is deserted and far less rewarding for the tourist than Darjeeling.

[In his *India etc.* 22nd ed. of 1982, John Murray gave Simla about five times the coverage that Baedeker did in 1914. One wonders whether Baedeker's man actually got there, so little detail does he provide. One also wonders *how many* intrepid German tourists actually ventured thus far, red book in hand – only to find the place overrun by the Brits. And remember that Baedeker published his *Indien* in 1914, not a propitious year for Anglo-German relations!

The other English hill station, **Ootacamund**, was given rather better coverage in *Indien* than was Simla:]

29M. Ootacamund. – HOTELS incl. Shoreham Hot, a family hotel prettily situated on a hill not far from Charing Cross, Coonoor Rd., P. 7R. (single rooms only out of season, P. 5R.); Royal Hot., Government Garden Rd., 10 Rm., P. 7-10R. (out of season 5-8R.). RICKSHAW, with two coolies, expensive; no tariff.

Ootacamund, in the Engl. abbreviation *Ooty,* the most important hill station in S. India, 2250m. above sea-level, is the summer residence of the Governor of Madras, with many European villas and gardens. It lies in a broad, undulating upland valley which opens to the W., between two arms of the *Dodabetta* (2730m.), the highest point of the Nilgiri Hills. The mean annual temperature is 14°C. One should beware the coldness of the nights, contrasting with the strong sunlight by day. There is an active social life here during the season (April-September). The most important public buildings are *St Stephen's Church,* the *Municipal Offices,* the *Post Office,* the *Bank* and the *Nilgiri Library.* To the S. of these, the *Market,* a *native bazaar*, the Parade Ground and some playing fields, separated to the W. from an artificially dammed *lake* (2200m.) by a causeway planted with willows. *Lake Road,* which encircles the lake, is the thoroughfare frequented by polite society. Of great beauty are the deep clarity of the sky and the rich vegetation, created principally by the introduction of foreign trees and shrubs.

To the N., above the other houses, is *Government House*, which is open from early morning until evening. The large trees come from Europe, Japan and, especially, Australia: for instance, the splendid Acacia melanoxylon and the giant Eucalyptus on the E. edge of the garden. On the terraces, beds filled with rich European flowers. - ½hr. NE., above the Botan. Garden, on the slope of the Dodabetta, the *Cinchona Plantation*, inaugurated in 1861, is the first successful attempt, after many setbacks, to introduce the Peruvian cinchona tree. Fine view.

10min. from the guest-houses (l. up the road after the exit), a small settlement of the *Toda,* one of the enigmatic original races which have remained in the Nilgiri district.

The total number of the Toda is no more than 600-700. Their settlements ("mand") always consist just of a few wooden huts, shaped like half barrels, with palm straw roofs. The people are well-formed, having good heads of hair and almost European features (aquiline nose). They wear a cloak shaped like the [ancient Greek] himation. They live from buffalo breeding (Bos bubalus). In every village is a holy *milk house*; the priest performs the sacred ritual of milking. In some villages one finds also a conical *temple* with a bronze idol in the form of a buffalo bell; an enclosed cattle-pound belongs to the temple. Polyandry is prevalent: several brothers may marry the same woman. The Toda are proof against Christianity. At Ootacamund they are avaricious, being accustomed to visits from strangers.

[There have been some tantalising references to the Himalayas, but a closer look must wait, until we have seen what Baedeker had to say about India's former capital…]

31. Calcutta.

STATIONS. The main sta. is at *Howrah,* where the main lines of the East Indian Railway arrive. The East Bengal Railway has two stations: *Sealdah Station* for Barrackpur-Damukdia-Darjeeling, Naihati-Lalgola-Katihar etc.; and *Beliaghata Station* for Diamond Harbour etc. – STEAMER PIERS along Strand Road.

Hotels (not commensurate with the city's importance): Great Eastern Hotel, 1-3 Old Court House St., P. about 12R; Grand Hotel, 15-17 Chowringhee Rd., 66 Rm., P. 8R., out of season 6-7R.; Spence's Hotel, 4 Wellesley Place. – For longish stays, there are several good *boarding houses* run by ladies.

Restaurants: Bristol Restaurant, corner of Chowringhee Rd. and Dharamtolla St., good; Bristol Grill, 5 New China Bazaar, near the Exchange, frequented at lunchtime by business people, good; Federigo Peliti, 11 Government Place, E. side, Castellazzo Bros., 18 Chowringhee Rd., both also pastry-cooks; Palace Rest., Esplanade Rd.

Hackney carriages: 1st cl., 8a. per mile, 2nd cl. 6a., each succ. hr. 8a., 6a.; all day (9hrs.) 5R., 3R.8a. – *Motor taxis* may be found in the inner city near the hotels.

Trams: running along the main roads of the city, S. to N. (past the hotels in Chowringhee Rd. and Old Court House St.), and along the more important lateral roads.

Shipping lines and agencies: *Peninsular & Oriental Steam Navigation Co.,* R.A.A.Jenkins, 19 Strand Rd., main connection to Europe via (40¼hrs. by train) Bombay, also twice a month via Colombo; *Austrian Lloyd*, C. Schmidtmann, 80 Dalhousie Square, SW. corner (twice monthly to Madras-Colombo); *British India Steam Navigation Co.,* Mackinnon, Mackenzie & Co., 16 Strand Rd., every fortnight to Madras-Colombo, 3 times a week to Rangoon. – Agency for *North German Lloyd,* Schröder Smidt & Co., 6-7 Old Court House St.

Post & Telegraph: *General Post Office*, Dalhousie Square; *Central Telegraph Office*, Old Court House St.

Travel agents: *Thos. Cook & Son,* 9 Old Court House St. (also bank and exchange office).

Banks: *National Bank of India,* 104 Clive St.; *Bank of Bengal*, 3 Strand Rd.; *Chartered Bank of India, Australia and China*, Clive St.; *Hongkong & Shanghai Banking Corporation*, [yes, HSBC here in 1914!!], Dalhousie Sq., S.; *Deutsch-Asiatische Bank*, 32 Dalhousie Sq., S. side.

Consulates: Germany: *Count Karl Luxburg,* consul-general, 16 Ballygunge Store Rd., at Simla in the summer; *H.R.Schuler*, consul, 9 Clive Row. – Austro-Hungary: *J.J.Czerwenka,* consul-general, 36 Theatre Rd.

Clubs. *Bengal Club*, 33 Chowringhee Rd., Esplanade, the most select club; *United Service Club,* 31 Chowringhee Rd. – *Deutscher Verein,* 13 Elysium Row.

Shops etc. – Bookseller: *Thacker, Spink & Co.*, the largest in India, 5-6 Government Place, N. side; branch in Park St. – Photographers: *Johnston & Hoffmann,* 22 Chowringhee Rd.; *Bourne & Shepherd*, 8 Chowringhee Rd. – Gold and silverware: *Hamilton & Co.,* 8 Old Court House St.; *Cooke & Kelvey*, in the same road. – European and tropical clothing: *Whiteaway, Laidlaw & Co.*, Chowringhee Rd.; *Hall & Andersen*, Chowringhee Rd. and Park St.; tailors: *Clarke, Ranken, Phelps & Co.,* all three in Old Court House St. – Provisions: *F.Schonert,* 4 Government Place, near Thacker's bookshop, esp. for kitting-out for major trips; also, the restaurants mentioned above.

Daily newspapers: *The Englishman, The Statesman* (the premier paper in Bengal); *Indian Daily News; The Hindu Patriot* (a native paper in English).

Scientific and educational establishments. – The university is merely an examining body, with its headquarters in the *University Senate House*, College Sq. Of the institutions affiliated to it, the nearer ones are: *Presidency college* for Engl. literature, history and philosophy (720 students), the *Sanskrit College* (120 stud.), the *Medical College of Bengal* (550 stud.) etc.; the *City College*, 13 Mirzapur St., teaches English, mathematics, physics, chemistry, philosophy, history, Sanskrit, Bengali, Persian etc. (over 1000 stud.). In other parts of the city, *Doveton College*, for Engl. literature, maths and sciences, Sanskrit, Persian and Arabic (200 stud.). *St Xavier's College* (R.C.) has 350 students. The educational instititute *La Martinière* is supported by the same means as the establishment of the same name in Lucknow. The *Civil Engineering College* (350 stud.) also forms part of the university. – Learned societies: *Asiatic Society of Bengal,* 57 Park St., with a valuable library; *Indian Research Society,* 32 Greek Row. – Libraries: *Imperial Library* (100,000 vols.) and the libraries of the above-named colleges, and of the Indian Museum.

Theatres: *Empire Theatre,* Corporation St.; *Royal Theatre,* Chowringhee Rd., near the Grand Hotel; *Opera House*, Lindsay St.

Churches: *St Paul's Cathedral, St John's; St Andrew's,* Scottish Presbyterian; *Old Mission Church; St Thomas's* and the Portuguese church, the *cathedral* of the archbishopric since 1886, both R.C.; *Armenian Church; Greek Church.* – Jewish *synagogue.*

Climate: dry and cool during the time from Nov. to the end of Feb., otherwise hot and humid. The mean annual temperature is 26.1°C. The hottest month is May, with 38.9° as the maximum, the coldest January with 8.9° as the minimum temperature. On average there are 118 days of rain per annum, almost exclusively during the summer. The annual precipitation is in the order of 2m. The drinking water is regarded as particularly unwholesome. – Hospitals: *Medical College Hospital* with 600 beds; *Presidency General Hospital*, for Europeans only; *Eden Hospital*, for women. – Chemist: *Bathgate & Co.*, 17 Old Court House St., obliquely opp. the Great Eastern Hotel.

For a limited visit: 1st day: visit *Government House*; always open, (conducted tour) and walk through the business quarter; in the afternoon, drive through the Maidan (park; sunset by the Hooghly). – 2nd day: *Indian Museum;* open 10-5, Sat., Sun., Mon., Tues., Wed. free, Fri. 4a.; Thurs. morning for students, Thurs. afternoons for women only); in the afternoon, the *Botanical Gardens.* – If the traveller is not acquainted with the Hathi Sing Temple at Ahmedabad, he should visit the *Jain Temple* also.

Calcutta, the most populous city and the most important trading centre in India, capital of the province of Bengal and, until 1912, of the Indian Empire, seat of a high court and many educational establishments, lies at lat. 22° 33' N., long. 88° 19' E., about 140km. from the sea, but only 6m. above sea-level, on the l. bank of the *Hooghly*, the westernmost estuarial arm of the Ganges which, at high tide, permits ships up to 8.5m. draught to enter. The city covers an area of 85sq.km. and, with its 1,222,300 inhab., stands second in Asia only to Tokyo, (though the latter has admittedly a population twice the size). Calcutta proper, lying E. of Upper Circular Rd., and bounded to the S. by Lower Circular Rd., numbers 890,000 inhab. The rest is contained in the surrounding suburbs and the sister town of *Howrah* on the r. bank (179,000 inhab.), to which a 450m. pontoon bridge leads across. Only one third of the population was born in Calcutta; two thirds are immigrants, chiefly from Bengal, then from the rest of India and other parts of Asia; the men outnumber the women by 50%. Hindus make up 65% of the population, Mohammedans 29.4% and Christians 4%. Among the 13,000 Europeans, barely 1/7 are non-English (Germans, few Austrians, French, Italians, many Greeks). The garrison consists of a battalion of infantry, and artillery battery, a company of the Submarine Mining Corps of British troops, and a regiment of native infantry in Fort William; also, an infantry regt. and a half-squadron of native troops at Alipur.

The name of the fishing village *Kalikata*, where Job Charnock, at the behest of the British East India Company, founded a settlement in 1696, and built Fort William to protect it, is said to be a cult centre of the goddess Kali. Its favourable position, at the head of the section of the Ganges navigable for sea-going ships, soon made the town mistress of all trade on the Ganges. Despite hostility from the Nawab of Bengal, it developed so quickly, that its territory was made a presidency as early as 1707, and its population was estimated at 400,000 in 1752. The capture of the town and destruction of the Fort by the Nawab Siraj-ud-Daula in the summer of 1756 interrupted its prosperity only briefly. Already in January 1757, Lord Clive won the town back and finally conquered the Nawab in June. In 1773-81, the present *Fort William* was built on the model of Vauban, and made impregnable by the razing of the native villages around it. Simultaneously, the Governor of Bengal, Warren Hastings, was made Governor-general, to whom the governors of Bombay and Madras were subordinated.

Calcutta is the natural gateway for trade with the whole of N. India, and it still maintains its superiority over Bombay, despite the latter's better position for trade with Europe. Its share of India's total trade is more than 38%. Just as Bombay is the cotton centre, Calcutta is the jute centre, where it comprises almost 3/8 of the total export, both raw and processed. The same is true of tea, of which almost 72% of the Indian product passes through Calcutta. Other exported goods are opium, skins and hides, oil-seed, wheat and legumes, raw cotton, shellac, coal, raw silk, saltpetre, oils etc. The once thriving export of indigo has been constantly on the decrease since the invention of artificial dyeing substances. More than half of Calcutta's total exports go to Europe, firstly to England (⅓ of the total), then Germany, which buys more than all the other European countries put together. North America (United States) stands between England and Germany, and immediately after the latter comes China. The most important imports are: cotton goods, gold and silver, metals, oil, sugar, salt, machinery, woollen goods, hardware, tallow, drinks, clothes, drugs and railway materials. – Recently, industries have been springing up, employing more than ⅓ of the population, jute-spinning in particular. The factories lie mostly in the suburbs and in Howrah where, apart from jute- and cotton-spinning mills, there are foundries and ropeworks.

The interest of the traveller to Calcutta is attracted almost exclusively to the European quarters of the city, which display in an impressive and splendid fashion the brilliant development of the British-Indian colonial empire. The centre-piece is undoubtedly Government House, the Viceroy's palace. It divides the business quarter with its lively traffic (reminiscent almost of London), from the broad grassy expanse of the Maidan. Noble public buildings rise all around, the older ones dating from the beginning of the XIXth c., their classical style sharply emphasising their European origins, the later ones in Gothic or Renaissance style, with some small concession to Indian forms. Monuments to governors-general and war heroes proclaim the glory of the British power and rule. The river teems with sea-going ships of all nations, and with numerous smaller craft. The image of a city that trades with the whole world is completed by shipyards, warehouses, and tall factory chimneys.

The most important business streets meet at Dalhousie Square, the main sq. and park of the city in the XVIIth c., with gardens and a large pond in the middle. To the SE., on the corner of Old Court House St., is the *Central Telegraph Office,* a brick building of 1873-78. To the W. of this, the *Deutsch-Asiatische Bank* [German-Asiatic bank] and, on the square, the *Dalhousie Institute*, a hall of honour built in 1865, with the marble statues and busts of distinguished men (incl. a statue of Lord Hastings by John Flaxman, 1826), which are to be transferred later on to the Victoria Memorial Hall. The imposing *General Post Office,* on the W. side of the sq., and completed in 1870, with a 16m.-high Corinthian portico and a 67m.-high dome, stands on part of the site of the old Fort William; at its NE. corner, a tablet and an obelisk, restored in 1902, remind us of the 146 men and women who, at the behest of the Nawab, after the capture of the Fort on the 20th of June, 1756, were incarcerated in the dark prison, barely 24sq.m. in size, the so-called "Black Hole", the majority suffocating during the burning hot night. Along the N. side of the sq. runs the *Bengal Secretariat*; in front of this, a statue to *Sir Ashley Eden* (Lieut-governor of Bengal, 1877-82). The E. continuation of the street, the busy Bow Bazaar where, among other races, many Chinese and Mohammedan dealers offer their wares, leads to Sealdah Sta. – the streets issuing from the W. side of the sq. join Strand Rd, which runs along the entire river face of the city. On Strand Rd. is *Metcalfe Hall* (built 1840-44), in which the Imperial Library has been housed since 1903; no. 13 is the *Sailors' Home*; also, many shipping offices, storehouses and the piers for the large liners. Beyond the pontoon bridge… is the *Mint*, built in 1824-30, where the Indian coinage is minted…

Government House, an impressive structure and worthy of the King's representative, was built in 1797-1804 on the pattern of the English stately mansion Kedleston Hall (XVIIIth c.), at a cost of almost £1 mill. It is completely white, with a dome over the central portion, and possesses four corner wings radiating outwards, colonnades and a magnificent open staircase on the entrance side (N.), surrounded by the lawns and palm-clusters of a garden 2½ hectares in area. The usual carriage entry to the garden is on the W. side. The central building contains, on its first floor, reception rooms, the throne-room with Tippoo Sahib's throne, the Council Chamber, where the judiciary council meets, and the large official banqueting hall, with stucco columns and Chinese marble floor. The sumptuous ballroom is on the second floor. The wings contain the apartments of the Viceroy and his family. Rooms, corridors and staircases are adorned with numerous portraits of fomer viceroys and other historical figures. The windows to the S. offer fine views out over the Maidan…

The ***Maidan**, with its enormous expanse of lawn and numerous monuments, is Calcutta's pride: in its area (5 sq.km.) and character, it is equalled by no other park within a city anywhere in the world. *Fort William*, of which it was laid out as the glacis, obtrudes but little. Two roads, Ellenborough Course and Red Road, cut lengthwise through the main part of the Maidan. At the end of the former, opposite the portal of the Viceroy's palace, is a bronze statue of the Governor-general *Lord Lawrence* (1864-69) by Thomas Woolmer; to W. and E. of this, equestrian statues: W., *Lord Canning* (1856-62), by J.H.Foley and Th. Brock; E., *Lord Hardinge* (1844-48), by J.H.Foley. To the S., where Red Rd. begins, the jubilee monument to *Queen Victoria*, by G. Frampton (1902), which is to be set up later on the steps leading up to the Memorial Hall. On the E. lawn is the *Ochterlony Monument*, a column rising to a height of 50m., in honour of Sir David Ochterlony, for his outstanding services to the East India Company in war and peace, 1777-1828. (One can ascend the column, inside: key at the police station, Lall Bazaar St.; from the top, a fine view over Calcutta and its surroundings). E. of Red Rd., at the intersection of two side-roads, a bronze statue of the Governor-general *Lord Mayo* (1869-72), who was assassinated while on a visit to the Andaman Islands….

In Eden Gardens, a cricket ground and a pagoda from Prome, set up here in 1856. A military band plays at 6 p.m.… In the evenings, the Strand provides the spectacle of elegant society driving past in smart carriages with superb horses. Particularly fascinating is the view of the river and the port, busy with shipping, esp. at *sunset. In the SW. corner of Eden Gardens is a marble statue of the captain, *Sir William Peel,* who succumbed to the injuries he received during the defence of Lucknow…

The native quarters of the city, especially the whole N. and NE. half of Calcutta (“Black Town”), where a muddle of dirty winding alleys stretches between several broad main and transverse streets, have nothing to show us that might be compared with the country’s ancient cultural centres. The picturesque *Jain Temple* in the Halsi Bagan quarter, founded by the jeweller Rai Buddree, is one of the richest examples of the strangely and frivolously overloaded style of Jain architecture, with its colourful marble halls, pools and gardens.

On the r. shore of the Hooghly, best arrived at from Chandpal Ghat by steam-boat (½hr.; 8a. return), also from Garden Reach by the ferry, lie the *Botanical Gardens, founded in 1786, 100ha. in area, for their beauty among the finest in the entire Orient, laid out like an English park with wide expanses of lawn, splendid avenues of palms and groups of trees, flower-beds, pools and cascades, hothouses and an important herbarium. All the characteristic tropical plants are represented here. Famous is the *Banyan fig-tree (Ficus bengalensis), about 140 years old, the largest tree on earth, looking from a distance like a leafy hill, 26m. tall, with a main trunk 18m. thick and 562 aerial roots, the ends of which grow into the ground, being propagated by protective contrivances; its upper foliage is over 300m. in circumference and, at noon, shades an area of almost 7000 sq.m.

The **Indian Museum in Chowringhee Rd. contains the most important collections of antiquities, crafts and scientific objects in the country, and is worth several visits. Nowhere else can we enjoy such a complete view of the whole history of Indian art, whose development may here be pursued in all its directions. Since 1909, the Museum has been altered and a wing added. The re-arrangement of the exhibits is not yet complete. Superintendent: Dr N. Annandale.

On the ground floor, to the l. of the main entrance: the *Geological Collection;* in the palaeontological section, the fossils from the Siwalik layers by the Himalayas are of particular interest. – Beyond the courtyard is the *Zoological Collection,* which continues on the upper floor. Connected with this is the anthropological department, with models of Indian ethnic types and their dwellings.

On the ground-floor, r., the *collection of antiquities, the richest collection of ancient Indian carvings in existence. Forming its nucleus are the finds of the “Asiatic Society”, which originate from excavations undertaken by the Archaeological Survey of India; to these were later added the finds from Bharhut, Gandhara and Buddha Gaya. The chronological arrangement of objects has been since 1870 the responsibility of the Superintendent, Dr John Anderson, with the advice of the General Director, Alex Cunningham. The former also published the first catalogue (1883; in two parts, the first out of print; supplement by Dr Th. Bloch, 1R.). There is no more recent catalogue than this. The rich collection of coins is shown only to specialists (catalogues by Vinc. Smith for the Hindu dynasties, and by Nelson Wright for the Mohammedan dynasties).

[The above section on Calcutta appeared in *Baedekeriana* no. 17, Spring 1992. Before we allow Baedeker to take us at least within sight of the greatest mountain of all, we follow him briefly to the other end of the Himalayas, to a secluded and potentially dangerous area which, in 1914, was still part of India:]

Peshawar (pron. Peshour; 360m. above sea-level), capital of the Frontier Province, seat of the Chief Commissioner and of the Command of the 1st Division of the Northern Army, with 97,900 inhab. (¾ Mohammedan) and busy trade with caravans from Kabul, Bukhara, Yarkand etc., lies on the *Bara*, a tributary of the Kabul River, in a plain enclosed by mountains. To the N. and NW., the view embraces the foothills, rising one behind the other, of the Himalayas, and the Hindu Kush, whose snowy peaks are visible when the air is clear; to the W., the Safed Koh range, with its low outliers to the S., stretching E. as far as Attock.

The European Cantonment, which possesses gardens and avenues, as is customary, displays the special character of the advanced frontier guard. The barracks of the Eur. troops (2 regts. of infantry, 1 motorised battery) lie mainly to the N. and W., and behind them the barracks of the native troops (3 regts. of infantry, 1 of cavalry). – The native *City,* 3km. to the E., is surrounded by a low clay wall, whose gates are shut at night, and which is riddled with narrow streets. The timber-framed houses generally have flat roofs with parapets, where the women and children dwell. There is busy colourful life in the bazaars, in which the ethnic types, costumes and wares from Afghanistan, the lands bordering the Oxus, Tibet and Central Asia, intermingle with those of India. There is a good general view of the town and its surroundings from the flat roof of the *Ghor Katri,* a former Buddhist monastery in the NE. part of the town, now utilised as a caravanserai. A similar view may be had from the 28m.-high tower of a clay-built fort, outside the town wall to the N.

The old Hindu name for the territory, of which Peshawar is now the centre, was Gandhara. Around the time of Christ's birth, nomadic tribes from Inner Asia settled here, of whose kings (*Kushan dynasty;* I – IInd c. A.D.) *Kanishka,* who embraced Buddhism, is the most important. Numerous monasteries and other religious buildings came into being…

The *excursion to the **Khyber Pass**, the narrow and winding cutting through the *Safed Koh range*, used since antiquity, fortified by the Grand Moguls and much fought over in the Afghan wars of the XIXth c., offers us an extremely remarkable insight into the trading life of inner Asia. The caravans, which we encounter, come mainly from the countries bordering the Oxus (over the passes of the Hindu Kush and the Afghan capital Kabul, 290km. from Peshawar). They often consist of hundreds of heavily laden camels, whose shaggy winter coats strike the observer as curious. The drivers are usually Afghans, tall, robust people, bold of expression, wrapped in sheepskins, with round leather caps on their heads.

At the entrance to the Pass, 17km. or 1½hrs. drive from Peshawar, stands Fort Jamrud (509m.), a three-storeyed clay-built structure, to which one could also use the branch-line, if the train departure times were not so inconvenient. On the other side of the road, a large enclosed caravanserai with the Customs Post, where one must show one's permit, and the fortified barracks of the Khyber Rifles (an auxiliary corps under Brit. Officers, formed by agreement with the predatory Afridi tribes). The Pass road begins to ascend, though with several dips, between dark rocky walls, 180-300m. high, behind which higher mountains tower, jagged and interspersed with caves. On rocky spurs to l. and r. we see small mud-built forts, to which zig-zag paths lead up, some watch-towers and, at short intervals, double sentries of the Khyber Rifles. Finally, we follow a stream which flows off l. into a side valley. Continuing to ascend, and passing an Afridi village, we reach *Ali Masjid* (742m.; 16.5km. or 1½hrs. drive from Jamrud), a small mosque and caravanserai, dominated by a mountain peak surmounted by a crenellated fort. One is not usually permitted to proceed any further. It is the custom to give the horses 1hr's rest before the return journey, which must occur before 2.30 p.m. – The road worsens. The Pass narrows to a ravine. The last British post is *Landi Kotal* (1028m.; 16km. from Ali Masjid), whence the road descends steeply towards Afghanistan.

At *Dakka* (428m.), at the NW. end of the Pass, 53km. from Jamrud, the road reaches Kabul River, and follows it upstream to the W. – The river's E. valley-cutting down to the Indus, difficult of passage and joining the latter opp. Attock, was the oldest route to India, used by Alexander the Great and occasionally later, even though most conquerors from the W., such as Timur Leng in 1397, Babar in 1519 and Nadir Shah in 1738, may have come over the Khyber Pass.

The following, and last, piece in this book did not get into the original *Baedekeriana* sequence of articles, but I felt that, having let Baedeker take us to the summit of Mount Parnassus and Adam's Peak, we should now allow him to lead us to…

Darjeeling.

The station is 2077m. above sea-level.

HOTELS: *Woodland's Hot., P. 10-12R., with a magnificent view; belonging to it, Drum Druid Hot., P. 10R.; Gr.-H. Rockville (Mrs Monk), also good, same prices; Boscolo's Hot., 11 Rm., P. 7-8R., praised. – Several boarding houses and many apartments to rent.

TRANSPORT: rickshaws, dandees and ponies; horses at *Johns.* Excursions are best made by pony, accompanied by a *syce* (horse boy).

DOCTORS: the Civil surgeon; the doctor at the Sanatorium; *Dr Seal;* dentists, *Smith Brothers.* – CHEMISTS: *Smith Stanisstreet & Co., Partridge & Co., Robert & Co.* – SANATORIUM: *Eden Sanitorium,* [sic] for convalescents (8,6,4 or 2R. per day, incl. food and medical treatment). - BANK: Alliance Bank of Simla.

POST & TELEGRAPH (see plan B2).

SHOPS. Equipment from *Francis Harrison Hathaway & Co; Whiteaway, Laidlaw & Co.* – Tailors: *Hinguen & Bes.* – Photographers: *Burlington & Smith; Smith Stanisstreet & Co.; Paar* (Austrian). – Curiosities, Chinese porcelain, turquoise, coral and amber jewellery, objects in jade and agate and kukris from *Möwis* and *Petri,* and at the native bazaar, where one can however scarcely make purchases without knowledge of the prices.

CLIMATE. The best time to visit is from the end of October through to January, the mean temperature during this period being 10°C; in January, the temperature sometimes drops below 2°C, when one will spend the evenings by the fireside. During this time, the sky is generally clear and the air refreshing in its purity; snow seldom falls. February is likewise cold, but windy and misty. In May, the thermometer rises rapidly to 15°, in June to 16°, in July and August to 18°; in September it eases and then drops rapidly. Darjeeling is one of the rainiest areas in the Himalayas (annual precipitation 315cm.). The summer months are the wettest. But one is never free from rain and mist. Often, downpours, storms and thunder will result in a particularly fine day.

Darjeeling or Darjiling (1900-2300m.; in Tibetan "Rdo-rje-gling", i.e. land of the thunderbolt or sceptre of Lama), the best-known and most beautifully situated hill station in the Himalayas, with marvellous views of the latters' snow-covered high peaks, stretches out over about 5km. along the undulating terrain of a narrow mountain ridge, running N-S. This ridge branches at its N. end, descending precipitously to the *Ranjit*, a tributary of the Tista. The widely scattered houses, framed in, and half hidden among, noble pines, oaks, chestnuts and maples, are most attractive to the eye, also at night because of the large number of electric lights. Despite the high altitude, roses, geraniums, violets and fuchsias are in bloom almost all through the winter. The establishment of the health resort dates from the year 1835, after the English government bought the territory from the Maharaja of Sikkim. The place developed rapidly, after the opening of the railway, and it now numbers 17,000 inhab., of whom about 10,300 are Hindu, 4500 Buddhists, 1159 Christians and 1050 Mohammedans. During the summer months, the Governor of Calcutta resides in Darjeeling with his officials, the population then rising to 24,000. A European regiment is based here. The town is constantly developing also as the centre for tea-growing, and trade with Sikkim, Tibet, Nepal and Bhutan. In recent years it has been the base for the English campaigns against Tibet, especially the one in 1904 under Colonel Younghusband, which led to the capture of Lhasa.

The chief tourist attraction of Darjeeling is its proximity to the main range of the eastern Himalayas ("home of the snow"; Sanskr. *Hima,* "winter, snow" and *alaya.* "dwelling"), which surpasses in altitude all other mountain ranges on earth. The total area of the Himalayas, from the Indus gorge (73° 21' E.) to the gorges of the Brahmaputra (95° 23'), is about 650,000 sq.km., i.e. more than Austria-Hungary. In the E. section, which commences with *Dhaulagiri* (8167m.) in W. Nepal, and then throws out 2 branches S., to the NW. and NE. of Darjeeling, there are 8 peaks of 8000m. or more, and another 40 or so which surpass 7600m. From Darjeeling, there is a majestic view of *Kangchenjunga* [sic] (or Kinchinjinga, Kinchinjanga) with its 2 peaks, 8580 and 8474m. which, after K2 in the Karakoram Range in Kashmir, counts as the third highest mountain on earth. The highest point on this earth is ***Mount Everest*** (8840m.), whose topmost summit is visible from Tiger Hill (see below); it was named in 1856 after the director of surveying and is not identical, as was earlier thought, to its spur *Gaurisankar* (7251m.). Forming part of the Everest group is also the fifth highest mountain, *Makalu* (8470m.), not visible from Darjeeling. The snow-line is at 4940m. on the S. slopes of the Himalayas, as opposed to 2700m. in our Alps.

The charm of the scenery at Darjeeling is increased by the fascination of the inhabitants, whose colourful variety may be observed especially in the Bazaar. The majority are Lepchas, a Mongol race which has emigrated from Tibet. They live in family units, scattered across the wooded mountains, and practising the most primitive forms of agriculture. They are stocky, with legs well-developed from mountain-climbing. Men and women dress almost identically and can be differentiated (since the men also are beardless) often only by the fact that men wear one pigtail and women two. They carry heavy loads by using a headband. The women like to adorn themselves with earrings, necklaces, and little boxes containing amulets, commonly of silver, decorated with turqoise, amber etc. Their uninhibited gaiety, especially among the girls and children, makes a welcome contrast to the deep seriousness and servility of the Hindus on the plains. The imaginative mythology of the Lepchas has been recorded in literature. Since the XVth c., the land has had Tibetan overlords and Buddhism as its religion, in the form of Lamaism. The monasteries and temples which lie in the mountains, often romantically set in protective forests, give the traveller the opportunity to become acquainted with the prayer wheels, prayer banners (both with the votive formula *om mani padme hum,* i.e. “oh thou jewel in the lotus flower, amen”, repeated thousand-fold), rosaries, portraits of holy men and other accessories for divine service in the priest-state of Tibet (barred to the outside world). – Bhutanis (Bhotias or Bhots), a rough and dirty mountain race from Bhutan, are often met with as litter-bearers and coolies. – The lively, adroit Nepalese from Nepal, slight of stature, are sought after as settlers on the tea plantations, craftsmen and servants; the curved knife, which they wear in their belts, is called the *kukri.* – Apart from representatives of smaller mountain tribes, dealers come in winter from Tibet to Darjeeling, where they live in tents. The Tibetans are of muscular build, like the Lepchas in their hair-style and jewellery; in their leather belts hang knives, chopsticks, wooden bowls, pipes, tobacco pouches etc. They bring ponies, yaks, sheep, goats, salt and musk, which they exchange for tobacco and manufactured articles.

The main street is Auckland Road, on which are situated the hotels and European shops. To the N., below the railway station, are the *Bazaar,* with the native stalls, and the *Market Place* (2076m.). To the W. of the station is the *Lowis Jubilee Sanatorium,* opened in 1887 for natives. To the NW., our eye is caught by the imposing *Eden Sanitorium,* set up high, for Europeans. It was opened in 1883 and named after Lieut.-Governor Sir Ashley Eden, who was responsible for developing Darjeeling. Further W., *Lloyd's Botanical Gardens* and the *District Jail.* – The S. continuation of Auckland

Rd. runs (rising to 2300m.) to the military cantonment of *Jalapahar,* with a large convalescent home.

The N. end of Auckland Rd. passes the *Darjeeling Club* and comes out into Chaurasta Sq., where the military band plays in summer. Walks branch off from here to E. and W. of Observatory Hill. The main walk, on the W. side, is called *The Mall.* Footpaths wind upwards to

****Observatory Hill** (2185m.). The view over the valleys and ridges of Sikkim to the Himalayan peaks, which enclose the Tista basin in a horseshoe, is of overwhelming splendour in clear weather. The distance (75-50km.) is roughly the same as that which separates the Rigi from the Bernese Alps, but the tremendous height of the Himalayan summits, rising clear above their lower spurs, precludes all comparison with Alpine views. Kangchenjunga is pre-eminent to the NNW. To the l. of it, rather nearer, stand Kabru (7321m.) and, even further forward, the fine Jannu (7714m.). to the r. of Kangchenjunga is Pandim (6712m.) and the splendid Siniolchum (6894m.). The glaciers can be made out with the help of binoculars. The passes stand out clearly, e.g., to the NE., the indentation of the Chola Pass (4419m.), which leads to the Chumbi valley in Tibet. The pavilion, which the attendant will open, contains a good photographic panorama (though the diagram at the bottom of the glass drum is wrongly orientated.). There is also a fine view into the deeply-cut valleys of the Rangit and the Tista, and of the wooded mountain landscape; on a mountain ridge to the N., we can make out the monastery of Pemiongchi.

The Mall goes to the NW. of Observatory Hill, past *St Andrew's Church,* built in 1871, and the new park, *Victoria Pleasance,* then the *Town Hall* and the *Amusement Club.* Further to the NW., the Governor's Residence, called the *Shrubbery,* built in 1879. Birch Hill Rd., 5km. long and offering several views, encompasses *Birch Hill* (2095m.), the low NW. outlier of the Darjeeling ridge. Walks lead to the top. On the N. side stands *St Joseph's College* (R.C., renovated in 1892), which has more than 200 pupils. – The NE. outlier, which branches off at Observatory Hill, is called *Lebong;* next to it is a British infantry cantonment.

EXCURSIONS. – Tiger Hill, about 5km. SE. and accessible in 1¼hrs. by pony, is frequented at sunrise, on account of the prospect it offers of Mount Everest (not visible from Darjeeling). One should set off early. The path goes via Jalapahar and Ghoom, then past the abandoned cantonment *Senchal*, of which virtually only the chimneys still stand, covered in moss, like strange columns. ***Tiger Hill** (2595m.) has a shelter on the summit. The panorama is more extensive than that from Observatory Hill. Mount Everest is on the NW. horizon at a distance of 172km., being the middle and second-highest of three snowy peaks which are visible to the l. of Phallut (3596m.), which is nearer, and part of the Kangchenjunga range.

Only his illumination by the first rays of the sun distinguishes him as the king of mountains…

Longer trips must be carefully prepared: one can obtain information and help from one's hotel landlord. Riding animals are needed (incl. a change of mount), coolies and provisions (best brought up from Calcutta). To use the Dak bungalows, one must seek permission from the Government Commissioner at Darjeeling. Provisions should be sent on ahead to the night quarters. The traveller is recommended to follow the ridge of the W. outlier of the mountain range in the direction of Kangchenjunga, which will bring him closer to the region of snows and, especially, give more splendid views of Mount Everest: 1st day, approx. 35km. up- and downhill to *Tonglu* (3070m.); 2nd day, 20km. to *Sandakpho* (3634m.); 3rd day, 18km. to *Phallut* (3600m.), in the NW. corner of the British territory. Instead of returning by the same route, one can pass through the Maharajah1's territory, thus becoming acquainted with the natural world and the life of the people in Sikkim; 4th day, *Dentam*; 5th day, *Pemiongchi,* the principal monastery in the land; 6th day, *Rinchimpong;* 7th day: return to Darjeeling.

The first scientific work about the Himalayas was published by the German *Hermann von Schlagintweit,* who explored them with his brother in 1855/56. In recent times, the range has annually been the objective of larger expeditions, either for scientific purposes, or for the pleasure of the most splendid mountaineering in the world. Up to the present time, few of the conquered peaks exceed 7600m. The following have particularly distinguished themselves: the American couple, Mr & Mrs *W.H.Workman* (almost annually since 1898), the Englishmen *Freshfield* (1899), *Conway* (1892) and *Dr Longstaff* (1907), the Norwegian *Rubenson* (1907) and others. Most of the reports are to be found in the English "Alpine Journal". Cf. also *Waddell's* "Among the Himalayas" (London, 1899; 22s.6d.) and *Freshfield's* "Round Kangchenjunga" (London, 1903; 22s.6d.).

[The above extracts from Baedeker's *Indien,* Leipsic, 1914, were translated from the German by the present author in 1986-90. As a matter of interest, John Murray produced his *India*, 1st ed. (Madras & Bombay only) in 1859. It ran to 22 editions!].

INDEX

The titles of articles are given in bold type

www.ingramcontent.com/pod-product-compliance
Ingram Content Group UK Ltd.
Pitfield, Milton Keynes, MK11 3LW, UK
UKHW012202240726
13966UKWH00002B/517

9 780956 528902